EXAM CRAM™

for NDS Design and Implementation CNE

David Johnson
Todd Meadors
John Michell

Exam Cram for NDS Design and Implementation CNE

© 1999 The Coriolis Group. All Rights Reserved.

Limits Of Liability And Disclaimer Of Warranty

Trademarks

The Coriolis Group, LLC
14455 N. Hayden Road, Suite 220
Scottsdale, Arizona 85260

480/483-0192
FAX 480/483-0193
http://www.coriolis.com

Library of Congress Cataloging-in-Publication Data
Johnson, David, 1970–
    Exam cram for NDS design and implementation CNE / by David Johnson, Todd Meadors, and John Michell
        p.   cm.
    ISBN 1-57610-353-6
    1. Electronic data processing personnel--Certification.   2. Novell software--Examinations Study guides.   3. NetWare (Computer file) I. Meadors, Todd.   II. Michell, John.   III. Title.
QA76.3.J6394   1999
005.7'1--dc21   99-32148
                                                          CIP

Printed in the United States of America
10 9 8 7 6 5 4 3 2 1

Publisher
Keith Weiskamp

Acquisitions Editor
Shari Jo Hehr

Marketing Specialist
Cynthia Caldwell

Project Editor
Toni Zuccarini

Technical Reviewer
Jim Boyes

Production Coordinator
Kim Eoff

Cover Design
Jesse Dunn

Layout Design
April Nielsen

CORIOLIS

14455 North Hayden Road, Suite 220 • Scottsdale, Arizona 85260

Coriolis: The Training And Certification Destination™

Thank you for purchasing one of our innovative certification study guides, just one of the many members of the Coriolis family of certification products.

Certification Insider Press™ has long believed that achieving your IT certification is more of a road trip than anything else. This is why most of our readers consider us their *Training And Certification Destination*. By providing a one-stop shop for the most innovative and unique training materials, our readers know we are the first place to look when it comes to achieving their certification. As one reader put it, "I plan on using your books for all of the exams I take."

To help you reach your goals, we've listened to others like you, and we've designed our entire product line around you and the way you like to study, learn, and master challenging subjects. Our approach is *The Smartest Way To Get Certified™*.

In addition to our highly popular *Exam Cram* and *Exam Prep* guides, we have a number of new products. We recently launched Exam Cram Live!, two-day seminars based on *Exam Cram* material. We've also developed a new series of books and study aides—*Practice Tests Exam Crams* and *Exam Cram Flash Cards*—designed to make your studying fun as well as productive.

Our commitment to being the *Training And Certification Destination* does not stop there. We just introduced *Exam Cram Insider*, a biweekly newsletter containing the latest in certification news, study tips, and announcements from Certification Insider Press. (To subscribe, send an email to **eci@coriolis.com** and type "subscribe insider" in the body of the email.) We also recently announced the launch of the Certified Crammer Society and the Coriolis Help Center—two new additions to the Certification Insider Press family.

We'd like to hear from you. Help us continue to provide the very best certification study materials possible. Write us or email us at **cipq@coriolis.com** and let us know how our books have helped you study, or tell us about new features that you'd like us to add. If you send us a story about how we've helped you, and we use it in one of our books, we'll send you an official Coriolis shirt for your efforts.

Good luck with your certification exam and your career. Thank you for allowing us to help you achieve your goals.

Keith Weiskamp
Publisher, Certification Insider Press

About The Authors

David Johnson is a manager at a large systems integration and maintenance company in Austin, TX. He served many years in the networking trenches, working his way up the food chain. When not working or writing, DJ enjoys billiards, food, cigars, and wine. DJ can be reached at **count0@texas.net**.

Todd Meadors is a Computer Information Systems (CIS) Instructor for DeKalb Technical Institute, a technical school outside Atlanta, GA. He teaches courses in networking and programming. He has a Master of Science degree in CIS from Georgia State University and an M.B.A. and B.B.A. from Mercer University. Todd also holds MCSE and CNE certifications. For fun, Todd enjoys weightlifting, playing with his kids, watching movies, reading noncomputer stuff, and spending two weeks at the beach each summer. He can be contacted by email at **ltmeadors@yahoo.com**.

John Michell is an independent Novell and Microsoft trainer, and the developer of Flashcards for Windows, the first study aid for people preparing to write certification exams. After several years in mainframe computer centers he spent some time in project management before discovering that his true avocation is training. When not training, writing, or creating the next Flashcards question set, he can be found making beer and wine or golfing. John can be reached at **jmichell@flashcards.com**.

Acknowledgments

First, of course, thanks to Ed Tittel and the staff at LANWrights for the opportunity to do something I really enjoy. Special thanks to MaryMary for managing this project with all of its unexpected twists and turns. Finally, thanks to Stephanie and Mama, the two "cats" in my life. Spending my days lounging is my new goal.

—*David Johnson*

Thanks to Ed Tittel at LANWrights for giving me the opportunity to write. Thanks to Mary Burmeister for guiding me on this project and to Kyle Findlay at LANWrights for handling my questions and invoices.

Thanks to Micki, my wife, who stuck by me during this project and picked up the slack when I couldn't. The "Y" sure is missing out on a bargain! Oh, Happy Mother's Day! A special thanks to my two kids, Zac and Jessie. They are good children and I appreciate them a bunch! Hang in there Zac, you're a smart boy! Hey Zac, I'm ready for the next Batman movie, are you? While I write this on the eve of Jessie's birthday, I'd like to say, "Happy Birthday, girl!" Save me some cake!

—*Todd Meadors*

I'd like to thank my wife Duff and my daughter Christine for putting up with my frequent absences and all the time I spend with computers. And I'd like to acknowledge the help and encouragement given me by my parents, Jack and Barbara Michell.

My thanks go also to Ed Tittel and Mary Burmeister at LANWrights for giving me a shot at this interesting endeavor of writing. It was fun, but harder work than I expected!

—*John Michell*

Contents At
A Glance

Table Of Contents

Introduction

Welcome to *Exam Cram for NDS Design and Implementation CNE*! This book aims to help you get ready to take—and pass—Novell certification Test 050-634, "NDS Design and Implementation." This Introduction explains Novell's certification programs in general and talks about how the *Exam Cram* series can help you prepare for Novell's certification tests.

Exam Cram books help you understand and appreciate the subjects and materials you need to pass Novell certification tests. *Exam Cram* books are aimed strictly at test preparation and review. They do not teach you everything you need to know about a topic, such as designing an NDS Directory tree, or all of the low-level details about how to create and populate User, Group, containers, and other objects in those Directory trees. Instead, we (the authors) present and dissect the questions and problems we've found that you're likely to encounter on a test. We've worked from Novell's own training materials, preparation guides, and tests, and from a battery of third-party test preparation tools. Our aim is to bring together as much information as possible about Novell certification tests.

Nevertheless, to completely prepare yourself for any Novell test, we recommend that you begin by taking the Self-Assessment immediately following this Introduction. The Self-Assessment will help you evaluate your knowledge base against the requirements for a CNE under both ideal and real circumstances.

Based on what you learn from that exercise, you might decide to begin your studies with some classroom training or by reading one of the many study guides available from Novell Press (an imprint of IDG Books Worldwide) or third-party vendors. We strongly recommend that you install, configure, and fool around with any software that you'll be tested on—especially NetWare 5 itself—because nothing beats hands-on experience and familiarity when it comes to understanding questions you're likely to encounter on a certification test. Book learning is essential, but hands-on experience is the best teacher of all.

Novell Professional Certifications

Novell's various certifications currently encompass six separate programs, each of which boasts its own special acronym (as a would-be certificant, you need to have a high tolerance for alphabet soup of all kinds):

➤ **CNA (Certified Novell Administrator)** This is the least prestigious of all the certification tracks from Novell. Candidates can demonstrate their skills in any of a number of areas of expertise. This certification requires passing one test in any of five tracks (three are specific to NetWare versions 3.x, 4.x, and 5; two are specific to GroupWise versions; for the purposes of this book, we assume the NetWare 5 track is the one for you). Table 1 shows the required test for the CNA certification. For more information about this program and its requirements, visit **http://education.novell.com/cna/**.

➤ **CNE (Certified Novell Engineer)** This is the primary target for most people who seek a Novell certification of one kind or another. Candidates who wish to demonstrate their skills in installing and managing NetWare networks make up its primary audience. This certification is obtained by passing six or seven tests, including five or six (depending on which track you pursue) required core tests and a single elective. Table 1 shows the required and elective tests for CNE certification in the NetWare 5 track. For more information about this program and its requirements, visit **http://education.novell.com/cne/**.

➤ **MCNE (Master CNE)** Candidates for this certification program must first prove their basic expertise by obtaining CNE certification. To obtain MCNE status, candidates must pass four to six additional tests in any of seven specialized areas. This is Novell's most elite certification. For more information about this program and its requirements, visit **http://education.novell.com/mcne/**.

➤ **CIP (Certified Internet Professional)** This certification program is designed for individuals who seek to step into one or more of a variety of professional Internet roles. These roles include that of Certified Internet Business Strategist, Certified Web Designer, Certified Web Developer, Certified Internet Manager, and Certified Internet Architect. To qualify, candidates must pass anywhere from one to five required tests, depending on which role they seek to fill. For more information about this program and its requirements, visit **www.netboss.com**.

Table 1   Novell CNA And CNE Requirements*

CNA

Only 1 test required	
Test 050-639	NetWare 5 Administration

CNE

All 5 of these tests are required	
Test 050-639	NetWare 5 Administration
Test 050-632	Networking Technologies
Test 050-640	NetWare 5 Advanced Administration
➤ Test 050-634	NDS Design and Implementation
Test 050-635	Service and Support
Choose 1 elective from this group	
Test 050-629	Securing Intranets with BorderManager
Test 050-628	Network Management Using ManageWise 2.1
Test 050-641	Network Management Using ManageWise 2.6
Test 050-636	intraNetWare: Integrating Windows NT
Test 050-618	GroupWise 5 Administration
Test 050-633	GroupWise 5.5 System Administration

* This is not a complete listing. We have included only those tests needed for the NetWare 5 track. If you are currently a CNE certified in NetWare 4, you need only take the CNE NetWare 4.11 to NetWare 5 Update test (Test 050-638) to be certified in NetWare 5.

➤ **CNI (Certified Novell Instructor)** Candidates who wish to teach any elements of the Novell official curriculum (and there's usually an official class tied to each of the Novell certification tests) must meet several requirements to obtain CNI certification. They must take a special instructor training class, demonstrate their proficiency in a classroom setting, and take a special version of the test for each certification topic they wish to teach to show a higher level of knowledge and understanding of the topics involved. For more information about this program and its requirements, visit **http://education.novell.com/cni/**.

Novell also offers a Master CNI (MCNI) credential to exceptional instructors who have two years of CNI teaching experience, and who possess an MCNE certification as well.

➤ **CNS (Certified Novell Salesperson)** This is a newer Novell certification and focuses on the knowledge that sales professionals need to master to present and position Novell's various networking products accurately and professionally.

To obtain this certification, an individual must pass a self-study class on sales skills and Novell products, as well as take regular product update training when it becomes available. This level of certification is intended to demonstrate a salesperson's ability to position and represent Novell's many products accurately and fairly. For more information about this program and its requirements, visit **http://education.novell.com/ powersell/**.

Certification is an ongoing activity. Once a Novell product becomes obsolete, Novell certified professionals typically have 12 to 18 months during which they may recertify on new product versions. If individuals do not recertify within the specified period, their certifications become invalid. Because technology keeps changing and new products continually supplant old ones, this should come as no surprise to anyone. Certification is not a one-time achievement, but rather a commitment to a set of evolving tools and technologies.

The best place to keep tabs on Novell's certification program and its various certifications is on the Novell Web site. The current root URL for all Novell certification programs is **http://education.novell.com/certinfo/**. But if this URL doesn't work, try using the Search tool on Novell's site with "certification" or "certification programs" as a search string. You will then find the latest, most up-to-date information about Novell's certification programs.

Taking A Certification Exam

Alas, testing is not free. Each computer-based Novell test costs $95, and if you don't pass, you may retest for an additional $95 for each try. In the United States and Canada, tests are administered by Sylvan Prometric and by Virtual University Enterprises (VUE). Here's how you can contact them:

➤ **Sylvan Prometric** Sign up for a test through the company's Web site at **www.slspro.com**. In the United States or Canada, call 800-233-3382; outside that area, call 612-820-5706.

➤ **Virtual University Enterprises** Sign up for a test or get the phone numbers for local testing centers through the Web page at **www.vue.com**. In the United States or Canada, call 800-511-8123 or 888-834-8378; outside that area, call 612-897-7370.

To sign up for a test, you need a valid credit card, or contact either company for mailing instructions to send them a check (in the U.S.). Only when payment is verified, or a check has cleared, can you actually register for a test.

To schedule a test, call the number or visit either of the Web pages at least one day in advance. To cancel or reschedule a test, you must call before 7 P.M. pacific standard time the business day before the scheduled test time (or you may be charged, even if you don't show up for the test). To schedule a test, please have the following information ready:

➤ Your name, organization, and mailing address.

➤ Your Novell Test ID. (Inside the United States, this means your Social Security number; citizens of other nations should call ahead to find out what type of identification number is required to register for a test.)

➤ The name and number of the test you wish to take.

➤ A method of payment. (As we've already mentioned, a credit card is the most convenient method, but alternate means can be arranged in advance, if necessary.)

Once you sign up for a test, you'll be informed as to when and where the test is scheduled. Try to arrive at least 15 minutes early. You must supply two forms of identification—one of which must be a photo ID—to be admitted into the testing room.

All tests are completely closed-book. In fact, you will not be allowed to take anything with you into the testing area, but you will be furnished with a blank sheet of paper and a pen or, in some cases, an erasable plastic sheet and an erasable pen. We suggest that you immediately write down all the information you've memorized for the test. In *Exam Cram* books, this information appears on a tear-out sheet inside the front cover of each book. You'll have some time to compose yourself, to record this information, and even to take a sample orientation test before you begin the real thing. We suggest you take the orientation test before taking your first test, but because they're all more or less identical in layout, behavior, and controls, you probably won't need to do this more than once.

When you complete a Novell certification test, the software will tell you whether you've passed or failed. Results are broken into topical areas that map to the test's specific test objectives. Even if you fail, we suggest you ask for—and keep—the detailed report that the test administrator should print for you. You should use this report to help you prepare for another go-round, if needed.

If you need to retake a test, you'll have to schedule a new test with Sylvan Prometric or VUE and pay another $95.

The first time you fail a test, you can retake the test the next day. However, if you fail a second time, you must wait 14 days before retaking that test. The 14-day waiting period remains in effect for all retakes after the first failure.

Tracking Novell Certification Status

As soon as you pass one of the applicable Novell tests, you'll attain Certified NetWare Administrator (CNA) status. Novell also generates transcripts that indicate which tests you have passed and your certification status. You can check (or print) your transcript at any time by visiting the official Novell site for certified professionals through its login page at **http://certification.novell.com/pinlogin.htm**. As the name of the Web page (pinlogin) is meant to suggest, you need an account name and a Personal Identification Number (PIN) to access this page. You'll receive this information by email about two weeks after you pass any exam that might qualify you for CNA or CNE status.

At the Novell certification site, you can also update your personal profile, including your name, address, phone and fax numbers, email address, and other contact information. You can view a list of all certifications that you've received so far and check a complete list of all exams you've taken.

Benefits Of Novell Certification

Once you pass the necessary set of tests (one for CNA, six or seven for CNE, four to six more for the MCNE), you'll become certified (or obtain an additional certification). Official certification normally takes anywhere from four to six weeks, so don't expect to get your credentials overnight. When the package for a qualified certification arrives, it includes a set of materials that contain several important elements:

➤ A certificate, suitable for framing, along with an official membership card.

➤ A license to use the appropriate Novell certified professional logo, which allows you to use that logo in advertisements, promotions, and documents, and on letterhead, business cards, and so on. As part of your certification packet, you'll get a logo sheet, which includes camera-ready artwork. (Note that before using any artwork, individuals must sign and return a licensing agreement that indicates they'll abide by its terms and conditions.)

➤ A subscription to the *NetWare Connection* magazine, which provides ongoing data about testing and certification activities, requirements, and changes to the program.

➤ Access to a special Web site, commensurate with your current level of certification, through the **http://certification.novell.com/pinlogin.htm** login page. You'll find more than your own personal records here—you'll also find reports of new certification programs, special downloads, practice test information, and other goodies not available to the general public.

Many people believe that the benefits of Novell CNA or CNE certification go well beyond the perks that Novell provides to newly anointed members of these elite groups. For years, job listings have included requirements for CNA, CNE, and so on, and many individuals who complete the program can qualify for increases in pay and/or responsibility. As an official recognition of hard work and broad knowledge, any of the Novell certifications is a badge of honor in many IT organizations, and a requirement for employment in many others.

How To Prepare For An Exam

Preparing for any NetWare-related test (including "NDS Design and Implementation") requires that you obtain and study materials designed to provide comprehensive information about the product and its capabilities that will appear on the specific test for which you are preparing. The following list of materials will help you study and prepare:

➤ The objectives for the course that relates to Test 050-634 appear in the information that Novell provides for Course 575 "NDS Design and Implementation." You can read these objectives on the Novell Web site at **http://education.novell.com/testinfo/objectives/575tobj.htm**. These will also define the feedback topics when you take the test, so this document should be an essential part of your planning and preparation for the exam. You might even want to print a copy and use it along with your other study materials.

➤ General information about Novell tests is also available, including what type of test will be delivered for each topic, how many questions you'll see on any given test, the minimum passing score (which Novell calls a *cut score*) for each test, and the maximum amount of time allotted for each test. All this information is compiled in a table called "Test Data" that you can read at **http://education.novell.com/testinfo/testdata.htm**.

In addition, you'll probably find any or all of the following materials useful as you prepare for the "NDS Design and Implementation" test:

➤ **Novell Course 575: NDS Design and Implementation** Novell Education offers a five-day class that covers the materials for this test at a level intended to permit anyone who's taken the 560 class (NetWare 5 Administration) and the 565 class (Networking Technologies) to completely master this material. Although Novell recommends these courses as prerequisites, they are not required to sign up for 575 (or to take the corresponding exam, 050-634).

➤ **Novell Press Study Guide** Novell Press offers a book titled *Novell's CNE Study Guide for NetWare 5,* by David James Clarke IV (ISBN 0-7645-4543-4) that covers all the objectives for Test 050-634, plus tests 050-639, NetWare 5 Administration, and 050-640, NetWare 5 Advanced Administration, in complete detail. The Novell study guides complement this book well, and we highly recommend them. We also recommend checking out another new Novell Press title for this subject called *Novell NDS Developer's Guide* by Chris Andrew, Bill Bodine, et al (ISBN 0-7645-4557-4) that adds a developer's perspective to the materials in the other book.

➤ **The Novell Support Connection CD** This monthly CD-based publication delivers numerous electronic titles on topics relevant to NetWare and other key Novell products and topics, primarily, "Monthly Update" CDs (there are two at the time of this writing). Offerings on these CDs include product facts, technical articles and white papers, tools and utilities, and other information.

A subscription to the Novell Support Connection costs $495 per year (a $100 discount is available to all CNEs and MCNEs as one of the benefits of certification), but it is well worth the cost. Visit **http://support.novell.com** and check out the information under the "Support Connection CD" menu entry for details.

➤ **Classroom Training** Although you'll find Novell Authorized Education Centers (NAECs) worldwide that teach the official Novell curriculum, unlicensed third-party training companies (such as Wave Technologies, American Research Group, Learning Tree, Data-Tech, and others) offer classroom training on NDS Design and Implementation as well. These companies aim to help you prepare to pass Test 050-634. Although such training runs upwards of $350 per day in class, most of the individuals lucky enough to partake (including your humble authors, who've even taught such courses) find them to be quite worthwhile.

➤ **Other Publications** You'll find direct references to other publications and resources in this book, but there's no shortage of information available about NDS Design and Implementation. To help you sift through the various offerings available, we end each chapter with a "Need To Know More?" section that provides pointers to more complete and exhaustive resources covering the chapter's subjects. This should give you some idea of where we think you should look for further discussion and more details, if you feel like you need them.

By far, this set of required and recommended materials represents a nonpareil collection of sources and resources for NDS Design and Implementation and related topics. We anticipate that you'll find that this book belongs in this company. In the following section, we explain how this book works, and we give you some good reasons why this book counts as a member of the required and recommended materials list.

About This Book

Each topical *Exam Cram* chapter follows a regular structure, along with graphical cues about important or useful information. Here's the structure of a typical chapter:

➤ **Opening Hotlists** Each chapter begins with a list of the terms, tools, and techniques that you must learn and understand before you can be fully conversant with that chapter's subject matter. We follow the hotlists with one or two introductory paragraphs to set the stage for the rest of the chapter.

➤ **Topical Coverage** After the opening hotlists, each chapter covers a series of topics related to the chapter's subject title. Throughout this section, we highlight topics or concepts likely to appear on a test using a special Exam Alert layout, like this:

> This is what an Exam Alert looks like. Normally, an Exam Alert stresses concepts, terms, software, or activities that are likely to relate to one or more certification test questions. For that reason, we think any information found offset in Exam Alert format is worthy of unusual attentiveness on your part. Indeed, most of the information that appears on The Cram Sheet appears as Exam Alerts within the text as well.

Pay close attention to any material flagged as an Exam Alert. Although all the information in this book pertains to what you need to know to pass the exam, we flag certain items that are especially important. You'll find what appears in the meat of each chapter to be worth knowing, too, when preparing for the test. Because this book's material is highly condensed, we recommend that you use this book along with other resources to achieve the maximum benefit.

In addition to the Exam Alerts, we have provided tips that will help you build a better foundation for NDS Design and Implementation knowledge. Although the information may not be on the exam, it's certainly related and will help you become a better test-taker.

This is how tips are formatted. Keep your eyes open for these, and you'll become an NDS Design and Implementation expert in no time!

➤ **Practice Questions** Although we talk about test topics throughout each chapter, this section presents a series of mock test questions and explanations for both correct and incorrect answers. We also try to point out especially tricky questions by using a special icon, like this:

Ordinarily, this icon flags the presence of a particularly devious inquiry, if not an outright trick question. Trick questions are calculated to be answered incorrectly if not read more than once, and carefully, at that. Although they're not ubiquitous, such questions make occasional appearances on the Novell tests. That's why we say test questions are as much about reading comprehension as they are about knowing your material inside out and backwards.

➤ **Details And Resources** Every chapter ends with a "Need To Know More?" section, which provides direct pointers to Novell and third-party resources offering more details on the chapter's subject. In addition, this section tries to rank or at least rate the quality and thoroughness of the topic's coverage by each resource.

If you find a resource you like in this collection, use it, but don't feel compelled to use all the resources we cite. On the other hand, we recommend only resources we use on a regular basis, so none of our recommendations will waste your time or money. But purchasing them all at once probably represents an expense that many network administrators and would-be CNAs, CNEs, and MCNEs might find hard to justify.

The bulk of the book follows this chapter structure slavishly, but there are a few other elements that we'd like to point out. Chapter 10 includes a sample test that provides a good review of the material presented throughout the book to ensure you're ready for the exam. Chapter 11 is an answer key to the sample test that appears in Chapter 10. We suggest you take the sample test when you think you're ready for the "real thing," and that you seek out other practice tests to work on if you don't get at least 77.5 percent of the questions correct. In addition, you'll find a Glossary, which explains terms, and an index that you can use to track down terms as they appear in the text.

Finally, the tear-out Cram Sheet attached next to the inside front cover of this *Exam Cram* book represents a condensed and compiled collection of facts and tips that we think you should memorize before taking the test. Because you can dump this information out of your head onto a piece of paper before taking the exam, you can master this information by brute force—you need to re-member it only long enough to write it down when you walk into the test room. You might even want to look at it in the car or in the lobby of the testing center just before you walk in to take the test.

Novell Terms

While studying for your NDS Design and Implementation test, you may come across terms that we represent a certain way in our material, but that are represented differently in other resources. Some of these are as follows:

➤ **NetWare Administrator** You may see this referred to as NWAdmin in some resources; however, NWAdmin is not acknowledged by Novell as a copyrighted term. Try not to confuse NetWare Administrator with NETADMIN, which is the text-based version of NetWare Administrator available in earlier versions of NetWare.

➤ **Network board** A network board is also called a network interface card (NIC), network adapter, network card, and network interface board. Novell uses the term *network board* most often. However, the network board vendors usually refer to network boards as NICs.

➤ **Application Launcher** You may see this called the Novell Applica-tion Launcher and sometimes abbreviated as NAL.

➤ **Novell Directory Services (NDS)** You may also see this service re-ferred to as NetWare Directory Services (it even appears as such on Novell's own Web site, **www.novell.com**). However, the official trade-mark name is Novell Directory Services.

➤ **NDS tree** The NDS tree is also called the Directory tree and some-times it's simply referred to as the Directory (with a capital D).

One general source of confusion (as is the case with NDS) is that some-times an "N" in an acronym is thought to stand for "NetWare" when it really stands for "Novell." As long as you know how to work the utility, you should be okay—the name isn't a huge issue.

How To Use This Book

If you're prepping for a first-time test, we've structured the topics in this book to build on one another. Therefore, some topics in later chapters make more sense after you've read earlier chapters. That's why we suggest you read this book from front to back for your initial test preparation. If you need to brush up on a topic or you have to bone up for a second try, use the index or table of contents to go straight to the topics and questions that you need to study. Beyond helping you prepare for the test, we think you'll find this book useful as a tightly focused reference to some of the most important aspects of the "NDS Design and Implementation" test.

Given all the book's elements and its specialized focus, we've tried to create a tool that will help you prepare for—and pass—Novell Test 050-634, "NDS Design and Implementation." Please share your feedback on the book with us, especially if you have ideas about how we can improve it for future test-takers. We'll consider everything you say carefully, and we'll respond to all suggestions.

Send your questions or comments to us at **cipq@coriolis.com**. Please remember to include the title of the book in your message; otherwise, we'll be forced to guess which book you're writing about. Also, be sure to check out the Web pages at **www.certificationinsider.com**, where you'll find information updates, commentary, and certification information.

Thanks, and enjoy the book!

Self-Assessment

Based on recent statistics from Novell, as many as 400,000 individuals are at some stage of the certification process but haven't yet received a CNA, CNE, or other Novell certification. We also know that easily twice that number may be considering whether to obtain a Novell certification of some kind. That's a huge audience!

The reason we included a Self-Assessment in this *Exam Cram* is to help you evaluate your readiness to tackle CNE (and even MCNE) certification. It should also help you understand what you need to master the topic of this book—namely, Exam 050-634, "NDS Design and Implementation." But before you tackle this Self-Assessment, let's talk about concerns you may face when pursuing a CNE, and what an ideal CNE candidate might look like.

CNEs In The Real World

In the following section, we describe an ideal CNE candidate, knowing full well that only a few real candidates will meet this ideal. In fact, our description of that ideal candidate might seem downright scary. But take heart: Although the requirements to obtain a CNE may seem pretty formidable, they are by no means impossible to meet. However, you should be keenly aware that it does take time, requires some expense, and consumes substantial effort to get through the process.

More than 160,000 CNEs are already certified, so it's obviously an attainable goal. You can get all the real-world motivation you need from knowing that many others have gone before, so you'll be able to follow in their footsteps. If you're willing to tackle the process seriously and do what it takes to obtain the necessary experience and knowledge, you can take—and pass—all the certification tests involved in obtaining a CNE. In fact, we've designed these *Exam Crams* to make it as easy on you as possible to prepare for these exams. But prepare you must!

The same, of course, is true for other Novell certifications, including:

➤ **MCNE (Master CNE)** This certification is like the CNE certification but requires a CNE, plus four to six additional exams, across eight different tracks that cover topics such as network management, connectivity, messaging, Internet solutions, plus a variety of hybrid network environments.

➤ **CNA (Certified Novell Administrator)** This entry-level certification requires passing a single core exam in any one of the five possible NetWare tracks, which include NetWare 3, NetWare 4/intraNetWare, and NetWare 5, plus GroupWise 4 and GroupWise 5.

➤ **Other Novell certifications** The requirements for these certifications range from two or more tests (Certified Novell Instructor, or CNI) to many tests, plus a requirement for minimum time spent as an instructor (Master CNI).

The Ideal CNE Candidate

Just to give you some idea of what an ideal CNE candidate is like, here are some relevant statistics about the background and experience such an individual might have. Don't worry if you don't meet these qualifications, or don't come that close—this is a far from ideal world, and where you fall short is simply where you'll have more work to do:

➤ Academic or professional training in network theory, concepts, and operations. This includes everything from networking media and transmission techniques through network operating systems, services, protocols, routing algorithms, and applications.

➤ Four-plus years of professional networking experience, including experience with Ethernet, token ring, modems, and other networking media. This must include installation, configuration, upgrade, and troubleshooting experience, plus some experience in working with and supporting users in a networked environment.

➤ Two-plus years in a networked environment that includes hands-on experience with NetWare 4.x and, hopefully, some training on and exposure to NetWare 5 (which only started shipping in August 1998, so nobody outside Novell has years of experience with it—yet). Some knowledge of NetWare 3.x is also advisable, especially on networks where this product remains in use. Individuals must also acquire a solid understanding of each system's architecture, installation, configuration, maintenance, and troubleshooting techniques. An ability to run down and research information about software, hardware components, systems, and technologies on the Internet and elsewhere is also an essential job skill.

➤ A thorough understanding of key networking protocols, addressing, and name resolution, including the Transmission Control Protocol/Internet Protocol (TCP/IP) and Internetwork Packet Exchange/Sequenced Packet Exchange (IPX/SPX). Also, some knowledge of Systems Network Architecture (SNA), Digital Equipment Corporation Network (DECnet), Xerox Network System (XNS), Open Systems Interconnection (OSI), and NetBEUI is strongly recommended.

➤ A thorough understanding of Novell's naming, directory services, and file and print services is absolutely essential.

➤ Familiarity with key NetWare-based TCP/IP-based services, including Hypertext Transfer Protocol (HTTP) Web servers, Dynamic Host Configuration Protocol (DHCP), Domain Name System (DNS), plus familiarity with one or more of the following: BorderManager, NetWare MultiProtocol Router (MPR), ManageWise, and other supporting Novell products and partner offerings.

➤ Working knowledge of Windows NT is an excellent accessory to this collection of facts and skills, including familiarity with Windows NT Server, Windows NT Workstation, and Microsoft implementations of key technologies, such as Internet Information Server (IIS), Internet Explorer, DHCP, Windows Internet Name Service (WINS), and Domain Name Service (DNS).

Fundamentally, this boils down to a bachelor's degree in computer science, plus three or more years of work experience in a technical position involving network design, installation, configuration, and maintenance. We believe that less than half of all CNE candidates meet these requirements, and that, in fact, most meet less than half of these requirements—at least, when they begin the certification process. But because all 160,000 people who already have been certified have survived this ordeal, you can survive it too—especially if you heed what our Self-Assessment can tell you about what you already know and what you need to learn.

Put Yourself To The Test

The following series of questions and observations is designed to help you figure out how much work you must do to pursue Novell certification and what types of resources you may consult on your quest. Be absolutely honest in your answers, or you'll end up wasting money on exams you're not yet ready to take. There are no right or wrong answers, only steps along the path to certification. Only you can decide where you really belong in the broad spectrum of aspiring candidates.

Two things should be clear from the outset, however:

➤ Even a modest background in computer science will be helpful.

➤ Hands-on experience with Novell products and technologies is essential for certification success. If you don't already have it, you'll need to get some along the way; if you do already have it, you still need to get more along the way!

Educational Background

1. Have you ever taken any computer-related classes? [Yes or No]

   If Yes, proceed to question 2; if No, proceed to question 4.

2. Have you taken any classes on computer operating systems? [Yes or No]

   If Yes, you'll probably be able to handle Novell's architecture and system component discussions. If you're rusty, brush up on basic operating system concepts, especially virtual memory, multitasking regimes, program load and unload behaviors, and general computer security topics.

   If No, consider some basic reading in this area. We strongly recommend a good general operating systems book, such as *Operating System Concepts*, by Abraham Silberschatz and Peter Baer Galvin (Addison-Wesley, 1997, ISBN 0-201-59113-8). If this title doesn't appeal to you, check out reviews for other, similar titles at your favorite online book-store.

3. Have you taken any networking concepts or technologies classes? [Yes or No]

   If Yes, you'll probably be able to handle Novell's networking terminology, concepts, and technologies (brace yourself for occasional departures from normal usage). If you're rusty, brush up on basic networking concepts and terminology, especially networking media, transmission types, the OSI reference model, networking protocols and services, and networking technologies, such as Ethernet, token ring, Fiber Distributed Data Interface (FDDI), and wide area network (WAN) links.

   If No, you might want to read several books in this topic area. The two best books that we know of are *Computer Networks, 3rd Edition*, by Andrew S. Tanenbaum (Prentice-Hall, 1996, ISBN 0-13-349945-6) and *Computer Networks and Internets*, by Douglas E. Comer (Prentice-Hall, 1997, ISBN 0-13-239070-1). We also strongly recommend Laura

Chappell's book *Novell's Guide to LAN/WAN Analysis* (IDG/Novell Press, 1998, ISBN 0-7645-4508-6), because of its outstanding coverage of NetWare-related protocols and network behavior. In addition, Sandy Stevens and J.D. Marymee's *Novell's Guide to BorderManager* (IDG/Novell Press, 1998, ISBN 0-7645-4540-X) is also worth a once-over for those who wish to be well-prepared for CNE topics and concepts.

Skip to the next section, "Hands-On Experience."

4. Have you done any reading on operating systems or networks? [Yes or No]

   If Yes, review the requirements stated in the first paragraphs after Questions 2 and 3. If you meet those requirements, move on to the next section, "Hands-On Experience." If No, consult the recommended reading for both topics. A strong background will help you prepare for the Novell exams better than just about anything else.

Hands-On Experience

The most important key to success on all of the Novell tests is hands-on experience, especially with NetWare 4.x, intraNetWare, and NetWare 5, plus the many system services and other software components that cluster around NetWare—such as GroupWise, Novell Directory Services (NDS), and the Netscape FastTrack Server—which appear on many of the Novell certification tests. If we leave you with only one realization after taking this Self-Assessment, it should be that there's no substitute for time spent installing, configuring, and using the various Novell and ancillary products upon which you'll be tested repeatedly and in depth.

5. Have you installed, configured, and worked with:

   NetWare 3.x? NetWare 4.x? NetWare 5? [Yes or No]

   The more times you answer Yes, the better off you are. Please make sure you understand basic concepts as covered in Test 050-639 and advanced concepts as covered in Test 050-640.

   You should also study the NDS interfaces, utilities, and services for Test 050-634, and plan to take Course 580, "Service and Support," to prepare yourself for Test 050-635. To succeed on this last exam, you must know how to use the Micro House SupportSource product, which costs more than $1,000 for a yearly subscription, but to which you'll have a week's exposure and after-hours access in Course 580.

You can download objectives, practice exams, and other information about Novell exams from the company's education pages on the Web at **http://education.novell.com**. Use the Certification|Test Info link to find specific test information, including objectives, related courses, and so forth.

If you haven't worked with NetWare, NDS, and whatever product or technology you choose for your elective subject, you must obtain one or two machines and a copy of NetWare 5. Then, you must learn the operating system and IPX, TCP/IP, and whatever other software components on which you'll be tested.

In fact, we recommend that you obtain two computers, each with a network board, and set up a two-node network on which to practice. With decent NetWare-capable computers selling for under $600 apiece these days, this shouldn't be too much of a financial hardship. You can download limited use and duration evaluation copies of most Novell products, including NetWare 5, from the company's Web page at **www.novell.com/catalog/evals.html**.

For any and all of these Novell exams, check to see if Novell Press (an imprint of IDG Books Worldwide) offers related titles. Also, David James Clarke IV has recently completed NetWare 5 upgrades to his outstanding *CNE Study Guide* series. These books should be essential parts of your test preparation toolkit.

6. For any specific Novell product that is not itself an operating system (for example, GroupWise, BorderManager, and so forth), have you installed, configured, used, and upgraded this software? [Yes or No]

If the answer is Yes, skip to the next section, "Testing Your Exam-Readiness." If it's No, you must get some experience. Read on for suggestions on how to do this.

Experience is a must with any Novell product test, be it something as simple as Web Server Management or as challenging as NDS installation and configuration. Here again, you can look for downloadable evaluation copies of whatever software you're studying at **www.novell.com/catalog/evals.html**.

If you have the funds, or your employer will pay your way, consider checking out one or more of the many training options that Novell offers. This could be something as expensive as taking a class at a Novell Authorized Education Center (NAEC), to cheaper options that include Novell's Self-Study Training programs, their video- and computer-based training options, and even classes that are now available online. Be sure to check out the many training options that Novell itself offers, and that it authorizes third parties to deliver, at **http://education.novell.com/general/trainopt.htm**.

Before you even think about taking any Novell test, make sure you've spent enough time with the related software to understand how it may be installed and configured, how to maintain such an installation, and how to troubleshoot that software when things go wrong. This will help you in the exam, and in real life!

Testing Your Exam-Readiness

Whether you attend a formal class on a specific topic to get ready for an exam or use written materials to study on your own, some preparation for the Novell certification exams is essential. At $95 a try, pass or fail, you want to do everything you can to pass on your first try. That's where studying comes in.

We have included a practice test in this book, so if you don't score that well on the first test, you need to study more and then locate and tackle a second practice test. If you still don't hit a score of at least 77.5 percent after two or more tests, keep at it until you get there.

For any given subject, consider taking a class if you've tackled self-study materials, taken the test, and failed anyway. The opportunity to interact with an instructor and fellow students can make all the difference in the world, if you can afford that privilege. For information about Novell courses, visit Novell Education at **http://education.novell.com** and follow the Training|Training Options link.

If you can't afford to take a class, visit the Novell Education page anyway, because it also includes pointers to a CD that includes free practice exams (it's called "The Guide" CD, and you can read more about it at **http://education.novell.com/theguide/**). Even if you can't afford to spend much at all, you should still invest in some low-cost practice exams from commercial vendors, because they can help you assess your readiness to pass a test better than any other tool. The following Web sites offer practice exams online for less than $100 apiece (some for significantly less than that):

➤ **www.bfq.com** Beachfront Quizzer

➤ **www.certify.com** CyberPass

➤ **www.stsware.com** Self-Test Software

7. Have you taken a practice exam on your chosen test subject? [Yes or No]

If Yes, and your score meets or beats the cut score for the related Novell test, you're probably ready to tackle the real thing. If your score isn't above that crucial threshold, keep at it until you break that barrier.

If No, obtain all the free and low-budget practice tests you can find (see the previous list) and get to work. Keep at it until you can break the passing threshold comfortably.

 Taking a good-quality practice exam and beating Novell's minimum passing grade, known as the cut score, is the best way to assess your test readiness. When we're preparing ourselves, we shoot for 10 percent over the cut score—just to leave room for the "weirdness factor" that sometimes shows up on Novell exams.

Assessing Readiness For Exam 050-634

In addition to the general exam-readiness information in the previous section, there are several things you can do to prepare for the "NDS Design and Implementation" exam. As you're getting ready for Exam 050-634, visit the Novell Education forums online. Sign up at **http://education.novell.com/general/forumlogin.htm** (you'll need to agree to their terms and conditions before you can get in, but it's worth it). Once inside these forums, you'll find discussion areas for certification, training, and testing. These are great places to ask questions and get good answers, or simply to watch the questions that others ask (along with the answers, of course).

You should also cruise the Web looking for "braindumps" (recollections of test topics and experiences recorded by others) to help you anticipate topics you're likely to encounter on the test. The Novell certification forum at **http://www.saluki.com:8081/~2/** is a good place to start, as are the Forums at **www.theforums.com**, and you can produce numerous additional entry points by visiting Yahoo! or Excite and entering "NetWare braindump" or "Novell braindump" as your search string.

When using any braindump, it's OK to pay attention to information about questions. But you can't always be sure that a braindump's author will always be able to provide correct answers. Thus, use the questions to guide your studies, but don't rely on the answers in a braindump to lead you to the truth. Double-check everything you find in any braindump.

Novell exam mavens also recommend checking the Novell Support Connection CDs for "meaningful technical support issues" that relate to your test's topics. Although we're not sure exactly what the quoted phrase means, we have also noticed some overlap between technical support questions on particular products and troubleshooting questions on the tests for those products. For more information on these CDs, visit **http://support.novell.com** and click on the "Support Connection CD" link on that page.

Onward, Through The Fog!

Once you've assessed your readiness, undertaken the right background studies, obtained the hands-on experience that will help you understand the products and technologies at work, and reviewed the many sources of information to help you prepare for a test, you'll be ready to take a round of practice tests. When your scores come back positive enough to get you through the exam, you're ready to go after the real thing. If you follow our assessment regime, you'll not only know what you need to study, but when you're ready to make a test date at Sylvan or VUE. Good luck!

Novell Certification Exams

Terms you'll need to understand:

√ Radio button

√ Checkbox

√ Exhibit

√ Multiple-choice question formats

√ Careful reading

√ Process of elimination

√ Adaptive tests

√ Form (program) tests

√ Simulations

Techniques you'll need to master:

√ Assessing your exam-readiness

√ Preparing to take a certification exam

√ Making the best use of the testing software

√ Budgeting your time

√ Guessing (as a last resort)

Exam taking is not something that most people anticipate eagerly, no matter how well prepared they may be. In most cases, familiarity helps offset test anxiety. In plain English, this means you probably won't be as nervous when you take your fourth or fifth Novell certification exam as you'll be when you take your first one.

Whether it's your first exam or your tenth, understanding the details of exam taking (how much time to spend on questions, the environment you'll be in, and so on) and the exam software will help you concentrate on the material rather than on the setting. Likewise, mastering a few basic exam-taking skills should help you recognize—and perhaps even outfox—some of the tricks and snares you're bound to find in some of the exam questions.

This chapter, besides explaining the exam environment and software, describes some proven exam-taking strategies that you should be able to use to your advantage.

Assessing Exam-Readiness

Before you take any more Novell exams, we strongly recommend that you read through and take the Self-Assessment included with this book (it appears just before this chapter). The Self-Assessment can help you gauge how your knowledge base stacks up against the requirements necessary for obtaining a CNE. Further, it can help you pinpoint areas of your background or experience that may be in need of improvement, enhancement, or further learning. If you get the right set of basics under your belt, obtaining Novell certification will be that much easier.

Once you've gone through the Self-Assessment, you can remedy those topical areas where your background or experience may not measure up to an ideal certification candidate. What's more, you can also tackle subject matter for individual tests at the same time, so you can continue making progress while you're catching up in some areas.

After you've worked through an *Exam Cram*, reviewed the supplementary materials, and taken the practice test, you'll probably know when you're ready to take the real exam. We strongly recommend that you keep practicing until your practice scores top the 77.5 percent mark (although you might want to give yourself some margin for error, because in a real exam situation, stress plays more of a role than when you practice). When you can consistently earn high scores on practice tests, you should be ready to go. If you get through the practice exam in this book without attaining 77.5 percent, you should continue to take other practice tests and study the materials until you master the information. You'll find details about other practice test vendors in the

Self-Assessment, along with pointers about how to study and prepare. But for now, let's discuss what happens on exam day.

The Exam Situation

When you arrive at the testing center where you scheduled your exam, you'll need to sign in with an exam coordinator. He or she will ask you to show two forms of identification, one of which must be a photo ID. After you've signed in and your time slot arrives, you'll be asked to deposit any books, bags, cell phones, pagers, or other items you brought with you. Then, you'll be escorted into a closed room. Typically, the room will be furnished with anywhere from one to half a dozen computers, and each workstation will be separated from the others by dividers designed to keep you from seeing what's happening on someone else's computer.

You'll be furnished with a pen or pencil and a blank sheet of paper or, in some cases, an erasable plastic sheet and an erasable pen. You're allowed to write down anything you want on both sides of this sheet. Before the exam, you should memorize as much of the material that appears on The Cram Sheet (in the front of this book) as possible. You can then write that information on the blank sheet as soon as you're seated in front of the computer. You can refer to your rendition of The Cram Sheet anytime you like during the test, but you'll have to surrender the sheet when you leave the room.

Most test rooms feature a wall with a large picture window. This allows the exam coordinator to monitor the room, to prevent exam-takers from talking to one another, and to observe anything out of the ordinary that might go on. The exam coordinator will have preloaded the appropriate Novell certification test—for this book, that's Test 050-634—and you'll be permitted to start as soon as you're seated in front of the computer.

All Novell certification exams allow a certain maximum amount of time in which to complete your work (this time is indicated on the exam by an onscreen counter/clock, so you can check the time remaining whenever you like). Test 050-634, "NDS Design and Implementation," is what Novell calls a *form test* or a *program test*. This test consists of a set of 68 questions and you may take up to 105 minutes to complete it. The cut score, or minimum passing score, for this test is 620 out of 800 (or 77.5 percent).

All Novell certification exams are computer generated and use a combination of questions that include several multiple-choice formats, interactive illustrations (sometimes called *exhibits*), and simulations. In short, Novell provides plenty of ways to interact with the test materials. These tests not only check your mastery of facts and figures about NDS design and implementation, but they also require you to evaluate multiple sets of circumstances and requirements. Sometimes, you'll be asked to give more than one answer to a question (in these cases, though, Novell almost always tells you how many answers you'll need to choose). Sometimes, you'll be asked to select the best or most effective solution to a problem from a range of choices, all of which may be correct from a technical standpoint. Taking such a test is quite an adventure, and it involves real thinking. This book shows you what to expect and how to deal with the potential problems, puzzles, and predicaments.

Most Novell tests, including "NDS Design and Implementation," that cover specific software products employ a sophisticated user interface, which Novell calls a *simulation*, to test your knowledge of the software and systems under consideration in a more or less "live" environment that behaves just like the original.

Many Novell tests, but *not* the "NDS Design and Implementation" exam, employ more advanced testing capabilities than might immediately meet the eye. Although the questions that appear are still multiple choice and so forth, the logic that drives them is more complex than form or program tests (like this exam), which use a fixed sequence of questions.

Eventually, most Novell tests will employ *adaptive testing*, a well-known technique used to establish a test-taker's level of knowledge and product competence. Adaptive exams look the same as form tests, but they interact dynamically with test-takers to discover the level of difficulty at which individual test-takers can answer questions correctly. Normally, when new tests are introduced in beta form (and for some time even after the beta is over), they are form tests. Eventually, most of these tests will be switched over to an adaptive format. That is, once Novell has run its question pool past enough test-takers to derive some statistical notion of how to grade the questions in terms of difficulty, it can then restructure the question pool to make a test adaptive.

On adaptive exams, test-takers with differing levels of knowledge or ability see different sets of questions. Individuals with high levels of knowledge or ability are presented with a smaller set of more difficult questions, whereas individuals with lower levels of knowledge are presented with a larger set of easier questions. Even if two individuals answer the same percentage of questions correctly, the test-taker with a higher knowledge or ability level will score higher because his or her questions are worth more.

Also, the lower-level test-taker will probably answer more questions than his or her more-knowledgeable colleague. This explains why adaptive tests use ranges of values to define the number of questions and the amount of time it takes to complete the test. Sooner or later, we expect this test, 050-634, to become adaptive as well.

Adaptive tests work by evaluating the test-taker's most recent answer. A correct answer leads to a more difficult question (and the test software's estimate of the test-taker's knowledge and ability level is raised). An incorrect answer leads to a less difficult question (and the test software's estimate of the test-taker's knowledge and ability level is lowered). This process continues until the test determines a test-taker's true ability level (presenting a minimum of 15 questions to all test-takers). A test concludes when the test-taker's level of accuracy meets a statistically acceptable value (in other words, when his or her performance demonstrates an acceptable level of knowledge and ability) or when the maximum number of items has been presented (in which case, the test-taker is almost certain to fail; no adaptive Novell test will present more than 25 questions to any test-taker).

Novell tests come in one form or the other—either they're form tests or they're adaptive. Therefore, you must take the test in whichever form it appears; you can't choose one type over another. If anything, it pays off even more to prepare thoroughly for an adaptive test than for a form test. The penalties for answering incorrectly are built into the test itself on an adaptive test, whereas the layout remains the same for a form test, no matter how many questions you answer incorrectly.

In the following section, you'll learn more about what Novell test questions look like and how they must be answered.

Exam Layout And Design

Some exam questions require you to select a single answer, whereas others ask you to select multiple correct answers. The following multiple-choice question requires you to select a single correct answer. Following the question is a brief summary of each potential answer and why it's either right or wrong.

Question 1

> What type of network traffic is generated to ensure that NDS objects are consistent in the replica list?
>
> ○ a. Limber
>
> ○ b. Heartbeat
>
> ○ c. Extended schema
>
> ○ d. Server Status Check

The correct answer is b. Heartbeat ensures integrity of the objects in NDS across replicas. Limber makes sure a server's name and internal address are consistent. Therefore, answer a is incorrect. The extended schema has nothing to do with network traffic. Therefore, answer c is incorrect. Server Status Check is started by a server with no replica. Therefore, answer d is incorrect.

This sample question format corresponds closely to the Novell certification test format—the only difference on the test is that questions are not followed by answers. In the real test, to select an answer, you position the cursor over the radio button next to the correct answer (in this case, answer b) and then click the mouse button to select the answer.

Let's examine a question that requires choosing multiple answers. This type of question provides checkboxes rather than radio buttons for marking all appropriate selections.

Question 2

> What are the repair operations that can be performed within NDS Manager? [Choose the four best answers]
>
> ❑ a. Repair Volume Object
>
> ❑ b. Repair Local Database
>
> ❑ c. Repair Replica Database
>
> ❑ d. Repair Network Address
>
> ❑ e. Repair Replica

The correct answers are a, b, d, and e. The repair operations that can be performed in NDS Manager are Repair Volume Object, Repair Local Database, Repair Network Address, and Repair Replica. Repair Replica Database is not a valid option. Therefore, answer c is incorrect.

For this type of question, more than one answer is required. As far as the authors can tell (and Novell won't comment), such questions are scored as wrong unless all the required selections are chosen. In other words, a partially correct answer does not result in partial credit when the test is scored. For Question 2, you have to check the boxes next to items a, b, d, and e to obtain credit for a correct answer. Notice that picking the right answers also means knowing why the other answers are wrong.

Although these two basic types of questions can appear in many forms, they constitute the foundation on which most of Novell's certification test questions rest. More complex questions include *exhibits*, which are usually screenshots of some kind of network diagram or topology, or *simulations*, which mock up some NetWare administrative utility, installation program, or other system component. (This test, 050-634, contains simulations, but no exhibits.) For some of these questions, you'll be asked to make a selection by clicking on a checkbox, entering data into a text entry box, or clicking on a radio button on a simulated screen. For others, you'll be expected to use the information displayed on a graphic to guide your answer to a question. Because software is involved, familiarity with important NetWare 5 administrative tools and utilities is the key to choosing the correct answer(s).

Other questions involving exhibits use charts or network diagrams to help document a workplace scenario that you'll be asked to troubleshoot or configure. Careful attention to such exhibits is the key to success. Be prepared to toggle frequently between the exhibit and the question as you work.

Test-Taking Strategy For Form And Adaptive Tests

When it comes to either kind of Novell test—be it a form test or an adaptive test—one principle applies: Get it right the first time. You cannot elect to skip a question and move on to the next one when taking either of these types of tests. In the form test, the testing software forces you to go on to the next question, with no opportunity to skip ahead or turn back. In the adaptive test, the adaptive testing software uses your answer to the current question to select whatever question it plans to present next. In addition, you can't return to a question once you've answered it on an adaptive test, because the test software gives you only one chance to answer each question.

On an adaptive test, testing continues until the program settles into a reasonably accurate estimate of what you know and can do, taking anywhere between 15 and 25 questions. On a form test, you have to complete an entire series of questions, which usually takes an hour or longer and involves many more questions than an adaptive test (68 questions for Test 050-634).

The good news about adaptive tests is that if you know your stuff, you'll probably finish in 30 minutes or less; in fact, Novell never schedules more than 60 minutes for any of its adaptive tests. The bad news is that you must really, really know your stuff to do your best on an adaptive test. That's because some questions are difficult enough that you're bound to miss one or two, at a minimum, even if you do know your stuff. Therefore, the more you know, the better you'll do on an adaptive test, even accounting for the occasionally brutal questions that appear on these exams.

Of course, it's also true on a form test that you must know your stuff to do your best. But for us, the most profound difference between a form test and an adaptive test is the opportunity to cover a broader range of topics and questions on the form test versus the randomness of the adaptive test. If the adaptive test engine happens to hit a hole in your knowledge base early on in the testing process, that can make it harder for you to pass, as the test engine probes your knowledge of this topic. On a form test, if some questions hit a hole, you can assume that other questions will appear that you'll be able to answer.

Either way, if you encounter a question on an adaptive test or a form test that you can't answer, you must guess an answer immediately. Because of the way the adaptive software works, you may have to suffer for your guess on the next question if you guess right, because you'll get a more difficult question next. On a form test, at least a lucky guess won't cost you in terms of the difficulty of the next question (but that doesn't mean the next question won't be a real skull-buster, too).

Test-Taking Basics

The most important advice about taking any test is this: Read each question carefully. Some questions may be ambiguous, whereas others use technical terminology in incredibly precise ways. Your authors have taken numerous Novell exams—both practice tests and real tests—and in nearly every instance, we've missed at least one question because we didn't read it closely or carefully enough.

Here are some suggestions on how to deal with the tendency to jump to an answer too quickly:

➤ Make sure you read every word in the question. If you find yourself jumping ahead in the question impatiently, read the question again.

➤ As you read, try to restate the question in your own terms. If you can do this, you should be able to pick the correct answer(s) much more easily.

➤ Some questions may be long and complex, to the point where they fill up more than one screen's worth of information. You might find it worthwhile to take notes on such questions and to summarize the key points in the question so you can refer to them while reading the potential answers to save yourself the effort of ping-ponging up and down the question as you read.

➤ Some questions may remind you of key points about NetWare tools, terms, or technologies that you might want to record for reference later in the test. Even if you can't go back to earlier questions, you can indeed go back through your notes.

Above all, try to deal with each question by thinking through what you know about NetWare 5, NDS, the administrative utilities, and other aspects of the system—its characteristics and behaviors—plus all the facts and figures involved. By reviewing what you know (and what you've written on your information sheet), you'll often recall or understand things sufficiently to determine the answers to the questions you'll encounter on the test.

Question-Handling Strategies

Based on exams we've taken, some interesting trends have become apparent. For those questions that take only a single answer, usually two or three of the answers will be obviously incorrect, and two of the answers will be plausible—of course, only one can be correct. Unless the answer leaps out at you (if it does, reread the question to look for a trick; sometimes those are the ones you're most likely to get wrong), begin the process of answering by eliminating those answers that are most obviously wrong.

Things to look for in obviously wrong answers include spurious menu choices or utility names, nonexistent software options, and terminology you've never seen. If you've done your homework for an exam, no valid information should be completely new to you. In that case, unfamiliar or bizarre terminology probably indicates a totally bogus answer. In fact, recognizing unlikely answers is probably the most significant way in which preparation pays off at test-taking time.

Numerous questions assume that the default behavior of some particular utility is in effect. If you know the defaults and understand what they mean, this knowledge will help you cut through many potentially tricky problems.

Mastering The Inner Game

In the final analysis, knowledge breeds confidence, and confidence breeds success. If you study the materials in this book carefully and review all the practice questions at the end of each chapter, you should become aware of those areas where additional learning and study are required.

Next, follow up by reading some or all of the materials recommended in the "Need To Know More?" section at the end of each chapter. The idea is to become familiar enough with the concepts and situations you find in the sample questions that you can reason your way through similar situations on a real test. If you know the material, you have every right to be confident that you can pass the test.

You should also visit (and print or download) the Test Objectives page for Course 575: NDS Design and Implementation (**http://education.novell.com/ testinfo/objectives/575tobj.htm**). Here, you'll find a list of 19 specific test objectives that will help guide your study of all the topics and technologies that Novell thinks are relevant to the 050-634 test. In fact, you can use this as a kind of road map to help guide your initial studying and to help you focus your efforts as you gear up to take your practice test(s)—and then, for the real thing when you're ready.

After you've worked your way through this book and the Test Objectives page, take the practice test in Chapter 10. This will provide a reality check and help you identify areas to study further. Make sure you follow up and review materials related to the questions you miss on any practice test before scheduling a real test. Only when you've covered all the ground and feel comfortable with the scope of the practice test should you take the real one.

If you take the practice test and don't score at least 77.5 percent correct, you'll want to practice further. Novell provides free practice tests on its "The Guide" CD. To obtain this CD, you must contact a local NetWare Authorized Education Center (NAEC) and request that one be sent to you. For more information on how to obtain this CD, you can use the Training Locator on the Novell certification pages at **http://education.novell.com** to locate the NAEC(s) nearest you.

Armed with the information in this book and with the determination to augment your knowledge, you should be able to pass the "NDS Design and Implementation" test. However, you need to work at it; otherwise, you'll spend the exam fee more than once before you finally pass. If you prepare seriously, you should do well. Good luck!

Additional Resources

A good source of information about Novell certification tests comes from Novell itself. Because its products and technologies—and the tests that go with them—change frequently, the best place to go for test-related information is online.

If you haven't already visited the Novell Education site, do so right now. The Novell Education home page resides at **http://education.novell.com** (see Figure 1.1).

> *Note: This page might not be there by the time you read this, or it might be replaced with something new and different, because information changes on the Novell site. Should this happen, please read the sidebar titled "Coping With Change On The Web."*

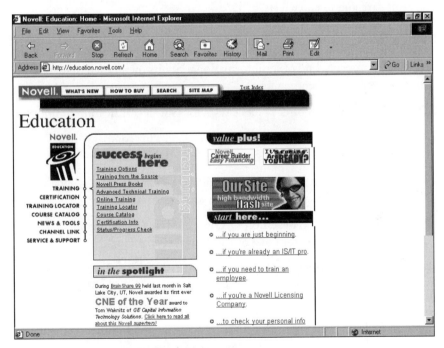

Figure 1.1   The Novell Education home page.

The menu options on the left side of the home page point to the most important sources of information in these pages. Here are some suggestions of what to check out:

➤ **Training** Use this link to locate an NAEC in your vicinity, to learn more about available training, or to request "The Guide" CD (which includes practice tests, among other materials).

➤ **Certification** This option is the ultimate source of all information about the various Novell certifications. Use this menu entry to find a list of the courses and related tests, including test objectives, test data, a testing FAQ (a list of frequently asked questions about Novell's testing policies, strategies, and requirements), and more.

➤ **News & Tools** Check this item to get news about new tests, updates to existing tests, obsolete tests that have been retired, and information about software and practice tests.

These are just the high points of what's available on the Novell Education pages. As you browse through them—and we strongly recommend that you do—you'll probably find other informational tidbits mentioned that are every bit as interesting and compelling.

The following vendors offer practice tests for Novell certification topics:

➤ www.certify.com is the Cyber Pass Web site. This company makes "CNEQuizr."

➤ www.stsware.com is the Self-Test Software Web site. This company makes practice tests for most of the Novell curriculum.

➤ www.bfq.com is the Beach Front Quizzer Web site. This company makes practice tests for most of the Novell curriculum.

➤ www.syngress.com is the Syngress Software Web site. This company has a set of NetWare 5 practice exams in the works. Visit the Web site for more information.

You can find still more sources of practice exams on the Internet if you're willing to spend some time using your favorite search engines.

Here's the bottom line about testing readiness: If you don't score 77.5 percent or better on the practice test in this book, you'll probably be well served by buying one or more additional practice tests to help you prepare for the real thing. It may even be cheaper than taking the Novell test more than once, and it will certainly increase the pool of potential questions to use as practice.

Coping With Change On The Web

Sooner or later, all the information we've shared with you about the Novell Education pages and the other Web-based resources mentioned throughout the rest of this book will go stale or be replaced by newer information. In some cases, the URLs you find here might lead you to their replacements; in other cases, the URLs will go nowhere, leaving you with the dreaded "404 File Not Found" error message. When that happens, don't give up.

There's always a way to find what you want on the Web if you're willing to invest some time and energy. Most large or complex Web sites—and Novell's qualifies on both counts—offer a search engine. On all of Novell's Web pages, a Search button appears along the top edge of the page. As long as you can get to Novell's Web site (it should stay at **www.novell.com** for a long time), you can use this tool to help you find what you need.

The more focused you can make a search request, the more likely the results will include information you can use. For example, you can search for the string

```
training and certification
```

to produce a lot of data about the subject in general, but if you're looking for the objectives for Test 050-634, "NDS Design and Implementation," you'll be more likely to get there quickly if you use a search string similar to the following:

```
050-634 AND objectives
```

Also, feel free to use general search tools—such as **www.search.com, www.altavista.com,** and **www.excite.com**—to look for related information. Although Novell offers great information about its certification tests online, plenty of third-party sources of information and assistance are available that need not follow Novell's party line. Therefore, if you can't find something where the book says it lives, start looking around. If worse comes to worst, you can always email us. We just might have a clue.

NDS Overview

Terms you'll need to understand:

- √ Novell Directory Services (NDS) or the Directory
- √ Objects
- √ Properties
- √ Schema
- √ Values
- √ [Root] object
- √ Container objects
- √ Leaf objects
- √ Common name
- √ Context
- √ Distinguished name
- √ Relative distinguished name
- √ Typeful and typeless names
- √ Trustee
- √ Rights
- √ Inheritance and the Inherited Rights Filter (IRF)
- √ Security equivalence
- √ Effective rights

Techniques you'll need to master:

- √ Understanding the NDS Directory, its role, and its benefits
- √ Learning the NDS object types
- √ Understanding NDS object naming
- √ Using NDS names with commands
- √ Implementing NDS
- √ Using NetWare Administrator to manage objects
- √ Comparing NDS to the bindery
- √ Understanding NDS security and maintenance

Novell Directory Services (NDS) is a database that provides you with the capability to manage, secure, and utilize network resources in an efficient and organized manner. NetWare 5 servers store the NDS database on their hard disks and make the resources in the database available to clients when the clients connect to the network. NDS also provides centralized management of the database. Managing NDS is one of the most important roles you, as an administrator, will have. One of the tools used to manage NDS is NetWare Administrator.

In this chapter, you'll learn what NDS is, its purpose, and its benefits. In addition, you'll learn about the objects that make up NDS, how they're named, how to use the NDS names with commands, and how to create objects using NetWare Administrator. Then, you'll learn how to implement NDS. We'll also compare NDS to the bindery (the NetWare 3.x resource database) and provide a brief overview of NDS security and maintenance.

What Is The NDS Directory?

NDS is a database collection of all the resources that can be used in a Novell network. Novell refers to NDS as the *Directory* or *Directory tree*. The Directory is hierarchical, or tree-like, in nature and provides a method of organizing network resources into manageable units. It's similar in function to the DOS/Windows file system structure.

> *Note:* *The NDS database is called the Directory. The capital D in Directory is to distinguish it from a DOS-based directory that holds other subdirectories and files.*

NDS stores the resources as *objects* in the database. Using NetWare Administrator, you'll create the objects in the Directory to match your organization. Now, let's look at the components of NDS. The Directory is composed of the following three components:

➤ Objects

➤ Properties

➤ Values

NDS Objects

An NDS object is used to represent a single piece of information, which may be made up of other smaller units of data. Each network resource appears as an object in the Directory. (NDS objects are covered in detail later in this chapter.) An object can be used to represent the following:

➤ **Physical resource** Physical resources include printers, users, workstations, and servers. Each of these will have an entry in the Directory.

➤ **Logical resource** NDS allows you to create objects that represent logical entities. For example, you can make users with similar functions members of the same Group object. The group doesn't physically exist, but it's used to logically associate users. This is typically done when implementing trustee rights. It's easier and more efficient to assign rights to a Group object than it is to assign rights to a lot of users individually.

Another example of a logical resource is a server volume. The physical volume can span over multiple hard disks or can occupy a portion of a single physical disk. A Volume object exists logically and represents the physical increment of hard disk storage.

A container is another example of an object that is a logical resource. A container logically groups other NDS objects.

 Think of an NDS object like a record in a database or traditional flat file system design.

NDS Properties

Each object in the Directory has properties associated with it. Properties are grouped together and in NetWare Administrator they are represented by tabs on an object's property page. Figure 2.1 shows a User object's Identification property page.

Every NDS object has a unique set of properties. For example, the following are some of a User object's properties:

➤ Last name

➤ Title

➤ Description

➤ Logon hours

➤ Password

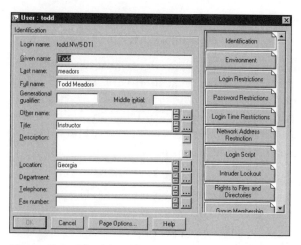

Figure 2.1   The Identification property page of a User object.

A Printer object, on the other hand, has these properties:

➤ Printer name

➤ Name of the print queue it serves

➤ Name of the print server that manages the Printer object

The properties in the Directory are defined in the *schema*. The schema is a set of procedures and rules that defines the structure of NDS objects, including the object name, required or optional attributes, and inheritance.

NetWare 5 comes with a pre-installed schema. You can elect to leave it as is (*base schema*), or you can change the schema (*extended schema*). Viewing and changing the schema is done through a NetWare 5 tool called NDS Manager. Figure 2.2 contains an example of a current schema shown in NDS Manager. (See Appendix A for more information about using NDS Manager.)

In Figure 2.3, you can see the attributes of a sample object—the User object. The Surname attribute of the User object is mandatory, which is why you must enter a Last Name value for each user you create in NetWare Administrator.

You can think of an NDS property as a field in a database or traditional flat file system design.

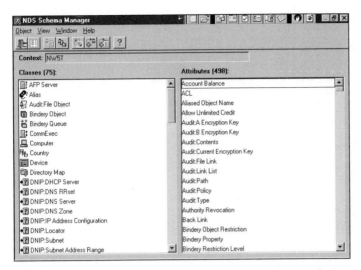

Figure 2.2   A view of the schema as seen with NDS Manager.

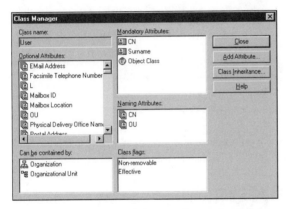

Figure 2.3   A view of the attributes for the User object via the Class Manager dialog box from the Schema Manager, which is part of NDS Manager.

NDS Values

Just as every object has a property, each property has one or more values. Refer back to Figure 2.1 and you can see that the Full Name field has a value of Todd Meadors. Some values are required by the schema and other values are optional. Objects of the same type have the same types of properties, but their values may be different. Different types of objects have different properties

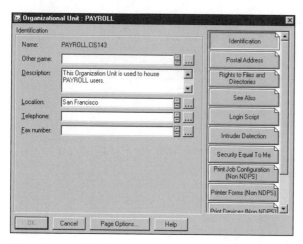

Figure 2.4   The Identification property page of an Organizational Unit object.

and, hence, different values. Figure 2.4 shows the properties of an Organizational Unit object. Notice how the values for this object differ from the values in the User object property page shown in Figure 2.1.

 You can think of a value as the actual data in a field in a database or traditional flat file system design.

In the following two sections, we'll explore the role of NDS and the benefits provided by NDS, respectively.

The Role Of NDS

NDS accepts requests for network resources by users on NetWare client workstations. The client requests the resource by name, and NDS searches for the object in the Directory tree. After the object is found, NDS attempts to determine the physical location of the resource. Then, it checks for several items based on the following criteria:

➤ Is the username valid?

➤ Does the user have the necessary rights required to access the network resource?

If the criteria are met, NDS connects the client to the resource. This process is known as the *request/response* sequence and occurs as follows:

1. A user at a client computer requests access to a network resource. The client computer issues a **GET NEAREST SERVER** packet.

2. The NetWare server that is physically closest to the user responds with a **GIVE NEAREST SERVER** packet.

3. The Directory on the server attempts to find the object's location in the tree. This is based on an indexing technique.

4. The physical location of the resource is found.

5. The client's username and password are validated.

6. The client's rights to the resource are verified.

7. The client gets connected to the requested network resource.

Now that we've had a chance to look at the role of NDS, let's take a look at the benefits provided by NDS.

Benefits Provided By NDS

When NDS is designed properly, the benefits are numerous. The following are just some of the benefits NDS offers:

➤ Centralized management of a network

➤ Accessibility by many client computers

➤ Quick access to network resources

➤ Object security

➤ Single-user login

➤ Logical organization of your network resources, regardless of the physical design

➤ X.500 naming standards

We cover these benefits in more detail in the following sections.

Centralized Network Management

NDS allows you to centralize management of the network. You can manage some aspects of NDS from a server using ConsoleOne and you can use certain NetWare Loadable Modules (NLMs) to maintain and check the health of NDS at the server. To access a server from a workstation, you run RCONSOLE from your workstation. You have to load REMOTE.NLM and provide a remote connection password, and then load RSPX on the server before you can use RCONSOLE on the workstation. To run REMOTE and RSPX on a server named NW-5, you'd enter the following at the server console:

```
NW-5: REMOTE
NW-5: RSPX
```

You can also fully administer NDS at a workstation using NetWare Administrator, which is an extremely powerful graphical tool. (See Appendix A for details about using NetWare Administrator.)

Accessibility By Many Client Computers

As mentioned, NetWare administrator is an extremely powerful graphical tool used to manage NDS from client workstations. You can run NetWare Administrator from any of the following client workstations:

➤ Windows 3.1

➤ Windows 95/98

➤ Windows NT Server

➤ Windows NT Workstation

 You can use NETADMIN (which is the text-based version of NetWare Administrator) on a DOS machine if you're running a NetWare 4 server. NETADMIN is not available on NetWare 5.

You have to install the Novell Client software to use NetWare Administrator on these workstations. The Client software is shipped with NetWare 5. The Client software for Windows NT Server/Workstation allows you to access Novell command-line utilities, such as **MAP, NDIR,** and **CAPTURE.**

Quick Access To Objects

NDS allows a user to quickly access objects in the Directory tree, because it uses an index method to look them up. This is similar to a table of contents or index in the back of a book. In NDS, you provide NDS the object name, and it finds the reference to the physical location of the object you requested.

Object Security

NDS promotes a strong security scheme because of inheritance. Rights flow down the NDS tree. By organizing objects in containers within containers, implementing security is easier. You apply the security at the container level.

Then, you put all the users that belong to the container in it. This minimizes your workload by allowing you to give and take away rights on a container basis rather than an individual basis.

Single-User Login

A user only needs to log in once to access any server in the Directory tree. This eliminates the need for a user to remember a username and password combination for every server to which they need access. In versions of NetWare prior to NDS, a user needed a username and password for each server.

Organization Of Network Resources

A major benefit of NDS is the capability it gives you to logically organize your entire organization. Regardless of the structure of your organizational chart, your physical topology, or your network, you can organize objects in NDS to fit your needs. This is done using container and leaf objects, which we cover in the "NDS Object Types" section later in this chapter.

X.500 Naming Standards

NDS conforms to the Open System Interconnection (OSI) X.500 standard for naming objects. The X.500 standard is compatible with the Internet. Object naming is discussed in the "NDS Object Naming" section later in this chapter.

> *Note: For more information on the X.500 naming standard, see the*
> *Exam Cram for Networking Technologies CNE book, also by Certification*
> *Insider Press, ISBN 1-57610-351-X.*

Now that you've had a chance to see the role of NDS and its benefits, let's take a look at the objects in greater detail.

NDS Object Types

As discussed, there are several types of NDS objects. They are as follows:

➤ The [Root] object

➤ Container objects

➤ Leaf objects

We'll look at each of these in more detail in the following sections.

The [Root] Object

The [Root] object is the top-level NDS object. It's analogous to the root, or \, in a DOS/Windows file system tree structure. The [Root] object is created when the server is installed. You cannot remove or rename the [Root] object.

There can be one and only one [Root] object in a given NDS Directory tree. It forms the basis for all other objects in the NDS tree. This object is always written with the square brackets around it. The [Root] object cannot be renamed, deleted, or moved with any NetWare tool.

In NDS, all other objects stem from the [Root] object—like branches on a tree, hence the name Directory tree. As mentioned, there can be only one [Root] object in an NDS tree; however, you can have multiple NDS trees. Figure 2.5 shows the objects under [Root], as seen via NetWare Administrator.

The [Root] object and the Directory tree names are different. The Directory name can be renamed using the DSMERGE utility.

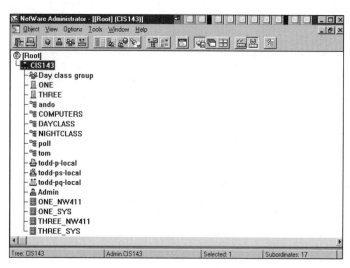

Figure 2.5   The [Root] object and the objects under it, as seen in NetWare Administrator.

Container Objects

As the name implies, container objects hold other objects, including container objects and leaf objects. They are analogous to directories/folders in the DOS/Windows environment. You would use a container object to represent your organization's divisions, departments, and workgroups. You can create three types of container objects:

➤ Country

➤ Organization

➤ Organizational Unit

The Country Object

The Country object is an optional container that is used to represent the country (or countries) where your network is located. You can use Country objects if your organization has divisions in multiple countries. This is an optional object, and when you name the Country object, you're limited to two characters. For example, US for the United States, UK for The United Kingdom, and FR for France. If you search the NetWare 5 documentation for "Naming Conventions-countries", you'll see a partial list of country names.

Country objects must be valid two-character country code abbreviations. A Country object can only be created in the [Root] object.

The Organization Object

This required object must be housed either in a Country object or directly within the [Root] object. You use this type of object to represent the name of your company or organization. For example, if you worked for My LAN Firm, you could name your Organization object literally My LAN Firm, spaces included. Another example would be for a nonprofit school named DeKalb Technical Institute, or DTI for short. The Organization object could be DTI.

You must have at least one Organization object. This is the first container that can have any leaf objects.

The Organizational Unit Object

An Organizational Unit object is created for the divisions or departments that exist within the overall organization. Therefore, Organizational Unit objects can only exist in the Organization object or other Organizational Unit objects. Example Organizational Unit object names include Payroll, Engineering, Production, and Marketing.

Table 2.1 shows the different container objects, what they can contain, and which containers can contain them.

Leaf Objects

Most of the objects in NDS are leaf objects. Network resources, such as users, printers, volumes, groups, servers, workstations, and print queues, are represented by leaf objects. Here are a few characteristics of leaf objects:

➤ Leaf objects can only be placed in Organizations or Organizational Units.

➤ Leaf objects cannot contain other leaf objects. Leaf objects are like files in DOS/Windows. Just as files contain data, leaf objects contain values.

➤ Container objects cannot be contained in leaf objects. In DOS/Windows, folders can contain other folders, but a folder cannot be contained in a file. The same rules apply.

Some of the more common leaf objects include the following:

➤ **Volume object** A volume represents either an entire disk or sections of one or more disks. Volumes are generally created at installation, but you can create a volume from the server console on free disk space. When you create a physical volume on free disk space, a logical Volume object is automatically created and placed in the same container that the server resides in. All system files get loaded to the SYS volume during installation, by default.

Table 2.1 Container objects and their characteristics.			
Container	**Can Contain**	**Can Be Contained In**	**Required**
Country object	Organization object	[Root]	No
Organization object	Organizational Unit objects and all leaf objects	[Root] or Country object	Yes
Organizational Unit object	Organizational Unit objects and all leaf objects	Organization and Organizational Unit objects	No

➤ **User object** The User object represents a user who can access network resources, such as files and printers. Every person who needs resources must have a valid User object. The name of a user's User object is his or her login name.

➤ **Printer object** The Printer object represents a printer on the network. This object allows users to print to a printer on the local area network (LAN).

➤ **Print Queue object** This object represents a storage area on the disk where the print jobs are held prior to printing. One of the Print Queue object's mandatory property values is the Print Queue Volume, which is the name of the Volume object on which the directory holding the print jobs exists.

➤ **Print Server object** This object represents the software that actually manages network printing.

➤ **Group object** This object represents a group of users who need common access to a resource.

➤ **Server object** This object represents the physical server. There's always a Server object in an NDS tree.

Note: *In NDS, the container that holds the object is called the object's parent. The object being held is called a child object. A container can be either a parent or child object. A leaf object is always a child object.*

Now that we've talked about the different object types, let's look at NDS object naming.

NDS Object Naming

The organization of the NDS tree impacts how NDS finds an object. Each object has a name, and NDS requires you to be precise when specifying the name of a resource. You also need to know the abbreviation codes for NDS objects. Table 2.2 contains a list of the various objects and their associated abbreviations.

Understanding the name of an object is imperative, because many command-line utilities, such as **LOGIN, CAPTURE, MAP,** and **CX,** require you to be fully name specific. One of the reasons NDS is particular about the name of an object is that NDS will not search the entire tree. This improves response time, because when you provide NDS with an object's complete name, NDS knows exactly where to look. For example, in Figure 2.6, there are two users named

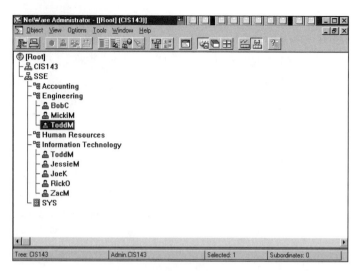

Figure 2.6   An NDS tree with identical users in different locations.

Table 2.2   A list of object abbreviation codes.

Object Name	Type	Abbreviation Code	Example
[Root]	Directory tree	Not applicable	Not applicable
Country object	Container object	C	C=US
Organization object	Container object	O	O=NOVELL
Organizational Unit object	Container	OU	OU=PAYROLL
All leaf objects	Leaf	CN (Common Name)	CN=ToddM

ToddM in different containers (one in Engineering and one in Information Technology). Therefore, you must specify the user's *context*, which is the location of an object in the NDS tree, so NDS knows to which object you're referring.

> *Note:* NDS *allows objects to have the same name as long as the objects are in separate containers.*

You need to be familiar with a few naming terms, including the following:

➤ **Common name** The name of a leaf object is referred to as its common name. In NetWare Administrator, the common name is the name next to the object's icon symbol.

Note: The maximum length of an object's name is 64 bytes, or characters.

➤ **Context** This is the actual position of the object in the NDS tree. The context of an object starts at the container in which the object is located and goes up, including all container objects to the [Root] object. This is similar to the path of a file name in DOS/Windows. In DOS/Windows, you refer to the name of a file by starting from the top, or root, and identifying each folder until you get to the file. In NDS, the name starts from the innermost object to the [Root] object, which is the reverse of how the files are referred to in DOS/Windows.

Note: Dots separate the container and leaf levels in NDS. This is an X.500 standard. The backslash (\) symbol is the separator in DOS.

➤ **Distinguished name** An object's distinguished name is the combination of its context and its common name. Distinguished names are unique. A distinguished name begins with a period, or dot, which signifies that the name must reference all containers all the way up to the [Root]. It fully distinguishes the object from any other object in the Directory. For example, in Figure 2.6, the user ToddM, in the Engineering department, has a distinguished name of:

`.CN=ToddM.OU=Engineering.O=SSE`

The other ToddM object has a distinguished name of:

`.CN=ToddM.OU=Information Technology.O=SSE`

The period between the names is used as a delimiter. This is analogous to a full pathname in DOS. Distinguished names are important, because if you don't account for the object's context using the distinguished name, the **LOGIN** command will fail. You'll see other commands that need the distinguished name in later sections.

 You cannot use periods at the end of distinguished names.

➤ **Current context** The current context is your current position in the NDS tree. The **CX**, or change context, command is used to set your current context in the NDS Directory tree. The **CX** command is comparable to the DOS **CD** command. If your current context is the same as the object's context, you can refer to the object by just the common name. For example, in Figure 2.6, if your current context is .Engineering.SSE, you could simply refer to the ToddM User object as ToddM.

➤ **Relative distinguished name** A relative distinguished name does not begin with a period; therefore, it does not necessarily reference the [Root]. The relative distinguished name is called relative because the name is used relative to your current context. When specifying a relative distinguished name, NDS creates a distinguished name from it. The relative distinguished name is added to the beginning of the current context.

Let's take a look at a few examples. If the relative distinguished name is CN=ToddM and the current context is OU=Engineering.O=SSE, the distinguished name is:

```
.CN=ToddM.OU=Engineering.O=SSE
```

On the other hand, if the relative distinguished name is CN=ToddM and the current context is OU=Information Technology.O=SSE, the distinguished name is:

```
.CN=ToddM.OU=Information Technology.O=SSE
```

 Remember this formula:

```
distinguished name = relative distinguished name +
    current context
```

Unlike distinguished names, relative distinguished names can have trailing periods at the end of their names. When NDS sees a trailing period, it'll remove one object from the left of the current context. It's like going up one level to the object's parent container. For example, let's say your context is OU=Accounting.O=SSE. After you enter the relative distinguished name CN=FredF., NDS takes the trailing period and removes one object on the left to create .CN=FredF.O=SSE. Another example is if your context is OU=XXX.OU=XX.O=X, and you enter the relative distinguished name CN=TM.., NDS will remove two objects from the left and create .CN=TM.O=X.

 You cannot use trailing periods with distinguished names. Trailing periods can only be used with relative distinguished names.

➤ **Typeful names** NDS typeful names use the abbreviations shown earlier in Table 2.2 to differentiate the various object types. The abbreviations are not mandatory. You've seen examples of typeful names earlier in this section. They are the examples that have the CN=*common_name*, OU=*organization_unit*, and O=*organization* prefixed before each object name. If you're using the typeful name, you must use the correct abbreviation followed by an equal sign and then the object name.

➤ **Typeless names** These NDS names refer to the objects without the abbreviation and equal sign. To illustrate, an example of a typeful name is:

```
.CN=DavidB.OU=Payroll.OU=Accounting.O=DeKalbTech
```

The typeless name for the same object is:

```
.DavidB.Payroll.Accounting.DeKalbTech
```

If you don't use typeful names, NDS attempts to calculate the attributes for the object. If NDS uses the wrong attribute, it cannot locate the object, which results in an error.

 Remember that with typeless names, you have *less* to *type* at the keyboard.

Using NDS Names With Commands

In this section, you'll learn to use common command-line utilities in conjunction with object names. The NetWare commands that you'll use with object names are **LOGIN**, **CX**, and **CAPTURE**. We'll cover each of these in more detail in the following sections.

The **LOGIN** Command

Let's look at how the object names are used with the **LOGIN** command. You use the **LOGIN** command at the workstation to perform many tasks, including:

➤ Logging into a specific server

➤ Logging in using context and typeful and typeless names

➤ Automatically setting the context at login

➤ Using objects with spaces in their names

We'll look at each of these in the following sections.

Logging Into A Specific Server

You can use the **LOGIN** command to log into a specific server. For example, to log into a server named DTI-2 with the username JoeK, you would type the following:

```
LOGIN DTI-2/JoeK
```

> *Note:* *You could also use the backslash (\) instead of the forward slash (/) to separate the server and username.*

The server name comes first, followed by the username. You could also leave off the server name, and NDS will log you into the nearest server. Of course, if you have a password, you'll have to enter that too.

Logging In Using A Typeful Distinguished Name

You can use the **LOGIN** command to log in using a typeful name. For example, a User object named AnnK exists in the Organizational Unit called Production, and Production exists in the Western Organization. To log into a server named CHEMICAL, she would enter the following command:

```
LOGIN CHEMICAL/.CN=AnnK.OU=Production.O=Western
```

Logging In Using A Typeless Distinguished Name

You can use the **LOGIN** command to log in using a typeless name. For example, a user object named DaveB exists in the Publishing Organizational Unit in the MBEnterprises Organization. To log into a server named MOUNTAIN, he would enter the following command:

```
LOGIN MOUNTAIN/.DaveB.Publishing.MBEnterprises
```

Automatically Setting The Context At Login

You can set the current context for users so that when they log in, they simply have to provide their common name. For a DOS-based workstation, this is done with an entry in the NET.CFG file, such as:

```
NAME CONTEXT=.OU=Engineering.O=SSE
```

Thus, when a user, for example, JohnB, issues the **LOGIN** command, he only has to enter his user login name, as follows:

```
LOGIN JohnB
```

Note that if the account had a value for the password property, John would be prompted to provide his password.

NDS uses **NAME CONTEXT** to locate the User object. For example, you have a user who happens to be the vice president of the company, and she doesn't want to have to enter the distinguished name when she logs in, as shown in the following command:

```
LOGIN .CN=MARYB.OU=Engineering.O=SSE
```

You can use the **NAME CONTEXT** statement in the NET.CFG file for a DOS connection to make her job easier. If she's a Windows client, however, you'd change the Context field on the Novell Login screen, as shown in Figure 2.7. To see the Context field tab from the Login screen, right-click on the Network Neighborhood icon, select NetWare Login, and click on the Advanced button. Make the necessary changes and click on OK to confirm. Now, the user only has to enter her username and password on the Novell Login screen. On either the DOS or Windows client, if the User object's context is not specified, the user will receive an error that states, "The login name is not in the specified context."

With version 3.1 of Novell's client for Windows 95/98, you can also right-click on the red Novell icon in the system tray to quickly access the NetWare Login program. This is also a handy way to view the properties of Novell Client32, which leads to another way to customize the Name Context setting.

Objects With Spaces In Their Names

You can use spaces in the name of an object; however, you must surround the whole NDS name with quotes when referring to the object with NetWare

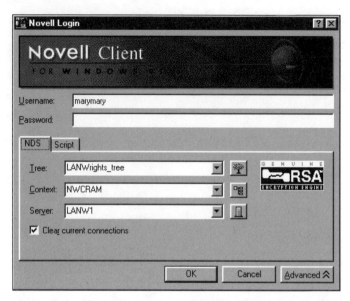

Figure 2.7   The Advanced settings on a Windows Client login screen.

command-line utilities. If you don't use the quotes around the entire name, you receive an error stating that NDS cannot find the object. For example, a correct entry is as follows:

```
LOGIN ".Zac Meadors.PRODUCTION.My LAN Firm"
```

In the following section, you'll learn how to use the **CX** command when using NDS object names.

The **CX** Command

The **CX**, or *change context*, command allows you to display either leaf and container objects in your current context in the NDS tree or set your current context to another container location in NDS. Now, we'll briefly discuss traversing the NDS tree with the **CX** command and displaying container and leaf objects with the **CX** command. (For detailed information about the **CX** command, see Appendix B.) To change your current context, you'd enter **CX** *container_name*. To see your current context, you'd simply type "CX" at the DOS prompt.

To go up one level higher in the tree to the parent object, you'd enter:

```
CX .
```

If you want to move up two levels, you'd enter:

```
CX ..
```

Suppose you wanted to go to a *sibling container*. (A sibling container is one that is a peer container.) For example, the container object CIS143 is the parent of the DAYCLASS, NIGHTCLASS, and EVENINGCLASS containers. DAYCLASS is a sibling container to NIGHTCLASS. If your current context is OU=.DAYCLASS.O=CIS143, you could go to NIGHTCLASS by typing in the following:

```
CX NIGHTCLASS.
```

Note that the preceding example uses the relative distinguished name and a trailing period. The next example uses the distinguished name:

```
CX .NIGHTCLASS.CIS143
```

To use the typeful name with the **CX** command, enter:

```
CX .OU=NIGHTCLASS.O=CIS143
```

> *Note:* *You must include a space after the **CX** command and prior to the period.*

The **CAPTURE** Command

The **CAPTURE** command is used on a workstation to trick the computer into thinking it has a local printer attached. You capture a local printer port and specify the logical printer or a Print Queue object that will hold the print requests until the printer is available. For example, let's say you have an NDS Printer object named HP_Laser, located in .OU=SouthEastern.O=TMI. In these examples, the server is called DTI-5. To enter a distinguished typeful name to correctly capture the printer for the local workstation, enter:

```
CAPTURE S=DTI-5 P=.CN=HP_Laser.OU=SouthEastern.O=TMI
```

To capture the same printer using a distinguished typeless name, you'd enter:

```
CAPTURE S=DTI-5 P=.HP_Laser.SouthEastern.TMI
```

To capture the printer using a relative typeless name, use the **CX** command to go to the container that holds the Printer object and then capture the printer, as shown in the following commands:

```
CX .SouthEastern.TMI
CAPTURE S=DTI-5 P=HP_Laser
```

For detailed information on the **LOGIN**, **CX**, and **CAPTURE** commands, see Appendix B of this book.

Implementing NDS

In this section, we'll take a look at a small company example. Assume a company named Short Stuff Enterprises (SSE) has several departments. The departments are:

➤ Accounting

➤ Engineering

➤ Human Resources

➤ Information Technology

Also, assume that each of these departments has users and printers. For SSE, each of the departments will be defined as Organizational Units; SSE is the parent container, and it's an Organization object. All the users in each department must be able to log in; therefore, there will be a User object created for each user. Human Resources users need to print, so the Print Server, Print Queue, and Printer objects are created in the HR Organizational Unit. There's also a SYS volume in the SSE Organization. Figure 2.8 shows an example of how this would look in NetWare Administrator.

Using NetWare Administrator To Create NDS Objects

In this section, you'll get firsthand experience creating two of the most common objects used in NDS: User and Organizational Unit objects. You'll also learn how to delete, move, and rename objects.

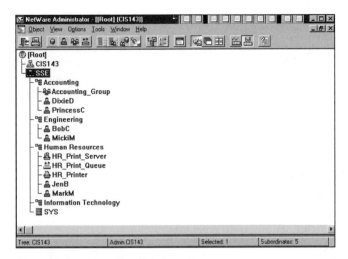

Figure 2.8 Short Stuff Enterprises.

Creating User Objects

To create a User object, follow these steps:

1. Open NetWare Administrator, select the container in which you want to create the user, and click on Object|Create.

2. Type "U" for User object, or use the scrollbar to locate the User object.

3. Type at least a Login Name and a Last Name and any additional information you want to enter.

4. Click on OK to finish.

 Alternatively, for Step 1, you could click on the Create User object icon in the taskbar, or right-click on the container, select Create, and choose User.

Creating Organizational Units

To create an Organizational Unit, follow these steps:

1. Open NetWare Administrator, select the container in which you want to create the Organizational Unit object, and click on Object|Create.

2. Type "O" to get to the Organizational Unit object, or use the scrollbar to locate the OU object.

3. Enter an Organizational Unit name and click on Create to finish.

Think "blue" is "true." What this means is when you click on an object in NetWare Administrator that is the object you are *truly* dealing with, it highlights the object in a blue background color. This helps minimize confusion. NetWare Administrator disables the ability to create an object if you click on a leaf object, but enables the ability to create an object if you click on a container object.

Deleting NDS Objects

Deleting an NDS object is rather simple:

1. Open NetWare Administrator and click on the object.

2. Select Object|Delete.

However, you cannot delete a container as long as there are objects in it. You can use the Ctrl or Shift key to highlight all the objects in a container, including the container itself, then click on Delete. You must highlight all the objects and the container or it won't work.

Moving Leaf Objects

To move leaf objects, follow these steps:

1. Open NetWare Administrator and click on the object.

2. Select Object|Move. The Move dialog box appears (see Figure 2.9).

 We refer to the browse button often in this book. Figure 2.9 points out the browse button.

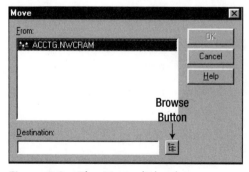

Figure 2.9 The Move dialog box.

3. Click on the browse button to the right of the Destination box. Browse the NDS Directory for the destination container you want.

4. Click on OK to confirm and the object gets moved.

 There are three ways to see an object's properties: double-click on the object, right-click and select Details, or click on Object|Details.

NDS Compared To The Bindery

Novell developed NDS for NetWare versions 4.x and higher. NDS replaces the bindery of previous versions. In NetWare version 3.x and earlier, the set of files that holds all the information about network resources is called the *bindery*. Each server holds its own bindery files. For a user to use a network resource on a NetWare 3.x server, the user must have a valid user login account name on that server and be *authenticated* by that server. If the user needs to log into a second NetWare 3.x server, the user must have a valid user login account name and be authenticated by that server as well.

Authentication is the process in which the server responds to a client's request for resources. When a user logs in, a request goes out for a server to validate that user and handle the user's requests. The server that's being logged into will respond to that request and validate the user's login name and password. Then, a network connection is made. By having a bindery for each server, you have more work to do than you would in an NDS environment. In a bindery situation, you have to add a user account to multiple servers for a user to access the necessary resources on different servers. This is where NDS is different. NDS allows a single user account login name for all the servers in the same NDS tree. NDS replicates the Directory to other servers in the same tree. Because all servers within a given tree have NDS in common, they are aware of each other and are able to validate any user login request. Even if a particular server doesn't have a copy of the Directory, it can forward the login request to another server. This server-to-server communication takes place in the background, and is transparent to the user. (Replication of the Directory is discussed in detail in Chapter 6.)

NDS Security

NDS allows you to secure your NDS objects and NDS properties. You might want some users to be able to view objects in a container, and you might want others to be able to look at just a user's phone number. You can implement both scenarios using NDS. But first, there are a few NDS security terms with which you need to be familiar:

➤ Trustee

➤ Rights

  ➤ Object rights

  ➤ Property rights

➤ Inheritance and the Inherited Rights Filter (IRF)

➤ Security equivalence

➤ Effective rights

We cover each of the preceding terms in detail in the following sections.

NDS Trustees

A *trustee* is an object that has been assigned access to another object. Trustees are added or deleted in the object's list of trustees. To view the trustees of a User object, select the object, right-click, and select Trustees Of This Object. Figure 2.10 shows the trustees for a User object named Buddy.

> *Note:* *The Object Trustees property is also called the Access Control List (ACL), and you'll sometimes see it referred to as the Object Trustees (ACL) property.*

Figure 2.10 NDS trustee list for an NDS object named Buddy.

NDS Rights

NDS rights are divided into two categories: object rights and property rights. NDS object rights control trustee access to the object itself. Specifically, object rights control viewing, deleting, and renaming an object. There are five NDS object rights, and they are listed in Table 2.3. You can also see some of them in Figure 2.10.

NDS property rights control what the trustee can do to the values stored within the properties of an object. Property rights allow a trustee to view, compare, search, and modify values in a property.

NDS object rights do not control NDS property rights, and NDS property rights do not control access to NDS object rights—with the exception of the Supervisor object right. If a trustee has the Supervisor object right, full control of all property rights is implied as well.

The NDS property rights are listed in Table 2.4 and shown in Figure 2.10.

With the Compare property right, you cannot see the contents of a property. It'll only return *true* or *false*, indicating whether a property is equal to a provided value.

When assigning property rights, you grant either All Properties or Selected Properties:

➤ **All Properties** This method allows you to grant rights for all the properties of an object at one time.

Table 2.3 NDS object rights.	
NDS Object Right	**Capability**
Supervisor	Gives a trustee complete control over an object including its properties.
Browse	Gives a trustee the ability to list and view objects in the tree.
Create	Gives a trustee the ability to create other objects in a container.
Delete	Allows a trustee to delete the object from the Directory.
Rename	Allows a trustee to change the name of an object—you actually are changing the name property.

Table 2.4 NDS property rights.	
NDS Property Right	**Capability**
Supervisor	Gives a trustee all rights to an object's property.
Compare	Allows a trustee to compare a given value to the value stored in the property.
Read	Allows a trustee to see the values in a property. Read implies Compare.
Write	Allows a trustee to add, rename, and modify a property's value. This implies the Add Self right also.
Add Self	Allows trustees to add and delete themselves as a value of a property.

➤ **Selected Properties** This method allows you to pick and choose to which properties a trustee has access. This comes in handy if you want someone to have access to one or a few properties instead of all the properties. For example, if you want a trustee to have access to another user's phone number, but not address, you could use this method.

Inheritance And The Inherited Rights Filter (IRF)

NDS rights flow down through the NDS tree. Remember that NDS uses the parent/child relationship, where containers hold other containers and leaf objects. With this in mind, Novell set up the NDS security mechanism so rights flow down from parent to child. This minimizes the amount of rights you have to assign on a trustee basis. If you design your NDS tree using division and/or department boundaries, you can take advantage of inheritance. If all your leaf objects are in one container, you might have to add and delete trustees to every object's ACL. This would be a security nightmare; therefore, NDS allows both object and property rights to be inherited, or flow down the tree.

 For property rights, only the All Properties rights can flow down. Rights assigned via Selected Properties are not inherited.

You can prevent rights from flowing down the NDS tree using one of the following methods:

➤ Block the inheritance using the Inherited Rights Filter (IRF).

➤ Assign the trustee different rights at a lower level in the NDS tree. By making a trustee assignment, you override the inheritance.

The IRF

The IRF is used to block the rights, which ultimately alter what a trustee can do at a lower level in the Directory. For example, in Figure 2.11, the [Root] object in a tree has the Supervisor, Browse, Create, Delete, and Rename rights, which are abbreviated as [SBCDR]. The rights flow down to the CIS143 and SSE Organizations. At the Engineering Organizational Unit, the IRF is used to block the Supervisor right; therefore, the users under the Engineering Organizational Unit only have the Browse, Create, Delete, and Rename rights—[BCDR].

You block the inherited rights by clicking on the Inherited Rights Filter button in the Trustees Of Object dialog box (shown in Figure 2.10). The resulting dialog box is shown in Figure 2.12.

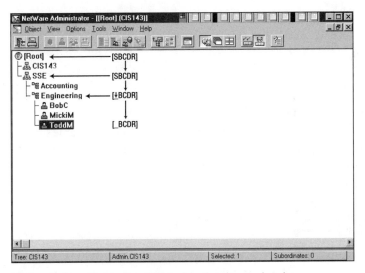

Figure 2.11 Using the IRF to block inherited rights.

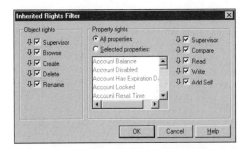

Figure 2.12 The Inherited Rights Filter dialog box.

New Trustee Assignments

The NDS rights can also be blocked by making an explicit trustee assignment at a level lower in the NDS tree. The new trustee assignment then becomes the rights that flow down from that point. See Figure 2.13 for an example. In this case, all the rights flow down until a new trustee assignment is made at the Engineering Organizational Unit that does not include the Supervisor and Create rights. This new assignment causes these rights not be inherited; therefore, the users under the Engineering Organizational Unit only have the Browse, Delete, and Rename rights (unless another trustee assignment is made at an even lower level in the tree).

Note: The IRF is called the Inherited Rights Mask (IRM) in earlier versions of NetWare.

The NDS Supervisor right can be blocked with the IRF; however, the Supervisor file system right cannot be blocked with the IRF. File system rights are not discussed in this book.

Security Equivalence

You can use the security equivalence feature to give an object the same security as another object. Additionally, a User object has an implied security equivalence to all parent containers—all the way up to and including the [Root] container object.

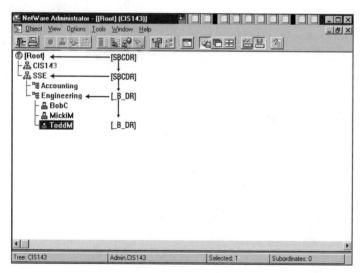

Figure 2.13 Making a trustee assignment at a lower level in the tree to change inheritance.

Effective Rights

The trustee's effective rights are what they can effectively do to objects at a certain point in the NDS tree. Effective rights can be:

➤ Inherited

➤ Filtered (blocked) by the IRF

➤ Granted through trustee assignment or group membership

➤ Created with security equivalence

Figure 2.14 shows the Effective Rights dialog box. To view this dialog box, click on the Effective Rights tab in the Trustees Of Object dialog box.

NDS Maintenance

You can maintain the NDS Directory using the server-based NLMs DSMERGE, DSREPAIR, DSDIAG, and DSTRACE. We'll cover these NLMs very briefly in this section, but for detailed information see Appendix B.

DSMERGE allows you to do the following:

➤ Check servers in the tree

➤ Check time synchronization

➤ Merge two NDS trees

➤ Rename an NDS tree

DSREPAIR is used to repair problems related to NDS database objects. The Directory can become corrupt, causing NDS to be unable to locate objects. Problems causing Directory corruption could occur because of sudden power outages or disk failures. To alleviate sudden power loss you could place an Uninterruptible Power Supply (UPS) on the server. This would give you enough

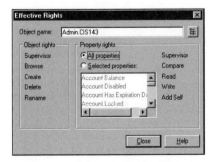

Figure 2.14   The Effective Rights dialog box.

time to gracefully shut down the server and minimize corruption of NDS. With DSREPAIR, you can perform the following operations:

➤ Repair the NDS tree in unattended mode.

➤ Repair time synchronization.

➤ Report synchronization status.

➤ View the repair log.

 Power outages can also cause volume corruption. You might have to run VREPAIR (Volume REPAIR) on the volume, too; the volume must be dismounted first.

The Directory Services Diagnostics (DSDIAG) NLM generates reports about the NDS tree, partitions, and servers. It can also help you to troubleshoot NDS problems. DSTRACE is used to check for Directory Services communication problems on the server.

Practice Questions

Question 1

> Which of the following are leaf objects? [Choose the two best answers]
>
> ❑ a. Volume
>
> ❑ b. Organizational Unit
>
> ❑ c. [Root]
>
> ❑ d. User

The correct answers are a and d. The Volume and User objects are NDS leaf objects. The Volume object represents logical storage on disk drives, and every person needing access to network resources must have a User object. An Organizational Unit is a container object and it holds leaf objects. Therefore, answer b is incorrect. The [Root] object is the top-level NDS object and is not a leaf object. Therefore, answer c is incorrect.

Question 2

> Which types of NDS rights allow a trustee to perform some type of action on an NDS object?
>
> ○ a. Property rights
>
> ○ b. Object rights
>
> ○ c. Inherited Rights Filter (IRF)
>
> ○ d. Effective rights

The correct answer is b. NDS object rights allow a person who has been granted rights (called the trustee) access to the object in some form. Property rights allow a trustee to access the values in a property. Therefore, answer a is incorrect. The Inherited Rights Filter (IRF) is used to filter, or mask, unwanted rights from flowing down in the NDS Directory tree. Therefore, answer c is incorrect. Effective rights are the true rights a trustee can use. Effective rights are what you can do after your NDS rights have been passed through the IRF or rights that have been explicitly granted. Therefore, answer d is incorrect.

Question 3

> You're a manager, and you're going on vacation. You want to temporarily assign a trusted employee the same rights you have so he can act as "manager" in your absence. What should you do to give this employee the same rights you have?
>
> ○ a. Give the other employee your login name and password.
>
> ○ b. Change the IRF to block Supervisor NDS rights.
>
> ○ c. Set Security Equivalence on the employee's User object to be the same as yours.
>
> ○ d. Create a new User object for the user with the same rights as yours.

The correct answer is c. By setting Security Equivalence on the User object to be the same as your User object, you're granting the trusted employee the same capabilities you have. If any issues come up while you are on vacation, the employee can perform the tasks you normally do. It's not a wise decision to give the employee your login name and password. No matter how much you trust someone, giving your User object's name and password to another individual is not advocated. Therefore, answer a is incorrect. If you change the IRF to block the Supervisor right, the employee would not be able to perform certain functions. Therefore, answer b is incorrect. You don't want to create a new User object for a temporary situation. Therefore, answer d is incorrect.

Question 4

> How many [Root] objects can be created in an NDS tree?
>
> ○ a. 0
>
> ○ b. 1
>
> ○ c. 64
>
> ○ d. An infinite number

The correct answer is b. There can be only one [Root] object, and it is automatically created when the first server is installed. The [Root] object cannot be deleted or renamed. The [Root] object differs from the name of the NDS tree, which can be renamed. Answer a is incorrect because there must be one [Root] object for each NDS tree. Answers c and d are both incorrect, because there can only be one [Root] container object created for an NDS tree.

Question 5

> Which of the following are considered typeless names? [Choose the two best answers]
>
> ❑ a. .CN=ToddMeadors.OU=TechnologyServices.O=BigCompany
>
> ❑ b. ZacMeadors.Production.LittleCompany
>
> ❑ c. MickiMeadors.HerCompany
>
> ❑ d. .CN=JessieMeadors.OU=Accounting.O=GirlsCompany

The correct answers are b and c. Typeless names do not have the abbreviation and equal sign in front of the object name. Answers a and d are incorrect, because they are typeful names. They have the abbreviation and the equal sign in front of the object name.

Question 6

> Which of the following are considered typeful names? [Choose the two best answers]
>
> ❑ a. .CN=ToddMeadors.OU=TechnologyServices.O=BigCompany
>
> ❑ b. ZacMeadors.Production.LittleCompany
>
> ❑ c. MickiMeadors.HerCompany
>
> ❑ d. .CN=JessieMeadors.OU=Accounting.O=GirlsCompany

The correct answers are a and d. Typeful names have the abbreviation and equal sign in front of the object name. Answers b and c are incorrect, because they are typeless names. They don't have the abbreviation and the equal sign in front of the object name.

Question 7

> Which of the following are distinguished names? [Choose the two best answers]
>
> ❏ a. CN=ToddMeadors.OU=TechnologyServices.O=BigCompany
>
> ❏ b. .ZacMeadors.Production.LittleCompany
>
> ❏ c. MickiMeadors.HerCompany..
>
> ❏ d. .CN=JessieMeadors.OU=Accounting.O=GirlsCompany

The correct answers are b and d. Distinguished names start with a period, which means they reference all the containers all the way up to the [Root] container. Distinguished names can be either typeful or typeless. Answers a and c are incorrect, because they do not have leading periods.

Question 8

> Which of the following are considered relative distinguished names? [Choose the two best answers]
>
> ❏ a. CN=ToddMeadors.OU=TechnologyServices.O=BigCompany
>
> ❏ b. .ZacMeadors.Production.LittleCompany
>
> ❏ c. MickiMeadors.HerCompany..
>
> ❏ d. .CN=JessieMeadors.OU=Accounting.O=GirlsCompany

The correct answers are a and c. Relative distinguished names do not start with a period. They are found relative to your current context. Relative distinguished names can be either typeful or typeless. Answers b and d are incorrect, because they have beginning periods.

Question 9

> Which of the following server commands or NLMs will fix the Directory after a power failure corrupts it?
>
> ○ a. DSDIAG
>
> ○ b. NetWare Administrator
>
> ○ c. DSREPAIR
>
> ○ d. DSFIXIT

The correct answer is c. DSREPAIR is a server-based NLM that allows you to repair the Directory if a problem exists. DSDIAG is used for NDS troubleshooting. Therefore, answer a is incorrect. NetWare Administrator is used to create, delete, and manage container and leaf objects from the workstation. Therefore, answer b is incorrect. There is no such command as DSFIXIT. Therefore, answer d is incorrect.

Question 10

> Which of the following allows you to rename the NDS tree?
>
> ○ a. DSMERGE
>
> ○ b. DSREPAIR
>
> ○ c. DSDIAG
>
> ○ d. DSTRACE

The correct answer is a. The DSMERGE utility is used to rename the NDS tree. You cannot rename [Root], but you can rename your tree. DSREPAIR is used to fix the Directory. Therefore, answer b is incorrect. DSDIAG is used to troubleshoot NDS. Therefore, answer c is incorrect. DSTRACE is used to watch for NDS problems. Therefore, answer d is incorrect.

Question 11

> You want to create a User object for a user. Which fields are you required to enter to create a User object? [Choose the two best answers]
>
> ❑ a. Login Name
>
> ❑ b. Given Name
>
> ❑ c. Last Name
>
> ❑ d. Title

The correct answers are a and c. To create a user, you must enter values for the Login Name and Last Name fields. This requirement is built into the base schema. You're not required to enter the Given Name or Title. Therefore, answers b and d are incorrect.

Question 12

> What is the maximum number of characters you can use to name an NDS object?
>
> ○ a. 1
>
> ○ b. 2
>
> ○ c. 32
>
> ○ d. 64

The correct answer is d. You can name an object with up to 64 characters. Therefore, answers a, b, and c are incorrect.

Question 13

What is the schema called after you modify it?

○ a. Base

○ b. Extended

○ c. Expanded

○ d. Secure

The correct answer is b. The schema that comes with NetWare is called the base schema. If you modify the base schema in some way, it's called the extended schema. The base schema is the non-modified form. Therefore, answer a is incorrect. There are no such things as expanded and secure schemas in NetWare. Therefore, answers c and d are incorrect.

Need To Know More?

 Hughes, Jeffrey F. and Blair W. Thomas. *Novell's Four Principles of NDS Design*. Novell Press, San Jose, CA, 1996. ISBN 0-7645-4522-1. Chapters 1 and 2 of this book contain information relevant to this chapter.

 Simpson, Ted L. *Hands-On NetWare*. Course Technology, Cambridge, MA, 1998. ISBN 0-7600-5861-X. Chapters 2 and 3 of this book contain information relevant to this chapter.

 For additional information about partitioning and NDS Manager, review the NetWare 5 online documentation. Use the keywords "NDS" and "object".

NDS Project
Preparation

Terms you'll need to understand:

√ Project manager

√ NDS expert

√ Server administrator

√ Connectivity specialist

√ Project approach

√ Design

√ Implementation

√ Design analysis

Techniques you'll need to master:

√ Understanding the benefits of successful NDS design and the impact on a network

√ Knowing the two primary influences on NDS design

√ Understanding the roles and responsibilities involved in the NDS design process

√ Using the phases of an NDS design project

One very important aspect of NDS design, particularly when studying for the NDS test, is understanding the project processes involved. In this chapter, we'll review the effects that your NDS design has on network operation and the various roles and phases of a design project.

NDS And The Successful Network

Because the Novell Directory Services (NDS) database acts as the central repository for network information, such as user and group accounts, printers, NetWare volumes, and servers, its design is important to the efficient operation of a network. This information serves as the infrastructure for the network, providing secure and effective operation. For all intents and purposes, all network services on an NDS network rely on NDS in some way. Because of this, an effective NDS design can increase a network's value and enhance its performance by allowing it to run more efficiently and securely. In addition, an effective NDS design can help provide a high level of fault tolerance.

Although a successful NDS design allows for better network performance, it should be noted that the inherent robustness of NDS means that it can effectively operate on any network—even one in which NDS operation is not a design consideration. For example, many NetWare 5 networks grew from existing technologies that did not incorporate the NDS design principles. NDS will operate well enough on these networks, but poorly designed NDS implementations impede network performance, decrease the network's manageability, and can affect access to network resources. As you'll learn later in this chapter, part of the design process for NDS is evaluating NDS operation on an ongoing basis to determine whether the best design is in place. This evaluation period should also be applied to networks that have grown into NDS from other technologies.

More often than not, inefficient NDS designs stem from a lack of knowledge, or application, of the NDS design principles. On the other hand, effective NDS designs are realized when those involved in the process understand the principles involved and create an implementation planned to achieve specific design goals.

Results Of Effective NDS Design

Perhaps the first question is: What results will I see if I follow the design goals and create a well-designed NDS implementation? First and foremost, an efficient design provides users easy access to network resources. This is done by consistently placing network resources in a logical position in the NDS tree, ensuring users are always aware of the location of resources and the steps required to access those resources.

An effective NDS design should include standards for naming, locating, and managing network resources. In addition, a successful NDS design allows network administrators to easily secure network resources from uninvited guests, and to assign administrative rights to key personnel for select branches or objects within the tree.

Of course, one of the most important aspects of effective Directory design is efficient, rapid access to network resources. As you'll learn throughout this text, through NDS design, you're able to place resources close to users and groups, increasing overall performance. The most effective Directory tree designs also include a high degree of fault tolerance, which minimizes the impact of an equipment failure. Following the "don't put all your eggs in one basket" adage, you can distribute your Directory over multiple servers, ensuring that, in the event that one fails, users will still be able to log in and access other network resources.

And, last but not least, a good NDS design scales easily to include additional users and services as the network grows. As you've probably experienced, the vast majority of networks grow over time. As the size of a company increases, the NDS tree must grow with it. Throughout this text, we'll look at how an NDS Directory's design is affected by merging two companies—Munson Media and Burmeister Publishing—and how a successful design easily expands to accommodate such acquisitions.

How Do You Do It?

On the highest level, a successful NDS design necessitates following a specific design process that identifies the benefits you expect to achieve for your organization. The design process must follow the standard design strategies discussed in later chapters of this book, and it determines the skill sets needed to accomplish the design. In addition, the process utilizes the structure of NDS to optimize its operation through partition replication and resource accessibility.

Of course, no single NDS design will work for every network. Because of this, a specific design must be created for each network. Along the same lines, as we mentioned earlier, a design cannot remain static while a network grows and changes. This makes periodically reevaluating your NDS design a necessity as well. During the reevaluation phase, you should elicit input not only from technically adept users, but from your average users as well. This will help you develop an accurate picture of how the network (and the NDS Directory) is performing.

There are two primary considerations when developing the highest levels of your NDS design: the organizational structure of your company and the physical layout of your network. If you start on your NDS design without considering your network layout, how your organization operates, or how NDS functions, you're setting your Directory design up for failure.

Because NDS operation is affected by your company's operational structure, one of the first steps in your design process is obtaining and reviewing your company's organizational chart. You must also determine the flow of work within the organization, who works with whom, and who needs access to which resources. In addition, you can identify the skills needed to complete and implement your NDS design. Then, the next logical step is to determine whether your organization has personnel that possess the skills required to complete the implementation. Finally, after you've identified the skills your team needs and put your team together, you'll need to manage the people involved in the design and implementation process to ensure that the process runs smoothly. The organizational design phase of the process is, in essence, the combination of determining the layout of the organization, understanding the workflow between individuals and departments, and utilizing the people within the organization who have the requisite skills.

The technical phase of the NDS design process involves designing the Directory tree to incorporate all the recommended design requirements and then optimizing the tree for efficient resource access throughout ongoing network conditions, including foreseen and unforeseen changes. To completely ensure your NDS tree functions at its optimal performance, you must consider both the operational and technical questions during design. Neither phase is independent of the other: A change in the organizational structure of a company will affect network performance and vice versa. A successful NDS design is a combination, or synthesis, of the two phases.

You must remember throughout the design process that your network will eventually change and your NDS design must be reevaluated at regular intervals. For this reason, your design plan should always include an evaluation phase.

Your NDS Project Team And Tasks

A large part of the organizational design phase consists of identifying the skills needed to design and implement your NDS tree, outlining the tasks required, and determining the personnel requirements. Most often, there are four major roles that take part in the NDS design and implementation process:

→ Project manager

→ NDS expert

→ Server administrator

→ Connectivity specialist

Each of the previous roles are discussed in the following sections. Although some organizations are large enough to justify at least one person in each of the design roles, there are many instances in which one person might have to wear multiple hats. To alleviate this problem, when possible, many companies hire consultants to assist their in-house staff with the NDS design project. If your organization is large enough and the consultants are available, user-side experts, such as printing experts, workstation experts, and application specialists, can assist with the design process.

What Does A Project Manager Do?

The NDS project manager is the coordinating and driving force behind the NDS design and implementation process. This role can be filled by a manager at any level of the IS department, preferably a senior manager of the administrators or server support staff. It's the project manager's primary responsibility to move the project along the set schedule and ensure timely completion. The project manager does this by maintaining the project's focus and schedule, as well as coordinating communication within the team and with others in the organization.

The project manager coordinates with the NDS expert on the team to ensure that the new implementation does not disrupt continuing network operations. In addition, the project manager is responsible for locating and acquiring the necessary resources and funding to complete the NDS design and implementation. The project manager then manages the design phase of the project and coordinates the implementation. To effectively manage the complete NDS design and implementation process, the project manager must be intimately familiar with all aspects of the company. The project manager's grasp of the "big picture" facilitates a successful NDS design. Along the same lines, the project manager must ensure that the new design is best suited to the organization's workflow and layout.

The project manager directs all phases of the project and coordinates communication among the team and upper management so they can discuss concerns and roadblocks as they appear. The project manager must also, after obtaining the resources and funding, manage the budget and project schedule. Of course, no project can run without efficient meetings, so it's the project manager's job to coordinate meetings and ensure they stay on track and do not extend beyond their allotted time. In addition to overseeing the project team and its tasks, the project manager should act as the liaison between the team and the rest of the company, educating the organization on the changes that will be made when the new NDS design is implemented.

As part of the project manager's responsibilities to oversee the entire project, the project manager must also evaluate software and determine the costs for implementation and operation, and the cost of licensing the software. The project manager should ultimately be concerned that the new design is effective and efficient, and services the user base. As part of the implementation process, the project manager must develop a timeline for project completion that includes administrator training, end-user training, implementation testing, a pilot rollout, and a complete process for the full rollout. Finally, after the project is complete, the project manager must ensure that users have adequate support.

What Does An NDS Expert Do?

An NDS expert is typically a person within an organization who has the most experience with NDS or has completed Novell-approved NetWare 5 and NDS training. Often, this particular role is fulfilled by a consultant or someone outside the core organization. This is because the NDS expert is ultimately responsible for the technical operation of the new design. In this role, the NDS expert must ensure that the new NDS design is complete and meets the entire organization's needs. Whereas the project manager handles all aspects of the project, the NDS expert often manages the inner-workings of the project team. The NDS expert must meet the project manager's timeline and ensure that each member of the project team is productive. It's also the NDS expert's job to design the NDS tree and the security that will be implemented.

Because the NDS expert handles the technical application of the design, he or she must manage the expectations of upper-management and other departments within the organization as they are presented by the project manager. The NDS expert also handles coordination of login scripts and other NetWare-specific considerations and manages the interaction between the groups involved in the project. Finally, the NDS expert must designate someone, often themselves, to document the design and the implementation of NDS.

What Does A Server Administrator Do?

On a project team, the server administrator is a person who works daily with the NetWare servers on the network. The server administrator must, first and foremost, ensure that the network continues operation and efficient performance throughout the project. After receiving the implementation strategy from the NDS expert, the server administrator handles the configuration of the time synchronization portion of the design. The server administrator also takes on the responsibility of planning the pilot rollout and ensuring its successful completion. Once the pilot rollout is complete and has been deemed successful, the server administrator handles the intricacies of the implementation and rollout to all departments in the organization.

Because server administrators have the greatest working knowledge of the company's NetWare servers, they manage the placement of the servers within the NDS tree and plan the process for adding and removing servers when necessary. In addition, they must be sure that the new design is backward compatible with existing workstations and servers on the network. They are also responsible for adding the new design to the disaster-recovery strategy used by the organization. Finally, the server administrator determines the disk space required for all existing servers and new servers as they are added to the NDS tree.

What Does A Connectivity Specialist Do?

Within the NDS project implementation team, the connectivity specialist manages the physical network itself. This includes all networking devices and connections, including the backbone, wide area network (WAN) connections, the relationships with the telecommunications companies, bridges, routers, and Internet connections. Because many of today's enterprise networks span WAN links, the connectivity specialist plays a key role in the implementation. In this role, the connectivity specialist manages the use of routing techniques, protocols, telecommunications, and the WAN structure and their effect on the NDS design. The connectivity specialist also makes decisions on whether to use a single protocol or multiple protocols based on the needs of the network.

Because the connectivity specialist handles the physical structure of the network, he or she is responsible for ensuring that network traffic throughput is maintained throughout the length of the project and after the complete implementation. The connectivity specialist should advise the implementation team on the use of existing and new routing issues, protocols, and WAN structure. The connectivity specialist must also advise the team on the implications of the NDS design on WAN traffic. This includes determining the efficiency of the new design and identifying possible bandwidth issues on the local area network (LAN) and WAN. To do this, the connectivity expert must establish current utilization levels and monitor utilization throughout the project. Finally, the responsibility for maintaining connectivity to other network hosts and operating systems belongs to the connectivity specialist.

Table 3.1 outlines the important points to remember regarding each of the major roles in the NDS design process.

Table 3.1 NDS design role responsibilities.		
Role	**Description**	**Responsibilities**
Project manager	Filled by any level of manager	Creates schedules and timelines
		Knows all areas of the company
		Maintains project focus
		Understands the big picture
		Coordinates communication amongst team members
		Manages the budget
		Handles resource identification and acquisitions
		Acts as a liaison between the project team and the company
NDS expert	Employee with most experience with NDS or a consultant	Manages the technical operation of the design
		Manages the inner-workings of the project team
		Monitors the timeline and ensures productivity
		Designs the NDS tree and security
		Designates documentation responsibilities

(continued)

Table 3.1 NDS design role responsibilities (continued).		
Role	**Description**	**Responsibilities**
Server administrator	Works daily with the NetWare servers	Ensures continued network operations
		Configures time synchronization
		Coordinates the pilot rollout
		Coordinates rollout to the organization
		Places servers in the NDS tree
		Updates the disaster recovery plan
		Manages disk space requirements
Connectivity specialist	Familiar with the network topology and connections	Understands efficient bandwidth utilization
		Knows the physical network
		Understands routers
		Works with the WAN connections
		Understands protocols

Project Tasks

As with all projects, the NDS design process includes specific phases and steps. Typically, an NDS project consists of four distinct phases and as many as seven steps. Throughout this section of the chapter, we'll examine the four phases of the project process and the various steps that make up each phase. It should be noted as we work through this process that it's a closed loop—the last phase of the project is used to determine the necessity of another project.

 The four phases and steps of the NDS design cycle are important to fully understand and remember.

Phase 1: Project Approach

As expected, the first phase of the project includes the first step: preparing for NDS design. This phase of the project involves gathering information pertinent to the NDS design and establishing project scope and schedule. In the project approach phase, the project team begins the process by interviewing the network users and technical personnel that will be most heavily impacted by the new design. The team, lead by the project manager, also gathers business operation information to facilitate the design process. During the project-approach phase, the project staff communicates with the affected personnel and is able to accurately set the expectations for the project, both for the end users and the implementation team. This ensures that the project rolls along with as few unexpected surprises as possible. This is also the phase in which the team members begin to fully understand their roles in the project.

Phase 2: Design

The design phase of the project includes both required and conditional steps, depending on the design being implemented. The decision to perform these conditional procedures is based solely on the need of the new design. There are also steps in this phase of the project that can be undertaken at any time during the phase, whereas others must follow in a specific order. The steps included in this phase of the project are:

1. Designing the NDS tree (required step)

2. Designing the partition and replica implementations for the tree (conditional step)

3. Planning the time synchronization strategy (conditional step)

4. Planning the user environment (required step)

Even though the preceding steps are all covered in detail in their respective chapters, we'll briefly discuss them here as well.

As mentioned, the first step in the design phase of the project is designing the Directory tree, which is covered in detail in Chapter 4. This process involves developing a naming standard for NDS objects and property values, and designing the upper and lower layers of the NDS tree. This step allows you to develop your NDS design to work efficiently and to create a tree that is easy to use and manage. After the tree design is established, the next step can be accomplished: designing the partition and replica implementations.

Covered in Chapters 5 and 6, NDS partitions and replicas are added to the design in the second step of this phase. Planning the partition strategy to be used and placing replicas on servers in the tree provides scalability, fault tolerance, and easy accessibility. Because not all NDS trees require partitions or replicas, this is a conditional step. Likewise, designing the time synchronization strategy is only necessary if a WAN link is involved in communication or there are more than 30 servers. This step, covered in Chapter 7, allows the project team to decide if the network can use the default time synchronization values or if the network would benefit from configured time synchronization.

When we get to Chapter 7, we'll discuss implementing time synchronization without placing undue stress on the network. When time synchronization is in place, you're assured that all servers agree on the date and time. This is necessary because the servers use this information by applying time stamps to events and other services, such as messaging applications and file systems.

The last step in this phase, planning the user environment, is required regardless of the type of NDS design that is being implemented. Discussed in Chapter 8 as the accessibility plan, planning the user environment involves developing login script standards, the security that will be used on the network, and policies for using Alias, Directory Map, and Profile objects. It's during this part of the process that standards for NDS security are established, file system structures are standardized, and guidelines are established to enable remote or traveling users to access the network.

Phase 3: Implementation

Comprised of only one step, the implementation phase (discussed further in Chapter 9) is when it all comes together. During this phase of the project, the design is implemented and fine-tuned. Many times, this phase of the process is divided into small parts, such as implementation testing, a pilot rollout, and then the final rollout.

Phase 4: Design Analysis

Technically not part of the implementation process, this particular phase involves continuous monitoring of the NDS tree compared to the operation of the organization. The design analysis phase should be included as part of the regular responsibilities of the network administrator. This type of analysis is often the result of normal management tasks, such as creating User and Group objects, configuring printing, determining security requirements, and ensuring the network is operating at its peak performance.

Table 3.2 outlines the phases of the design and implementation process and the steps involved in each.

Table 3.2	NDS design and implementation phases.	
Phase	**Name**	**Step**
1	Project Approach	Preparing for NDS design
2	Design	Designing the Directory tree
		Developing partition and replica implementations (conditional)

(continued)

Table 3.2	NDS design and implementation phases (continued).	
Phase	**Name**	**Step**
2	Design	Implementing time synchronization (conditional)
		Planning the user environment
3	Implementation	Implementing the design
4	Design Analysis	Monitoring the design and performance continually

Sample Company Description

Throughout the remainder of this book, we'll utilize an example company to illustrate the finer points of NDS design. In this section, we'll take an overview look at our company and how its various idiosyncrasies impact the design of the NDS tree.

To fully understand the implications of NDS design, we must consider combining two NDS trees. To do this, we'll merge two companies: Burmeister Publishing and Munson Media. Together, they'll make up MB Enterprises. Burmeister Publishing is a traditional publishing house based in San Francisco, CA, that focuses on computer-oriented books for retail and college use. In this role, it has also been contracted by many of the major hardware and software vendors for technical manuals and white papers. Burmeister Publishing currently has 300 employees and 65 printers located on a three-building campus. The buildings are interconnected using Fiber Distributed Data Interface (FDDI) and will eventually be connected to Munson Media via two dedicated T1 lines. Burmeister Publishing is made up of five major departments:

➤ Editing/Acquisitions (three servers)

➤ Executive/Administration (two servers)

➤ Information Services (three servers)

➤ Marketing (two servers)

➤ Production (two servers)

The company's 12 servers are evenly distributed amongst the departments, with Editing/Acquisitions and IS each having three, and all other departments having two each. Each department has two dedicated IS staff members to handle all issues that arise. Figure 3.1 shows Burmeister Publishing's organizational chart, and Figure 3.2 is its existing network layout.

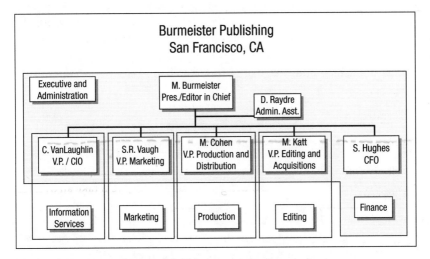

Figure 3.1 Burmeister Publishing's organizational chart.

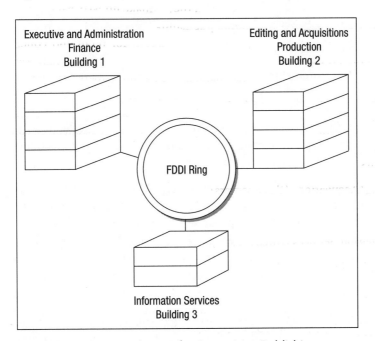

Figure 3.2 A network map for Burmeister Publishing.

Munson Media is a magazine and electronic publishing house located in two offices in Vancouver and Dallas. The electronic publishing division has grown significantly in the last two years and has spawned a Web-based training department. At this time, the two sites are connected via Frame Relay, but this will be upgraded when the merger takes place. The Dallas office houses the magazine facilities and the executive offices, whereas Vancouver handles the electronic publishing and Web-based training. The Dallas office contains the following departments:

➤ Executive/Administration

➤ Magazine Editing and Acquisitions

➤ Magazine Production

➤ Marketing

There are a total of 10 servers and 225 employees at this site. The company's organization is fairly flat, and the existing NDS tree reflects that. In Vancouver, the organization is somewhat more dynamic, and dedicated servers are in place for the following departments:

➤ IS and Internet (five servers)

➤ Online Production (seven servers)

➤ Support Call Center (three servers)

➤ Testing and QA (seven servers)

The Testing and QA department's servers map exactly to the Production department to ensure accurate testing of the online content. Figure 3.3 shows Munson Media's current organizational chart.

You've been hired as the Information Technology Manager for MB Enterprises and will act as the project manager during the merger to ensure the project runs smoothly. Your first responsibility in this role is to identify the personnel needed to perform the project and develop a budget. Although both companies have experienced network staff, you've decided to go outside to a consulting firm for the NDS expert. Fortunately, all offices are in technologically advanced cities and finding such an expert should be no problem. Because the Vancouver office houses the majority of the technical staff, you've decided to base your office there and run the project from that site. Figure 3.4 shows the network as it will exist after the merger is complete. Keep in mind, as you progress through this book, the specifics of each of the companies and how the various tools and techniques are used to ensure a successful NDS design.

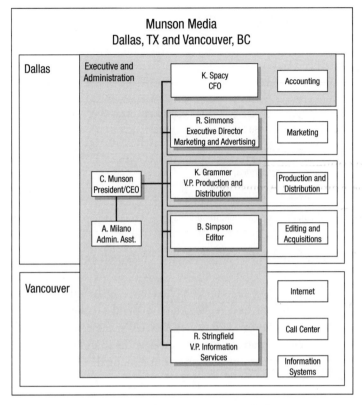

Figure 3.3   Munson Media's organizational chart.

Figure 3.4   The new MB Enterprises WAN.

Practice Questions

Question 1

> Which of the following project steps are considered conditional because of the structure of the NDS tree? [Choose the two best answers]
>
> ❑ a. Planning the user environment
>
> ❑ b. Implementing time synchronization
>
> ❑ c. Monitoring design and performance
>
> ❑ d. Developing partition and replica implementations

The correct answers are b and d. The decision regarding whether to implement time synchronization depends on the size and structure of the network: If there's a WAN link or more than 30 servers, time synchronization should be configured. Similarly, NDS partitions and replicas also depend on the NDS tree design, and not all implementations will utilize them. On the other hand, it's always necessary to develop a plan for the user environment and monitor the design and performance after the new design is implemented. Therefore, answers a and c are incorrect.

Question 2

> During which phase of the implementation process does the team communicate with the users and management most frequently?
>
> ○ a. Preparing for NDS design
>
> ○ b. Implementation
>
> ○ c. NDS design
>
> ○ d. Performance monitoring

The correct answer is a. During the preparation phase, the project team must talk with the users and management to determine the workflow in the organization and accurately design the NDS tree. Although communication must continue throughout the entire project, the team and users talk most frequently during the preparation phase. Therefore, answers b, c, and d are incorrect.

Question 3

Which of the following is most often a result of an inefficient NDS tree design? [Choose the two best answers]

❑ a. Increased network throughput

❑ b. Decreased network throughput

❑ c. Standardized naming systems

❑ d. Difficulty in locating network resources

The correct answers are b and d. When an NDS tree has been successfully designed, the users enjoy easier access to network resources and increased overall network performance. Conversely, poorly designed trees result in just the opposite. Therefore, answer a is incorrect. In addition, to successfully design an NDS tree, naming standards must be established to ensure all resources are easily identifiable. Therefore, answer c is incorrect.

Question 4

Which of the following are the two biggest driving factors in the design of an NDS tree? [Choose the two best answers]

❑ a. Organizational structure

❑ b. Building layout

❑ c. Network layout

❑ d. Company politics

The correct answers are a and c. The two primary considerations when developing the highest levels of your NDS design are the organizational structure of your company and the physical layout of your network. Although the layout of the buildings your company uses might affect network layout, it's not necessarily a consideration in NDS design. Therefore, answer b is incorrect. In a perfect world, company politics should have no bearing on NDS design. Therefore, answer d is incorrect.

Question 5

Which member of the design and implementation team is tasked with ensuring the project follows the timeline after it has been established?

- ○ a. Server administrator
- ○ b. Project manager
- ○ c. Connectivity specialist
- ○ d. NDS expert

The correct answer is d. In the role as second in command, the NDS expert must monitor the project process to ensure that the team sticks to the established timeline. Neither the server administrator nor the connectivity specialist deals with the project's timeline. Therefore, answers a and c are incorrect. Whereas the project manager is responsible for initiating the project and developing the timeline, the NDS expert is responsible for making sure it's completed. Therefore, answer b is incorrect.

Question 6

Which phase of the NDS design and implementation process is most often a part of normal network operation?

- ○ a. Design
- ○ b. Implementation
- ○ c. Project approach
- ○ d. Design analysis

The correct answer is d. The design analysis phase involves continuous monitoring of the NDS tree compared to the operation of the organization. The design analysis phase should be included as part of the regular responsibilities of the network administrator and is often the result of normal management tasks, such as creating users and groups, configuring printing, determining security requirements, and ensuring the network is operating at its peak performance. Although the other phases of the NDS project include steps that can be taken care of during normal operation, they do not directly apply. Therefore, answers a, b, and c are incorrect.

Question 7

Which of the following roles are useful to the NDS project but are not required for most implementations? [Choose the two best answers]

- ❏ a. Connectivity specialist
- ❏ b. Printing expert
- ❏ c. Application specialist
- ❏ d. Design specialist

The correct answers are b and c. End-user experts, such as printing experts and application specialists, can aid in the NDS design process, but they are not required roles in the normal design process. The connectivity specialist is a required role. Therefore, answer a is incorrect. Throughout the course of this chapter, we have not discussed a design specialist, and, in fact, the process does not include such a role. Therefore, answer d is incorrect.

Need To Know More?

 Clarke, David James, IV. *CNE Study Guide for Core Technologies.* Novell Press. San Jose, CA, 1996. ISBN 0-7645-4501-9. Chapter 3 deals with the NDS design process and preparing for that process.

 For additional information on planning for your NDS implementation, review the NetWare 5 online documentation. Use the keywords "NDS design".

Designing The Directory Tree

4

Terms you'll need to understand:

√ Container objects

√ Leaf objects

√ Common name

√ Distinguished name

√ Relative distinguished name

√ Context

√ Current context

√ Name context

√ Typeful (and typeless) naming

Techniques you'll need to master:

√ Showing a name as typeful or typeless

√ Using distinguished and relative distinguished names

√ Determining your current context

√ Setting the desired context in the client properties

√ Creating a naming standard

In this chapter, we discuss how objects in the Novell Directory Services (NDS) tree are named, the importance of naming standards, the two-stage process of designing a Directory tree, and the impact of administration philosophy on tree design.

Naming

Before we can discuss naming standards, you have to understand how NDS names are constructed. NDS objects are either *container objects* or *leaf objects*. Each NDS object name has two parts: its *common name* and its *context*. You can refer to the object with its complete location (its *distinguished name*) or its location relative to the workstation's current location (its *relative distinguished name*). This current location is known as the *current context*. Also, you can show the object name with object type identifiers (*typeful naming*) or without the identifiers (*typeless naming*). A workstation can be set to start in a particular context, known as its *name context*. We'll discuss each of these terms in the following sections.

Container Objects

Container objects are NDS objects that contain, or hold, other NDS objects. The purpose of container objects is to organize the objects in the tree into logical groupings for management and organizational purposes. The standard container objects are the Country, Organization, and Organizational Unit objects. An NDS container is like a folder in the file system, whereas an NDS leaf object is like a file.

Leaf Objects

Leaf objects represent physical or logical resources on the network. It's possible to assign values to many properties of leaf objects. Some properties are mandatory (that is, values must be provided for selected properties to create the object). Other values are optional, and some may be multivalued (for example, a user could have multiple telephone numbers).

One type of leaf object is the User object. Mandatory properties for the User object include Login Name and Last Name. Optional properties for the User object include the following:

➤ Name

➤ Group memberships

➤ Password

➤ Telephone number

➤ Mailbox ID

Other examples of leaf objects include Printer, Group, Volume, License Certificate, and IP Address objects.

Common Name

An object's common name is the name of the object, without information about the object's location in the NDS tree. It might be the name of a printer (such as LJ4_Accounting), a user (such as MJones), or any other object in the tree.

In Figure 4.1, the common name of the Postscript object is:

```
CN=Postscript
```

> *Note: Common names apply to leaf objects, not to containers.*

Context

An object's context defines where the object is found in the NDS tree. Context is shown as a listing of all the containers that hold the object, right up to the [Root] of the tree. In Figure 4.1, the context of the Postscript object is:

```
OU=AccountsPayable.OU=CorpServices.O=ABCFoods
```

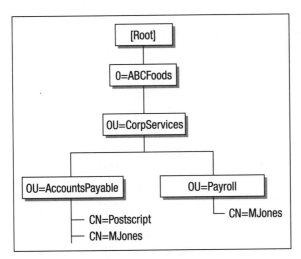

Figure 4.1   Objects in an NDS tree.

Think of a person, Mary Jones, working in the Accounts Payable department in the Corporate Services Division of the ABC Foods Corporation. There might be several people called Mary Jones, in different departments of the corporation. People can tell them apart by their location within the corporation. A person might say, "Is this report for Mary Jones in Accounts Payable, or Mary Jones in Payroll?" Here, the person's name, Mary Jones, is like the common name of an object, and the department name, the Accounts Payable department in the Corporate Services Division of the ABC Foods Corporation (to state it fully), is like an object's context.

Note: Figure 4.1 shows that there can be two objects with the same common name in the tree, as long as they are in different contexts.

Distinguished Name

When you combine an object's common name with its context, you are specifying its distinguished name. In our previous example, the distinguished name for the MJones object in Accounts Payable is

```
.CN=MJones.OU=AccountsPayable.OU=CorpServices.O=ABCFoods
```

and the distinguished name for the MJones object in Payroll is

```
.CN=MJones.OU=Payroll.OU=CorpServices.O=ABCFoods
```

 As you can see, there is a leading dot in the previous distinguished names. All distinguished names begin with a leading dot.

Name Context

When you log in to NetWare from your workstation, the client software must tell the login processor where to find your User object. The workstation will "point" to a certain location within the NDS tree, based on one of the property values of Client 32. This is known as the workstation's *name context.* You can specify the desired name context by clicking the Advanced button in the login dialog box, or by modifying the parameters in the properties of the client software. In Figure 4.2, the properties of the client software show that it will look for the context **corpservices.abcfoods** in the **abc_tree** NDS tree. Because no server is specified, the client will attach to the first server in that tree that responds to a login request.

Novell Client Configuration   `[?]` `[X]`

Default Capture	Protocol Preferences
Service Location	Advanced Settings
Client	Location Profiles	Advanced Login	Contextless Login

Preferred server: `[                    ]`

Preferred tree: `[abc_tree            ]`

Name context: `[corpservices.abcfoods]`

First network drive: `[F          ▼]`

Client Version: 3.0.0.0

`[    OK    ]`   `[  Cancel  ]`

Figure 4.2   Novell Client Configuration dialog box.

 Whereas it's possible to set the tree, server, and name context properties each time the client software is installed, it's more efficient to automate this step. Search the NetWare 5 online documentation for "NCIMAN.EXE" (Novell Client Install Manager) for information on how to do this.

We talk about the *client software* often in this chapter. Client software refers to a program running on a user's workstation that connects the workstation to the NetWare network. Novell makes several clients that understand NDS. Novell's first NDS-aware client was known as the Virtual Loadable Module (VLM) client—it was used to connect MS-DOS and Windows 3.x workstations to NDS. There are also several versions of Novell's Client 32 client software, which are used for connecting computers running MS-DOS, Microsoft Windows 3.x, Windows 95/98, and Windows NT to NetWare.

The Microsoft Windows operating systems provide their own 32-bit clients for NetWare, generically named Microsoft Client For NetWare Networks. Many of these clients understand NDS, but others (notably the version that shipped with the original version of Windows 95) do not.

> *Note: You must be running a Novell client to run NetWare Administrator or the Novell Application Launcher.*

Current Context

In normal conversation, when you are talking about people in the Accounts Payable department, you don't need to keep saying the name of the department. You know that the people you're talking to will understand which group you're talking about. In the same way, you can refer to objects in your workstation's *current context* just by the objects' common names, without mentioning the context information.

The client software on the workstation keeps track of current context information. Immediately after login, the workstation's current context is the same as the context of the User object. Subsequent actions by the user can change the current context.

 You can determine your current context by going to the workstation's command prompt and entering the **CX** command.

Relative Distinguished Name

In regular conversation, it's much more convenient to refer to Mary Jones, or Mary Jones in Accounts Payable, than to give the complete description—Mary Jones in Accounts Payable in the Corporate Services Division of the ABC Foods Corporation. Similarly, in specifying NDS objects, it's easier to refer to the relative distinguished name

```
CN=MJones
```

than to the distinguished name

```
.CN=MJones.OU=AccountsPayable.OU=CorpServices.O=ABCFoods
```

To use relative distinguished names, you specify the object name *relative* to the workstation's current context. For example, you could issue a **CAPTURE** command to the STANDARD printer in the current context:

```
CAPTURE P=CN=STANDARD
```

If the current context is

```
OU=CorpServices.O=ABCFoods
```

this would be equivalent to the following **CAPTURE** command:

```
CAPTURE P=.CN=STANDARD.OU=CorpServices.O=ABCFoods
```

Notice when you use a relative distinguished name, you do not use a leading dot. Some people use the following mnemonic to remember this: "With Relative Distinguished names, you Remove the Dot."

Whereas humans prefer to use abbreviations and to count on others to make assumptions about what group or department you're talking about, NetWare wants to be *sure* that it's using the correct objects all the time. Therefore, all names passed from the client software to NetWare must be distinguished names. The client software is responsible for converting relative distinguished names to distinguished names.

Upon receiving a relative distinguished name from a user, the client software constructs a distinguished name to pass to NetWare, by:

1. Starting with a dot

2. Including the relative distinguished name supplied by the user

3. Appending the context

Modifying The Distinguished Name Built By The Client

You can modify the distinguished name that will be created by the client software by including part of the final distinguished name in the text you supply to the client, or by telling the client not to use all of the current context. We discuss these two methods in the following sections.

Adding Information To The Text You Give The Client

If the current context is

```
O=ABCFoods
```

but the object you want to refer to is in the

```
OU=CorpServices.O=ABCFoods
```

container, you can give the client the information it needs to construct the correct distinguished name for the object by adding the needed container name to the object name, like this:

```
CAPTURE P=CN=STANDARD.OU=CorpServices
```

Note once again that there is no leading dot, indicating that we're specifying a relative distinguished name. The client software will follow the three steps listed in the previous section and construct the correct distinguished name:

```
.CN=STANDARD.OU=CorpServices.O=ABCFoods
```

Telling The Client Not To Use All Of The Current Context

If the current context is

```
OU=AccountsPayable.OU=CorpServices.O=ABCFoods
```

but the printer you want to refer to is in the

```
OU=CorpServices.O=ABCFoods
```

container, you can tell the client software not to use the left-most container(s) in the current context when constructing the distinguished name. To pass this information to the client software, just put a dot at the end of the relative distinguished name for each container you want omitted. Here's the command you would use:

```
CAPTURE P=CN=STANDARD.
```

Once again, the client software will follow the three steps in the previous section, removing the OU=AccountsPayable container and producing the correct distinguished name:

```
.CN=STANDARD.OU=CorpServices.O=ABCFoods
```

An NDS object name cannot have a dot at the beginning and a dot at the end. The leading dot means "this is a distinguished name," and the trailing dot means "when building a distinguished name from this relative distinguished name, remove the left-most container in the current context."

You need to know how to identify the correct relative distinguished name, given a context, that corresponds with a distinguished name.

Typeful Naming

Up to now, we have included type identifiers with all object and container names we have shown. In the name

```
.CN=MJones.OU=AccountsPayable.OU=CorpServices.O=ABCFoods
```

CN=, **OU=**, and **O=** are object attribute type identifiers. **CN=** shows that MJones is a common name, **OU=** shows that AccountsPayable and CorpServices are Organizational Unit objects, and **O=** shows that ABCFoods is an Organization object. This method of naming is time-consuming but leaves no doubt about the type of object being discussed.

Typeless Naming

Although it adds clarity to specify the object type with all its identifiers, it's almost never necessary to do so. The client software can make the correct assumption about the types of objects and containers in any name specified. Therefore, you can enter a command such as

```
CAPTURE P=STANDARD
```

instead of

```
CAPTURE P=CN=STANDARD
```

For a distinguished name, you can enter this command:

```
CAPTURE P=.STANDARD.CorpServices.ABCFoods
```

The client software assumes the right-most container is an Organization, the left-most part of the name is a common name, and any other containers are Organizational Units. The only situation in which this logic can cause errors is if the right-most container in the current context is a Country object. In that case, a user should enter both the **O=** and the **C=** type identifiers, as appropriate. This potential confusion is one of the reasons the use of the Country object is usually not recommended. (Country, Organization, and Organizational Unit objects are discussed in more detail later in this chapter, in the section entitled "Standards For Object Names.")

If the command had been one that refers to containers, not leaf objects, such as the Change Context (**CX**) command, then the left-most portion of the name supplied would be assumed to be an Organizational Unit. Unless the name supplied had only one part, in which case the object must be an Organization.

A name such as

`.STANDARD.CorpServices.O=ABCFoods`

is described as "mixed," because part of it is typeful and part is typeless.

Naming Standards

It's important to create naming standards as the first step in designing the NDS tree. After a tree has been in use for some time, it's very difficult to impose a new set of naming standards—existing objects with names that do not conform to the standards will have to be renamed, or exceptions will have to be made.

Capitalizing the fields in the parts of a name and the type identifiers is optional, for example, o=Abc, O=aBc, o=abC, O=ABC are all equivalent.

Benefits Of Clearly Defined Naming Standards

There are several benefits to having a clearly defined set of naming standards in place before designing an NDS tree. Here are some of them:

➤ **Meaningful server names** There's a tendency to use names for servers that are humorous or in fashion. However, names like Sneezy, Grumpy, and Doc, or Jupiter, Mars, and Saturn, convey no information. If an administrator is trying to respond to a server error message, it's much easier if the server name indicates its function and location. A name like S-CAL-ACCT5 is much more useful than a name like BILBO.

➤ **Ease of finding resources** If a user wants to print a document in a remote office, and is searching the NDS tree to find a printer there, having standardized names for containers and printers can help. If the standard for printer names includes both the printer type and its location, the user can choose

.P-LJ4-3W.Boise.Montana-Idaho.ABCFoods

and know that the printer is a LaserJet 4 on the West side of the third floor in the Boise office.

➤ **Ease of merging trees** Imagine a situation where an enterprise decides to allow several departments to install NetWare independently, planning to merge them later when wide area network (WAN) links are in place. Problems will arise with the merge if multiple departments have chosen the same tree name. Also, extra work will be necessary after the merge if the separate implementations used different names for the Organization object.

Standards For Object Names

It would make sense to develop standards for every possible object type in the tree, but the major benefits accrue from setting standards for the names of certain critical objects. Here is a list:

➤ **Tree name** All tree names should be unique across the enterprise, to permit merging of trees in the future. Departmental tree names should identify the department and location. ABC_Paris is an example of a regional tree name.

➤ **Country** The Country object is rarely used. If the enterprise spans national boundaries, it's preferable to create regional Organizational Units that identify countries, as in Figure 4.3. Usually the two-letter ISO standard country names are chosen. If you search the NetWare 5 documentation for "Naming Conventions-Countries," you'll see a partial list of country names.

Remember that if you choose to use the Country object, it must be located directly under the [Root], and it must follow the two-letter ISO standard for naming.

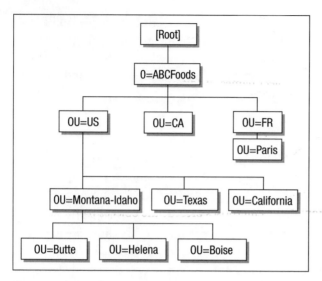

Figure 4.3 An NDS tree with country name Organizational Units.

➤ **Organization** The Organization object should have the same name in all trees, to facilitate future merging. The Organization object's name should be a recognized abbreviation of the name of the enterprise. Even in a very small departmental tree, all objects should be in Organizational Units under the Organization, again for ease of future merges.

➤ **Organizational Units in the upper layers** In the upper layers of the NDS tree (see the following section), Organizational Unit names indicate regions or locations. The names should be easily understood by users navigating through the tree.

➤ **Organizational Units in the lower layers** In the lower layers of the NDS tree, Organizational Unit names indicate administrative units of the enterprise, such as Accounting or Engineering, or standard names for grouping NDS objects, such as Apps for applications or Resources for printers and servers. Abbreviations commonly used in the enterprise are useful—HR for Human Resources, for example.

➤ **Servers** As mentioned previously, server names should indicate the server's function and location. It's not a good idea to indicate the version of the operating system on the server, because it would be very inconvenient to have to rename the server when a new version of the operating system is installed.

Multiple servers in a location can be distinguished by a numeral. In the example

S indicates that the object is a server, CAL shows it is in Calgary, and ACCT5 shows it is the fifth Accounting department server.

➤ **Volumes** All NetWare servers have a SYS volume—it would be pointless to rename their NDS object names. Additional volumes are traditionally called VOL1, VOL2, and so on, but this gives no indication as to their purpose. Some organizations name their volumes APPS, DATA, and MAIL. The scheme chosen should be standard across the enterprise, so users from other parts of the enterprise will know where to look for specific files.

➤ **Printers** The name used for a Printer object should indicate the printer's type and its location. Some enterprises precede the object's name with P- to indicate that the object is a printer.

 Do not make the common mistake of naming a printer after its current "owner." New users can be confused by references to "Terry's Printer" when Terry has moved on.

➤ **Users** It's common to create names for User objects from the user's first and last name. If a user's name is Mary Macdonald, common schemes would create MARYM or MMACDONA, usually restricting the length of the object name to eight characters for ease in creating home directories. Some organizations prefer to use an employee number as the object name, making it difficult for an intruder to guess a user's ID. It's preferable to ensure that no two User objects in the enterprise have the same name to avoid any confusion. Rules for ensuring uniqueness (that is, how you would name User objects for two users with the same name) should be included in the naming standard.

➤ **Groups** Group object names should indicate the purpose of the object. The name G-Payroll indicates members of the Payroll department. The name G-P-3W would then indicate the users who can use the third floor West printer.

➤ **Directory Maps** The name of a Directory Map object should indicate the name of the directory to which it's pointing. Preceding the name with DM- helps to indicate the object type. DM-PUBLIC might be the name of a Directory Map object pointing to SYS:PUBLIC on a particular server in a container.

➤ **Organizational Roles** These objects are like groups in that they list (though as occupants, not as members) the users who perform certain types of activities. The name of an Organizational Role object should indicate the activity or the name of the group that carries out that activity. It's useful to precede the name of the object with OR- to indicate the object type. OR-HELPDESK might be the name of an Organizational Role object whose occupants carry out help desk activities for users.

➤ **Workstations** When an enterprise uses Z.E.N.works, a Workstation object can be created for each workstation that is registered in NDS. This name is created automatically as part of the registration process. The administrator can define the rules that will be used to create the name. Typically, the name is a combination of a computer's name, address, and owner. For consistency of naming, the administrators should work together to define these rules.

Standards For Properties

Because information stored in NDS is available to anyone who can log into the network, there's a strong temptation to use NDS as a type of corporate human resources database. Be careful not to duplicate other databases in the enterprise, however. If this information is already captured in the corporate human resources database, storing it in NDS as well will simply cause duplication of effort and waste time resolving differences.

If the enterprise has decided to store human resources information in NDS, standards should be created listing which of the optional properties are to be specified and what the acceptable values are for those properties. At a minimum, standards should state how the user's name, title, department, location, email address, and telephone number should be entered.

How Decentralized Administration Can Affect Standards

As you'll see later, an enterprise can decide either to perform administration from a central site or to delegate administration to individuals in the regions. From the point of view of standards, decentralized administration can result in inconsistent adherence to standards, because administrators in the regions may create their own rules without reference to the central standards body. Organizations should expect such loss of consistency as one of the negative aspects of decentralizing administration.

The Upper Layers Of The NDS Tree

Like the file system, the NDS tree is an "inverted tree," which means that its root is at the top. So, when we talk about the upper layers of the tree, we mean the root of the tree (the [Root] object is always written [Root]) and the first few layers of containers below it—Country, Organization, and a small number of layers of Organizational Unit objects.

The enterprise for which you're designing the tree may have several geographic locations. The number of locations determines what you use to represent the upper Organizational Units.

Naming The Tree

A tree needs to have a name to differentiate it from other trees that are visible on the network. Although it's tempting to name the NDS tree after your favorite type of tree, names like Palm, Pine, and Maple provide no useful information to an administrator trying to decide on which tree to install a new server. Names like ABC_Tree and CalgaryTest are preferable. Spaces are not allowed in tree names.

 It's possible to rename a tree with the **DSMERGE** command. But, you'll have substantial work to do after renaming the tree if you have hundreds of workstations installed with the old tree name specified in the properties of their client software. It's best to get the name right at the start. In addition, the **DISPLAY SERVERS** console command only shows the first 12 characters of a tree name. Therefore, you should not exceed 12 characters when naming the tree.

Shape The Tree Like A Pyramid

NDS trees work best if they are shaped like a pyramid. There should not be a large number of Organizational Units inside a given container because trees that are too flat are awkward to manage and inefficient. To maintain the pyramid shape when the circumstances might lead you to create a flat design (for example, a newspaper publishing enterprise with 50 locations), create regional or "placeholder" Organizational Units. Novell's design guideline is to consider using regional Organizational Unit containers if a container has 10 to 15 subcontainers.

Tree Design For A Single Location

If an enterprise has only one location, many of the complexities of NDS design are avoided. In a small, one-location enterprise, you can use a simple design based on the administrative structure of the enterprise, as in Figure 4.4.

In the smallest networks (under 100 users), there's no benefit to be gained from creating any Organizational Units under the Organization object. Just create the Organization object and place all objects within that container.

Administrators are sometimes tempted to create extra Organizational Units because each one can have its own login script, allowing easy assignment of resources to the users in each container. This is not generally worthwhile. Resources can be used in the container's login script to assign resources to groups of users as needed. For example, the following line from a container's login script will assign the correct printer to the members of the Accounting department:

```
IF MEMBER OF "ACCOUNTING" THEN #CAPTURE P=ACCTG_PRINTER
```

Tree Design For Multiple Locations

If an enterprise has offices in multiple locations, experience has shown it's best to design the tree to consider the communications infrastructure of the network. This is because there's substantially more network traffic within the departments of an enterprise than between them. Therefore, instead of creating a Production Organizational Unit object that includes all Production

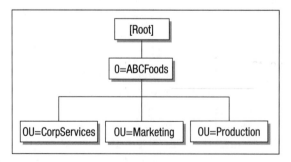

Figure 4.4   An NDS tree for a single-location enterprise.

department users in their many geographical locations, it's better to create a Production Organizational Unit object in each location. In Chapter 5, you'll learn that partitioning the NDS tree is easier, and network traffic because of partitioning is reduced, if the upper layers of the tree follow the physical structure of the network.

Following this philosophy, you should create Organizational Unit objects for each physical location in which the enterprise has an office. In Figure 4.5, Calgary, Dallas, and Paris are physical locations—that is, all the servers in these sites are on the same LAN, or at least have high-speed access to each other. If there are several sites in Calgary that are not connected by high-speed links, an Organizational Unit should be created for each of them—for example, Calgary-Sales and Calgary-Production.

You may find it useful to create a regional Administrator object or Organizational Role object to manage the objects in each location.

If there are many locations, implement placeholder Organizational Units to maintain the pyramid shape of the tree, as in Figure 4.6, where OU=Montana-Idaho,

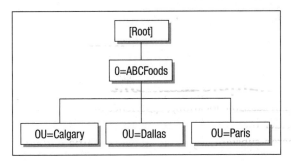

Figure 4.5   An NDS tree for a multiple location enterprise.

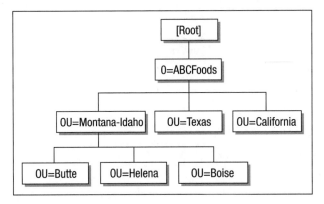

Figure 4.6   An NDS tree with placeholder Organizational Units.

OU=Texas, and OU=California are placeholder Organizational Units. The only objects likely to appear under these placeholder Organizational Units are the Administrator or Organizational Role objects.

 Know the various aspects of basing tree design on the communications infrastructure of the network. One of Novell's key design guidelines is to create the upper layers of the NDS tree based on geography (locations and WAN links).

The Lower Layers Of The NDS Tree

Whereas the design of the upper layers of the NDS tree is based on the geography or WAN infrastructure of the network, the design of the lower layers is based on how the network's resources are used. The general rule for the design of the lower layers is to group User objects and the resources they will need to access within the same Organizational Unit. Therefore, you would put all the User objects in a geographical area and the objects representing the file system volumes, the printers, and the applications the users will be using in a single container.

Because it's typical for all users in a particular department to need access to the same resources, the Organizational Units in the lower layers of the tree usually are named after an enterprise's divisions and departments, as shown in Figure 4.7.

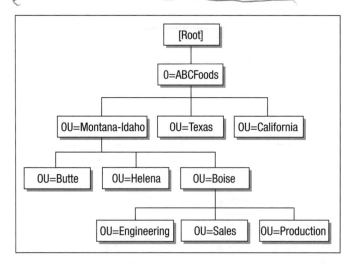

Figure 4.7   Administrative Organizational Units in the lower layers of an NDS tree.

Engineering, Sales, and Production are the departments in the Boise location; therefore, an Organizational Unit is created for each of them.

The considerations mentioned in the preceding section "Tree Design For A Single Location" apply here. In a location with just a few users, creating an additional Organizational Unit to house just three or four User objects is not justified. The only point in favor of such a choice would be to ensure that the structure would be the same in each of the enterprise's locations.

Designing For Easy Administration

When designing the NDS tree, the enterprise's management philosophy should be kept in mind. Some enterprises like to manage the business centrally, and some prefer to delegate authority to the enterprise's constituent parts. It's reasonable to mirror this philosophy in the administration of the NDS tree. In this section, we discuss both *centralized* and *decentralized* administration.

Centralized Administration

In a centralized administration design, the responsibility for management of the NDS tree is kept within a centrally located administration group, typically at corporate headquarters. This group will be responsible for the creation of all objects, from containers to User objects, and can be counted on to adhere to the corporate naming standards. (After all, they probably were part of the team that generated the standards.) Because of the geographical separation (and often time-zone differences) between the administrators and the end users, it's common that responsiveness to users' requests in a centralized administration environment is not as good as users might want.

> *Note: In smaller organizations, centralized administration may belong to an individual rather than a group.*

Usually, an Organizational Role object is created to list the members of this administration group, and the necessary NDS rights are assigned to the Organizational Role object.

Decentralized Administration

In a decentralized administration design, the responsibility for management of the NDS tree is distributed to administration groups located in the various regions. Generally, users are happier with this arrangement, because responsiveness to their requests tends to be better than in the centralized administration design. To implement a decentralized administration design, Organizational Roles are created under the regional or location Organizational Unit containers with only the rights to manage the objects below that point in the tree. As well as the possible loss of consistency in applying the previous naming standards, it's common to see more containers created in the decentralized administration than in the centralized administration design, because the decentralized administrators want to take account of local needs.

To implement decentralization, an Organizational Role object is created for the administrators of the regional or location Organizational Unit container, and the necessary NDS rights are assigned to that Organizational Role object. Usually, the Organizational Role for the overall administrators of the enterprise is given Supervisor object rights to the container.

> *Note: Once decentralized administration has been implemented,*
> *it's possible for one of the regional administrators to make the overall*
> *administrators unable to manage the container by simply removing the*
> *Organizational Role for the overall administrators of the enterprise*
> *from the list of trustees of the container. Implemented incautiously, this*
> *action could render that branch of the tree unmanageable.*

NDS Tree Design For The Sample Company

To give you an understanding of how these tree design rules can be applied, we will now design three trees: one each for the two original companies in the sample scenario (Munson Media and Burmeister Publishing), and one for the merged company, MB Enterprises.

The Burmeister Publishing Tree

Here is the description of Burmeister Publishing, from Chapter 3: Burmeister Publishing (BP) currently has 300 employees and 65 printers located in a three-building campus in San Francisco, CA. The buildings are connected using Fiber Distributed Data Interface (FDDI) and will eventually be connected to Munson Media via two dedicated T1 lines. BP is made up of five major departments: Executive/Administration, Marketing, Editing/Acquisitions, Production, and Information Services (IS).

This tree is very simple, as shown in Figure 4.8. We create five Organizational Units: one for each of the major departments. There's no need to pay attention to the network infrastructure here, because the FDDI links between the three buildings on the campus make this a single LAN.

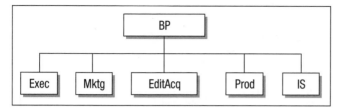

Figure 4.8 The Burmeister Publishing NDS tree.

The Munson Media Tree

The following is excerpted from the description of Munson Media in Chapter 3: Munson Media is a magazine and electronic publishing house located in two offices in Vancouver and Dallas. The Dallas office is comprised of the Executive/Administration, Magazine Editing and Acquisitions, Magazine Production, and Marketing departments. In Vancouver, the organization is somewhat more dynamic, and dedicated servers are in place for the Online Production (seven servers), Testing and QA (seven servers), IS and Internet (five servers), and Support Call Center (three servers) departments.

Because Munson Media's offices are in two locations, we need to create place-holder Organizational Units for each of them: OU=DAL and OU=VAN. Under these Organizational Units, we switch to administrative design and create Organizational Units for the departments (see Figure 4.9).

Before merging the Burmeister Publishing and Munson Media trees, we have to create the SF Organizational Unit, and move the administrative Organizational Units under it. See Appendix A for the steps required for this process, using NDS Manager.

Munson-Burmeister Enterprises will be located in three cities: San Francisco, Dallas, and Vancouver. The cities will eventually be connected by two T1 lines, and although this fact might persuade us to consider the two companies to exist at a single location for the purposes of NDS tree design, the initial design

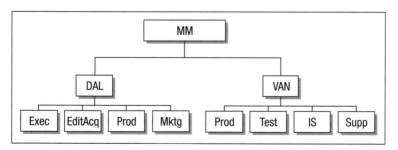

Figure 4.9 The Munson Media NDS tree.

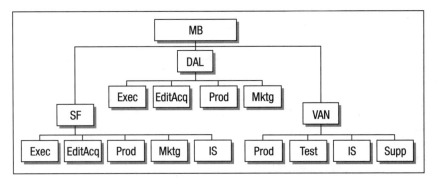

Figure 4.10 The MB Enterprises NDS tree.

will have to take the current situation into account. Therefore, the NDS tree in Figure 4.10 will need three placeholder Organizational Units: the two existing ones from the Munson Media tree and a new one, OU=SF, inserted from the Burmeister Publishing tree.

 Do you think there are too many Organizational Units in this NDS tree? Some NDS designers would say that the administrative Organizational Units under the placeholder Organizational Units are unnecessary. However, if you refer to the discussion in the preceding section "Tree Design For A Single Location," you'll notice that we've included the administrative Organizational Units expecting that each location will have its own administrator, who would probably want the extra flexibility provided by the administrative Organizational Units.

Practice Questions

Question 1

A workstation's current context is:

`OU=Sales.OU=Calgary.O=ABC`

What is the typeless distinguished name for the Printer object Postscript3 in the OU=Calgary.O=ABC context?

○ a. .CN=Postscript3.OU=Calgary.O=ABC

○ b. Postscript3

○ c. Postscript3.

○ d. .Postscript3.Calgary.ABC

The correct answer is d. The typeless distinguished name for the Printer object Postscript3 in the OU=Calgary.O=ABC context is .Postscript3.Calgary.ABC. .CN=Postscript3.OU=Calgary.O=ABC is the distinguished name for the object, but it's the typeful distinguished name. Therefore, answer a is incorrect. Postscript3 is the common name of the object, not the typeless distinguished name. Therefore, answer b is incorrect. Postscript3. is an accurate relative distinguished name for the object, but the question asks for you to identify a distinguished name. Therefore, answer c is incorrect.

Question 2

A workstation's current context is:

`OU=Sales.OU=Calgary.O=ABC`

What is the typeful relative distinguished name for the Printer object Postscript3 in the OU=Eng.OU=Calgary.O=ABC context?

○ a. .CN=Postscript3.OU=Eng.OU=Calgary.O=ABC

○ b. CN=Postscript3.OU=Eng

○ c. CN=Postscript3.OU=Eng.

○ d. .CN=Postscript3.OU=Eng.

The correct answer is c. CN=Postscript3.OU=Eng. is the typeful relative distinguished name for the Printer object Postscript3 in the OU=Eng.OU=Calgary.O=ABC context. .CN=Postscript3.OU=Eng.OU=Calgary.O=ABC describes the object accurately, but it's a distinguished name. Therefore, answer a is incorrect. CN=Postscript3.OU=Eng is a relative distinguished name that equates to the distinguished name .CN=Postscript3.OU=Eng.OU= Sales.OU=Calgary.O=ABC. Therefore, answer b is incorrect. .CN=Post-script3.OU=Eng. contains an invalid name—no distinguished name ends with a trailing dot. Therefore, answer d is incorrect.

Question 3

What is the current context of the MJones object in the figure?

○ a. .AccountsPayable.CorpServices.ABCFoods

○ b. .OU=AccountsPayable.OU=CorpServices.O=ABCFoods

○ c. AccountsPayable.CorpServices.ABCFoods

○ d. AccountsPayable.

○ e. None of the above

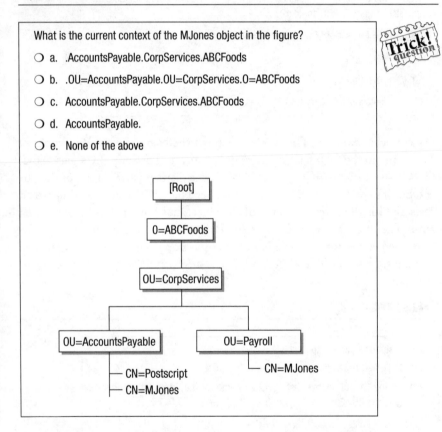

The correct answer is e. The term *current context* is used when referring to the current location of a client in the NDS tree, which is why this is a trick question. When referring to an object's location in the tree, the term *context* is used. Therefore, answers a, b, c, and d are incorrect.

Question 4

A workstation's current context is:

OU=Sales.OU=Calgary.O=ABC

Which of the following will result in the correct name for the Printer object Postscript3 in the OU=Eng.OU=Calgary.O=ABC context being passed to NetWare by the client software? [Choose the three best answers]

❑ a. Postscript3.OU=Eng.

❑ b. .Postscript3.OU=Eng.OU=Calgary.O=ABC

❑ c. Postscript3.

❑ d. Postscript3.Eng.

The correct answers are a, b, and d. Each of them, when combined with the current context following the rules for modifying the name built by the client software, results in the distinguished name .OU=Eng.OU=Calgary.O=ABC. Answer c is incorrect, because it would result in the distinguished name .Postscript3.Calgary.ABC.

Question 5

An NDS 5 server in the Paris office of ABC Foods is used primarily for file and print services. A small GroupWise post office and two Oracle database appli-cations run on it as well. Which of the following NDS names for the Server object best fit the following standard? [Choose the two best answers]

➤ Server names indicate their location and their primary function.

➤ Multiple servers in the same location should be differentiated by a numeric suffix.

❑ a. Android1

❑ b. PARIS-FS-2

❑ c. PARIS-FS1-GW -OR

❑ d. PARIS-GEN2

❑ e. PARIS-NW5-GEN2

The correct answers are b and d. PARIS-FS-2 and PARIS-GEN2 fit the stan-dards given. Android1 indicates neither the location nor the function of the server. Therefore, answer a is incorrect. PARIS-FS1-GW-OR indicates three functions carried out by the server, not its primary function. Therefore, answer c is incorrect. PARIS-NW5-GEN2 includes the version of the operating system in use, which is not included in the standard. Therefore, answer e is incorrect.

Question 6

Smallcorp is a 20-person manufacturing company located in a single location in London, England. The network administrator has just learned about NDS and has developed the tree design shown in the figure. Which of the following descriptions apply to the design? [Choose the three best answers]

❏ a. Correctly based on network geography

❏ b. Too many levels

❏ c. Allows for future expansion

❏ d. Allows different login scripts to be used for different employee types

❏ e. Easy to administer

```
                        [Root]
                          |
                    O=Smallcorp
                          |
                     OU=London
                          |
        ┌─────────────────┼─────────────────┐
  OU=Administration    OU=Sales        OU=Production
        │                 │                 │
   ┌────┴────┐       ┌─────┴─────┐     ┌─────┴─────┐
OU=Acctg OU=Execs OU=Inside OU=Outside OU=Doors OU=Windows
```

The correct answers are b, c, and d. The tree design shown in the figure has too many levels, allows for future expansion, and allows different login scripts to be used for different employee types. This does not mean this is a good design, but the descriptions do apply. The network has only one location, so basing the design on network geography is inappropriate. Therefore, answer a is incorrect. The tree is overly complex, has too many levels, and has too many administrative Organizational Units. Therefore, answer e is incorrect.

Question 7

Bigcorp is a 1,000-person manufacturing company organized into three corporate divisions: Administration, Sales, and Production. The network administrator has just learned about NDS and has developed the tree design shown in the figure. Which of the following descriptions applies to the design?

○ a. Low network traffic

○ b. Correctly based on network geography

○ c. Easy to partition

○ d. None of the above

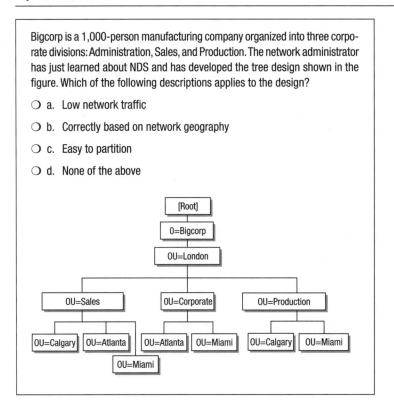

The correct answer is d. Because users in the same part of the organization tend to use the same set of resources, this design will result in excessive network traffic. Therefore, answer a is incorrect. A correct design based on network geography would create Organizational Units below O=BIGCORP for each of the sites (Calgary, Atlanta, and Miami). Therefore, answer b is incorrect. Partitioning is difficult if the design of the upper layers of the tree do not follow the network infrastructure. Therefore, answer c is incorrect.

Need To Know More?

 Henderson, Jim and Peter Kuo. *NetWare Directory Services Troubleshooting.* New Riders Publishing, Indianapolis, IN, 1995. ISBN 1-56205-443-0. An excellent source for NetWare administrators wanting to understand the intricacies of NDS. This book contains a good section on NDS design, and explains NDS's sometimes cryptic error messages.

 Hughes, Jeffrey F. and Blair W. Thomas. *Novell's Four Principles of NDS Design.* Novell Press, San Jose, CA, 1996. ISBN 0-7645-4522-1. This book contains a full description of the principles of NDS design. It's well-written and easy to understand.

 Hughes, Jeffrey F. and Blair W. Thomas. *Novell's Guide to NetWare 5 Networks.* Novell Press, San Jose, CA, 1999. ISBN 0-7645-4544-2. One of the first books on NetWare 5, this book covers a wide range of NetWare 5 topics, including a section on NDS design.

 http://developer.novell.com/research/appnotes.htm is the main page for Novell's AppNotes. This monthly publication contains many articles on all phases of NetWare, and has a search engine that can be used to find articles covering topics you're interested in. Do not search on NDS, however, because you'll retrieve almost every article! A couple of interesting articles are:

➤ Hughes, Jeffrey F. and Blair W. Thomas. "Enhancements to Novell Directory Services in NetWare 5." October 1998, p. 3.

➤ Lee, Ron. "Universal Guidelines for NDS Tree Design." April 1996.

NDS Partition Techniques

Know How to create a partition

Terms you'll need to understand:

√ Partition

√ [Root] default partition

√ Scalability

√ Fault tolerance

√ Partition boundary

√ Partition root object

√ Parent partition

√ Child partition

√ Novell Directory Services (NDS) Manager

√ Synchronization

Techniques you'll need to master:

√ Understanding the benefits of partitioning

√ Comparing the NDS partition to the file system partition

√ Determining when to partition

√ Understanding key partition terms and guidelines

√ Using NDS Manager (NDSMGR32.EXE)

√ Creating, merging, and moving partitions

√ Aborting a partition operation

√ Checking partition continuity

√ Viewing server partitions and partition information

√ Checking synchronization and repairing partitions

The Novell Directory Services (NDS) database tree can be partitioned to improve the overall performance of the network. Partitioning an NDS tree can also provide for scalability and fault tolerance of an NDS database. In this chapter, we'll review the basics of NDS partitions. Then, you'll learn when and how to partition an NDS tree, the benefits of partitioning a tree, and what you should do in case there are partition problems. First, let's look at an overall perspective on NDS partitioning.

NDS Partition Overview

A *partition* is a logical portion of the NDS database. A partition is made up of at least a single container object and all the objects that exist within that container object. Other objects that can exist in a container object include, for example, Organizational Unit, User, and Group objects.

Remember that NDS is hierarchical in nature with container objects (such as Organizational Unit objects) as parent objects, and leaf objects (such as User and Group objects) as child objects. Think of the NDS partitioning concept as hierarchical in nature, too. There are top-level partitions (the parents) that can have multiple subordinate objects beneath them (the children).

In a partition, the top-level container object is termed the *partition root object* and is not the same as the *[Root] container*. The [Root] container is the NDS object from which all other objects emerge. You do not have to create any additional partitions for NDS to have a partition. The [Root] container defines a partition boundary and is created automatically during server installation. When a server is first installed, a copy, or replica, of the NDS tree (the [Root] partition) is placed on the server. Any other partitions must be created manually by a network administrator using the NDS Manager tool, NDSMGR32.EXE. Figure 5.1 shows the default partition—the [Root] container.

NetWare 5 propagates the [Root] partition, and all other partitions, to a maximum of two other servers that are installed within a given partition. As soon as those servers are installed, they automatically receive a copy (replica) of the partition in which they are placed.

In the following sections, we'll explore the benefits of partitioning, compare the NDS partition to a file-system partition, and discuss key partition terms. We'll also determine whether a sample NDS tree needs partitioning. Finally, we'll explore several guidelines that you might find useful when partitioning.

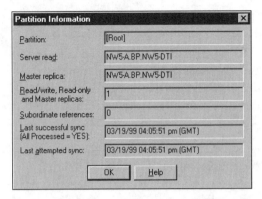

Figure 5.1   An NDS Manager screen showing the existence of the default [Root] partition.

Benefits Provided By Partitioning

By partitioning your NDS tree, you gain several benefits, including the following:

➤ **Scalability** Scalability refers to the degree to which NDS can be broken down into smaller pieces or partitions. If the NDS database is partitioned or split into several pieces, those pieces can be copied to other network servers. This allows for practically unlimited growth of the NDS database by giving you the ability to distribute the contents of the entire database and workload associated with NDS events among multiple servers. The degree of scalability your network has depends on how your network is organized. For example, if you have more than one location, you can break your NDS tree into several pieces and place a replica of a partition in another location.

➤ **NDS access via bindery services** In earlier NetWare local area networks (LANs)—before 4.x—that use bindery services, you can set up a partition and then replicate it, which allows NDS objects to be seen by bindery-based clients and older bindery-based applications.

➤ **Reduced response time** By partitioning the NDS tree, you can reduce the size of the NDS database that any one server must accommodate. This greatly improves searches of objects in the database, either in Windows or DOS-text mode. Accessing the browse list of network computers, printers, and folders in Network Neighborhood will be quicker, too.

➤ **Improved login authentications** After you partition the NDS tree, you can distribute the NDS database so it will be close to the users. This allows users' login requests to be authenticated by the server closest to them—called the *nearest server*. When a user attempts to log in, the login process issues a **GET NEAREST SERVER** request. The login process attempts to access the closest physical server. The nearest server responds with a **GIVE NEAREST SERVER** response and takes the responsibility of authenticating the user's name, password, time-of-day access, and so on. By localizing the NDS partition, users' login access times improve because the server at their local office or site authenticates them.

➤ **Fault tolerance** A well-designed NDS tree and properly planned partition boundaries allow the efficient placement of replicas on multiple servers. If a primary server goes down, one of the other servers that has a copy of the NDS partition can authenticate user logins and display objects, such as Printer, Server, and Organizational Unit objects.

➤ **Facilitate localized security administration** If you have multiple geographic locations connected via a wide area network (WAN) link, you can partition all the objects to one physical location. This allows network administrators at their local sites to manage security more effectively, because they only have to deal with their partitions. This reduces the amount of objects visible to the administrators and fewer objects require less support.

 Partitioning does not imply fault tolerance on the file system—only on the NDS database. To provide fault tolerance on the file system, you have to use disk mirroring or duplexing, a Redundant Array of Inexpensive Disks (RAID), or server mirroring.

NDS Partitions Compared To File System Partitions

An NDS partition is not the same as a file system partition. The NDS partition contains NetWare directory services objects. The file system contains folders (directories) and files. NDS Manager (NDSMGR32.EXE) manages NDS partitions, whereas Windows Explorer or DOS command-line utilities manage folders and files on the DOS and NetWare partitions. The NetWare partition is managed via NetWare Administrator (NWADMIN32.EXE) from a client or with server tools on the server. Remember that a NetWare server needs both a DOS and a NetWare partition configured on the hard disk. NDS Manager does not manage these types of partitions.

You can manage the file system partition in NetWare Administrator as well as in Windows Explorer. In NetWare Administrator, you can perform tasks such as creating, renaming, and deleting folders and files.

Determining The Need To Partition

Now that you understand the benefits of partitioning your NDS tree, let's look at the criteria that will help you decide whether to partition. The criteria used in this decision revolve around the following issues:

➤ Number of geographic locations

➤ Number of servers with partition replicas

➤ Number of NDS objects

If your network has multiple geographic locations, between 10 and 15 servers with partition replicas, or between 1,500 and 3,500 NDS objects, then it's a candidate for partitioning and later replication. However, if your network does not meet these criteria, then it's advantageous to maintain the NDS database with just the default [Root] partition instead of splitting your NDS tree into multiple partitions—you'll have less to manage. Figure 5.2 contains a flowchart that can help you decide whether to partition.

If you have a small LAN with no WAN connections and less than 3,500 NDS objects, you could just maintain the [Root] default partition to reduce the number of partitions you must manage. If you use only the default partition and you remove it, you are, in effect, deleting the whole NDS directory tree.

Note: *When you partition your NDS tree, it doesn't affect what the users see. The NDS tree looks the same to them whether it's partitioned or not.*

Key Partition Terms

If you've decided to partition your NDS tree, you need to be familiar with the following key terms:

➤ Partition boundary

➤ Partition root object

➤ Partition parent

➤ Partition child

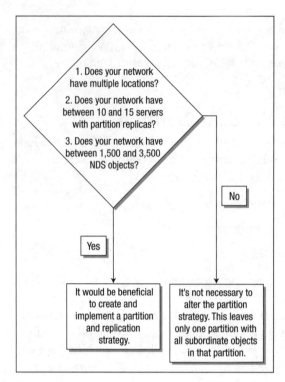

Figure 5.2 Partitioning decision flowchart.

Partition Boundary

A *partition boundary* is defined by a container object and any object that has that container as its parent. A partition can contain multiple containers; however, all NDS objects in a container belong to the same partition as the container. For example, assume a User object named Zac is located in an Organizational Unit called Production. If the Organizational Unit is in a partition, then the User object Zac is located in the same partition as Production. Zac cannot be located in any other partition; it can only reside in one partition at a time.

This is analogous to a file belonging to a folder, where the file is a User object and the folder is an Organizational Unit object. A file can only belong to one folder, and, while in one folder, it cannot be located in another folder.

With respect to partition boundaries, remember the following points:

➤ A partition can have multiple containers; however, a partition cannot extend into the boundary of another partition. Stated another way, a container or leaf object cannot be in multiple partitions.

➤ The optimal tree design should provide a pyramid shape—with more containers and leaf objects at the bottom of the tree than at the top. Because partition boundaries must follow container boundaries, it follows that the partitions will also ideally constitute a pyramid shape. The benefits of this strategy are fewer and more evenly distributed subordinate reference replicas, as we'll see in Chapter 6.

➤ You can only split a partition across container boundaries. If you have leaf objects, such as User, Printer, and Server objects, then you must create another container that holds them in order to split them into a partition.

 Think of a boundary as a logical circle drawn around the partition root object and encompassing everything beneath it.

Figure 5.3 shows a diagram of partition boundaries.

Partition Root Object

A partition takes the name of the top-level container from which it's partitioned. For example, assume an Organizational Unit container called Production is immediately under the [Root] partition. If you split, or partition, Production from the [Root] partition, then the partition name becomes Production. The Production container would be referred to as the *partition root object*. Any subordinate objects would now belong to the Production partition root object.

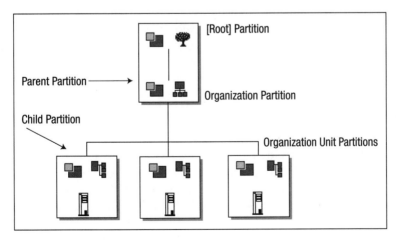

Figure 5.3 Partition boundaries.

The [Root] partition is the default NDS partition. The partition root object is any container that has been partitioned using NDS Manager. The [Root] partition and the partition root object are not the same thing. The partition root object is the container closest to [Root] that defines the top-level container of any given partition.

Partition Parent And Partition Child

A *parent partition* is a partition that is one level higher than a partition root object in an NDS tree. A *child partition* is a partition that is one level lower than a partition root object in an NDS tree. By creating a child partition, you're splitting one partition into two with all partition information staying on the same server that had the original, or parent, partition.

Because this parallels a Windows or DOS tree, let's take a look at an analogous example. Assume you have a folder called FolderA and it contains another folder called FolderB. You can say that FolderA is the parent of FolderB and FolderB is the child of FolderA. This is the same type of relationship that exists with parent and child partitions in an NDS tree. These relationships are hierarchical in nature. Figure 5.3, earlier in the chapter, shows parent and child partitions.

Understand the differences between parent partitions and child partitions.

Partition Guidelines

Partition guidelines are provided to help you define partition boundaries. The two main factors associated with partition guidelines with which you need to be concerned are as follows:

➤ Physical locations

➤ Partition size and partition quantity

Physical Locations

If your organization has multiple network sites with servers in remote locations, the general rule is not to span partition boundaries across a WAN link. However, this decision has an element of subjectivity to it. You might consider the following guidelines when determining whether to partition your NDS tree across a WAN link:

➤ If your WAN is slow (56Kbps or slower), do not partition across it. The partition replicas will attempt to equalize because of a process called *synchronization*. Most likely, a large amount of the WAN link's bandwidth will be allocated to synchronization and a much smaller amount of bandwidth dedicated to user requests.

➤ If your WAN link is fast and reliable (for example, a T1 or T3 connection), then the decision is a bit more nebulous. If there's a high demand for users to access data across the WAN link, then it's probably not a good idea to have your partitions span the WAN link. However, if there's a low demand to access data across the WAN link, then you *might* consider partitioning across the WAN link—but *only* if you find it's imperative.

 Do not create partitions that will span across a WAN link unless your WAN bandwidth is sufficient.

➤ If WAN bandwidth is an issue, you could create smaller partitions placed in a few locations. This reduces WAN traffic once synchronization occurs between partitions across the WAN link.

➤ You can implement a location-based tree design for networks that have multiple geographic locations connected by WAN links. In other words, you can create, for the upper layers of your pyramid-shaped tree, an Organizational Unit for each physical location, whether it's across the street or across the world. Therefore, if you have a department in a separate building and a division in a separate country, you can make partitioning and replication easier by creating an Organizational Unit object for each location. This simplifies partitioning and replication because the locations are already logically defined.

➤ There is one circumstance in which you might not want to implement a location-based design. If you have a high-speed WAN connection, such as Fiber Distributed Data Interface (FDDI), you might not need to create separate Organizational Units for each location. If the WAN link is fast, it might appear that it's operating like a LAN, reducing the need for location-based partition boundaries.

➤ For lower-layer partitions, design the partitions around the divisions or departments and keep their resources, such as printers, servers, and applications, in divisional or departmental container objects. The location-based approach is also conducive to how users perform their daily activities. People typically use printers, applications, and servers in one geographic location, so you should keep those items in an Organizational Unit that you can partition.

➤ Also, for lower-layer partitions, try to keep all objects that are in one location in the same partition. Also, partition around the local server in each geographic area. This allows NDS to update on a local server and not across the WAN link.

We've reviewed the location factors that guide partitioning into an optimal network. You must also be aware that as your organization changes, you might need to revisit your partition and replication strategies. What is optimal today might not be optimal tomorrow. In the following section, we'll investigate the second factor related to partition guidelines—the size of the partition.

Partition Size And Quantity

The size of a partition can affect NDS synchronization and network response time. As a network administrator, you'll need to monitor the size and quantity of partitions in your NDS tree. For this discussion, we'll assume the server is a 100MHz Pentium-class PC with 64MB of RAM. Of course, if your server is faster, it could handle a larger size and quantity of partitions.

Note: *A NetWare 5 server needs a minimum of 64MB of RAM to run. As always, more is recommended.*

Follow these size guidelines for an optimal NDS tree:

➤ **Try to keep small partitions** Generally, the maximum number of NDS objects in a partition should range between 1,500 and 3,500 objects. A larger number of objects may result in synchronization problems as NDS attempts to synchronize a large number of updates related to user logins and other NDS object changes. As an organization grows, you may need to split a partition into child partitions to maintain this guideline.

➤ **Try to keep the [Root] partition small** It's best to keep only the [Root] object and the required Organization object container (the O=*Organization Name* object) at the very top level partition. Therefore, don't include a physical location in the default [Root] partition, because replication of the partition would be dispersed to other servers. Also, don't put any Organizational Unit objects (the OU=*Organizational Unit Name* objects) in the [Root] partition.

➤ **Maintain a small number of child partitions** Novell suggests no more than 35 child partitions for a single parent partition. If your site has more, you might want to modify your tree design. Partition operations such as creating, deleting, merging, and moving partitions affect child partitions. Also, be mindful not to have too many child partitions connected to their parent partitions across slow or unstable WAN links.

The advantages of having smaller partitions include the following:

➤ Enhances performance by putting resources near the users

➤ Diminishes network traffic because the partitions are smaller

➤ Encourages fault tolerance because you reduce the dependence on one server

➤ Reduces the size of the NDS database for any given server

However, there are also some disadvantages of having smaller partitions. Disadvantages include the following:

➤ Because the partitions are smaller, you have more of them, which increases the time it takes a network administrator to maintain the network.

➤ The complexity of the network increases because there are more partitions to deal with.

➤ There is a greater need for synchronizing the NDS database between partitions.

In the following sections, you'll learn how to implement and manage partitioning using NDS Manager.

Installing And Running NDS Manager

NDS Manager is used to partition and replicate an NDS tree. NDS Manager is executed using the NDSMGR32.EXE utility, which is located, by default, in the SYS:\PUBLIC\WIN32 directory. To *replicate* means to copy NDS data to a NetWare server. Partitioning and replication go hand-in-hand. This chapter covers partitioning, and Chapter 6 discusses replication.

NDS Manager replaces the Partition Manager tool that shipped with early versions of NetWare 4.x. NDS Manager first appeared in the NetWare 4.11 release, and the version shipping with NetWare 5 is consistent with the look and feel of the NetWare 4.11 version. NDS Manager provides support for the NetWare clients shown in the following list (which means you can run it from any of the following clients):

➤ Microsoft Windows 95/98

➤ Microsoft Windows NT

Like most Windows-based tools, NDS Manager is powerful and user-friendly. It allows an administrator to perform the following tasks from a client computer:

➤ Partition an NDS database.

➤ Replicate portions of the database.

➤ Repair the NDS database (which reduces the need to repair at the server or run RCONSOLE).

➤ Update the Directory Services NetWare Loadable Module (DS.NLM) to a newer version.

➤ Execute diagnostic software to ensure the integrity of the NDS tree structure.

➤ View the partition list and replica ring information.

Also, like most Windows-based tools, there are multiple ways to accomplish the same task. You can use two methods to execute NDS Manager:

➤ **Execute NDS Manager in standalone mode** You can run NDS Manager by double-clicking on NDSMGR32.EXE in the SYS:\PUBLIC\WIN32 folder on the workstation. You can also create a shortcut and place it on a client's desktop.

If you do not use the correct version of the client software, you'll encounter problems when trying to run NDS Manager. Because you'll be accessing a NetWare 5 server, you have to load the client for NetWare 5 onto the workstation (it comes on a separate CD shipped with NetWare 5). The error messages that will appear if you don't have the client loaded imply that some of the DLL files are corrupt. They are not necessarily corrupt; they're just incompatible with the client software you're running. You typically only see this problem if you try to access a NetWare 5 server with an earlier version of the client software.

➤ **Execute NDS Manager from NetWare Administrator (NWADMIN32)**
If you want to execute NDS Manager from within NetWare Administrator, you can copy a dynamic link library (DLL) file to the NetWare
Administrator SNAPINS folder. When NetWare Administrator starts,
it will read the contents of the SNAPINS folder and incorporate NDS
Manager under the NetWare Administrator's Tools menu. Follow these
steps to use NDS Manager from within NetWare Administrator:

1. Copy the NMSNAP32.DLL file located in SYS:\PUBLIC\WIN32
   to SYS:\PUBLIC\WIN32\SNAPINS.

2. Start NWADMIN32 (NetWare Administrator) located in
   SYS:\PUBLIC\WIN32.

To create a shortcut to NDS Manager and NetWare Administrator on the desktop, drag and drop the utilities (NDSMGR32.EXE
and NWADMIN32) to the workstation desktop. Then, you can
start the programs by clicking on the shortcuts.

Partitioning Using NDS Manager

Now, that we have discussed some of the theoretical aspects of partitioning
and how to install NDS Manager, let's take a look at the following hands-on
topics:

➤ Creating a partition

➤ Merging a partition with its parent

➤ Moving a partition

➤ Aborting a partition operation

➤ Checking partition continuity

➤ Viewing server partitions

➤ Viewing partition information

➤ Viewing partition hierarchy

➤ Checking synchronization

➤ Repairing a partition

Creating A Partition

The create partition option allows you to split your NDS database so it can be replicated to NetWare servers later. Doing this creates a child partition that is subordinate to the parent partition. For example, you might create a partition if your organization grew and you needed multiple business units. You could then replicate those units to local division or department servers placed near the users and printers. To create a child partition within NDS Manager, follow these steps:

1. Open NDS Manger (NDSMGR32.EXE) in one of the two ways discussed earlier in this chapter.

2. Make sure you have the Tree View selected (View|Tree). This is located on the NDS Manager toolbar.

3. Highlight the container you want to create as a child partition by clicking on the object. This container must already be created. Typically, you would choose an Organization or Organizational Unit container object.

4. Click on Object|Create Partition. (Alternatively, you can right-click on the container and choose Create Partition, or click on the Create Partition icon in the toolbar.)

5. The Create Partition dialog box appears and asks you to confirm your request. Click on Yes.

6. Next, you're informed that the preconditions for the operations have been met. To continue with the create process, click on Yes.

7. The last screen indicates that processing is done. Click on Close. Your request is processed.

Figure 5.4 shows a sample screenshot of a partition that has already been created. Notice the little symbol to the left of the tree and the Organization container symbol. That symbol indicates that the container is a partition.

Merging A Partition

When you merge a partition, what you're really doing is merging the child partition to the parent partition. The child partition is removed, but the container is not. You might merge if an organization or business unit combined or merged with another. You could then delete redundant objects in NetWare Administrator.

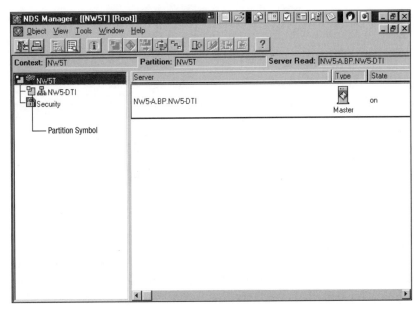

Figure 5.4   The result of a create partition operation.

 You cannot delete a container object in NetWare Administrator if it's a partition root object.

Before merging a child with a parent partition, it's wise to check the synchronization on both partitions. After a partition is merged with its parent, you can go into NetWare Administrator and manage the leaf objects (including deleting and renaming objects). This is demonstrated later in this chapter. To merge a child partition with its parent partition, follow these steps:

1. Open NDS Manager (NDSMGR32.EXE).

2. Highlight the child partition you want to merge with its parent.

3. Click on Object|Partition|Merge. (Alternatively, you can click on the Merge icon on the toolbar, or right-click on the partition and choose Merge.)

4. The Merge Partition dialog box appears. Click on Yes to confirm your request.

5. Next, you're informed that the preconditions for the operations have been met. To continue with the merge process, click on Yes.

6. The last screen indicates that processing is done. Click on Close. Your request is processed.

After the merge process is completed, a screen similar to Figure 5.5 appears. Notice there's now one partition again.

   Note: Make sure that all the servers that contain the partition are online before merging a child with a parent partition.

Moving A Partition

To move a partition to another container, you'll use the partition move operation. You might move a partition to another location if an organization or department that is part of the partition moved to another site. To move a partition, proceed with these steps:

1. Open NDS Manager (NDSMGR32.EXE).

2. Highlight the child partition you want to move.

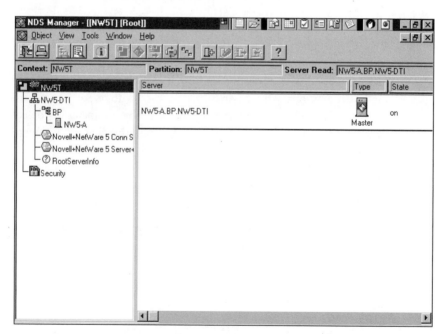

Figure 5.5   The result of merging a child with its parent partition.

3. Click on Object|Partition|Move. (Alternatively, you can right-click on the partition and click on Move, or click on the Move button on the toolbar.)

4. Click on the browse button (to the far right of the To Context field) and the screen shown in Figure 5.6 appears.

5. Choose the container to which you want to move the container. It will confirm your request, so click on OK.

6. Next, you're informed that the preconditions for the operations have been met. To continue with the move process, click on Yes.

7. The last screen indicates that processing is done. Click on Close. Your request is processed.

When moving a partition container, remember the following rules:

➤ The container object being moved must be a partition.

➤ If the destination container does not exist, you must create it in NetWare Administrator.

➤ The container object being moved can have no child partitions.

Note: *It's not possible to move a container in NetWare Administrator. This is considered a partition operation and must be done from NDS Manager.*

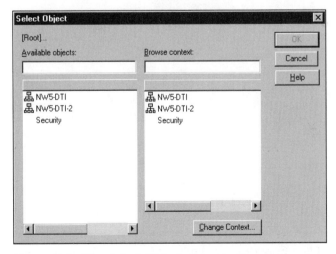

Figure 5.6 The Select Object dialog box appears when you click on the browse button.

Aborting A Partition Operation

You can abort a create partition operation, merge partition operation, or move partition operation, as long as the operation that you are aborting has not committed to the database. Otherwise, it has already completed. To abort an operation, go into NDS Manager, choose the partition where the operation is running, and select Object|Partition|Abort Operation. Complete the request by clicking the appropriate boxes.

You might want to abort an operation if you get synchronization or database errors right after a partition operation. Or, you could use an abort operation when you simply want to stop an operation.

Checking Partition Continuity

You can check the continuity of a partition to help determine if any of the partitions' replicas are getting synchronization errors. To check partition continuity, right-click on a partition and select Partition Continuity. A screen similar to Figure 5.7 appears. In this example, the replica on the right has no errors. If it did have errors, the server replica icon would have an exclamation point. Chapter 6 discusses replication in more detail.

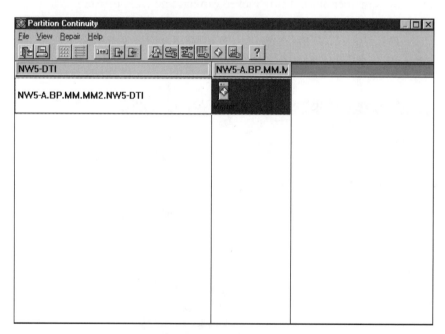

Figure 5.7 The Partition Continuity screen.

Viewing Server Partitions

To view the partitions on a server, select the Server object in NDS Manager. The partitions appear in the right pane of the screen. Figure 5.8 shows the partitions on the NW5-A server.

Viewing Partition Information And Partition Hierarchy

You can view the information about a partition by selecting the partition and then clicking on Object|Information. Alternatively, you can click on the Information icon on the NDS Manager toolbar or right-click on the partition and select Information.

You can also view the partition hierarchy. This shows the parent and child relationships. You accomplish this by double-clicking on partition objects, just as you would by double-clicking on folders in Windows Explorer to see other folders and files.

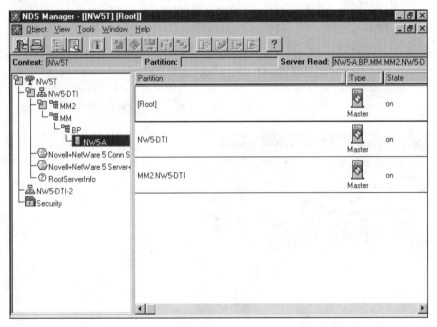

Figure 5.8   Viewing server partitions.

Checking Synchronization

Checking the status of a partition is an important function. If a partition has errors, you want to repair them. To check for synchronization problems, go into NDS Manager, select a partition, then select Object|Check Synchronization. Another alternative is to click on the Check Synchronization option on the toolbar, or right-click on the container and choose Check Synchronization. Answer the questions that appear appropriately. Figure 5.9 shows a satisfactory synchronization check. It shows a partition that was checked within tolerance levels.

Repairing A Partition

You can run repair operations from NDS Manager. Select the partition in question and run Partition Continuity from the Object menu. Alternatively, you can get to Partition Continuity from the Check Synchronization screen, or right-click on a partition and select Partition Continuity. Then, you select Repair on the Partition Continuity screen. You can run various repair operations from here.

The following list names the repair operations and provides a brief explanation of each. A log file is generated by each repair operation:

➤ **Repair Replica** This entails checking the replicas on each server and validating them. You should perform a Repair Local Database first. This is the same as running DSREPAIR.NLM on the local server.

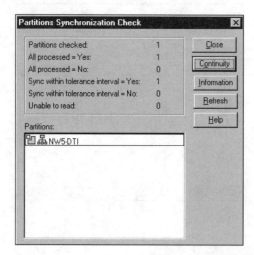

Figure 5.9 A successful synchronization check.

➤ **Repair Network Addresses** This is run to ensure that each server is broadcasting the proper Internetwork Packet Exchange (IPX) address on a LAN. This could also be run from the DSREPAIR.NLM on a server.

➤ **Repair Local Database** This can be executed to ensure integrity of the NDS database. Again, running DSREPAIR at the server console will work, too.

➤ **Repair Volume Objects** This operation verifies volumes, ensuring that a Volume object exists for each volume. When the operation finds a volume with no Volume object, it creates a Volume object for the volume.

 To execute DSREPAIR on a server named NW5-A, you would enter the following command:

`NW5-A: LOAD DSREPAIR`

Note that you do not have to type "LOAD" in NetWare 5 like you did in previous versions of NetWare—you can just type "DSREPAIR". This is true for the loading of all NLMs.

Figure 5.10 shows a sample log file. This was generated from a Repair Volume Object operation. Notice that you can save or print the log file.

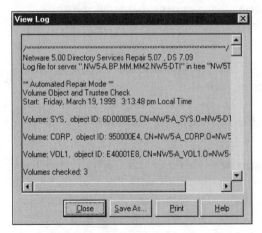

Figure 5.10 The View Log dialog box.

Sample Company Scenario

In this section, we'll take a look at a sample company scenario with respect to partitioning. Burmeister Publishing has several departments in San Francisco, and Munson Media has multiple departments in Dallas and Vancouver. These two entities will merge to create MB Enterprises. The following suggestions are offered to deal with the new company and partitions:

➤ **Place the [Root] partition in one of the cities** One of the cities will need to hold the [Root] partition. For example, you could place the [Root] partition in Vancouver because it has the most servers in the IS department. You will want to replicate it to other cities. Also, keep the [Root] partition small; this can be accomplished by creating other child partitions.

➤ **Create a partition for each of the cities** To follow Novell's guidelines and be consistent with the benefits described earlier, the partition boundaries should follow the physical layout of the network. Because the cities are connected by WAN links, creating a partition boundary at each city allows us to meet the following goals, which were mentioned earlier in this chapter:

  ➤ **Improve login authentications** Partition boundaries based on physical location facilitate replica placement on local servers and avoid synchronization traffic across the WAN link. This improves user login access times because the nearest server will manage the login process. Because all departments have multiple servers, access times should be fast for the users and give them acceptable performance.

  ➤ **Reduce response time** If each city is partitioned, the size of the NDS database stored at each city will be smaller than if they are all in one single partition. This will reduce response time for user requests for NDS resources and displaying the browse lists in Network Neighborhood.

  ➤ **Facilitate localized security administration** Each city can now have localized administration of security. Because Dallas does not have an IS staff, you might consider adding several network administrators at that site to facilitate localized administration. Those staff members can handle the local users' needs.

➤ **Create a partition for each department** The decision to partition each department is based on the number of objects within the lower-level departmental containers. As mentioned earlier, the guideline is to limit the number of objects in any given partition to no more than 3,500 objects (for typical server hardware).

Figure 5.11 shows an overview of our sample company scenario. Keep in mind, this is one possible solution, and as the needs of the company change, the partition plan might change, too.

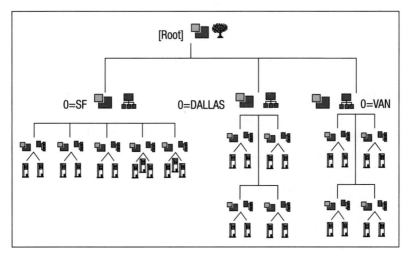

Figure 5.11 A possible result of partioning the sample company.

Practice Questions

Question 1

A child partition can belong to multiple parent partitions.

○ a. True

○ b. False

The correct answer is b; the statement is false. A child partition can only belong to one parent partition.

Question 2

Which tools allow you to partition the NDS tree? [Choose the two best answers]

❏ a. NDSMGR32.EXE

❏ b. NDSMGR32.BAT

❏ c. NMSNAP32.DLL

❏ d. NWADMIN32.EXE

The correct answers are a and d. You can partition the NDS tree with NDSMGR32.EXE (NDS Manager) and NWADMIN32.EXE (NetWare Administrator). However, to accomplish this in NetWare Administrator, you must copy the NMSNAP.DLL to the folder SYS:\PUBLIC\WIN32\SNAPINS. Then, you'll see the NDS Manager option on the Tools menu in NetWare Administrator. Answer b is incorrect, because of the incorrect .BAT extension. Answer c is incorrect, because NWADMIN32.EXE is the DLL file needed to see NDS Manager on NetWare Administrator's Tools menu.

Question 3

What is the name of the default partition that is created at installation?

○ a. ROOT

○ b. Partition root object

○ c. Child partition object

○ d. [Root]

The correct answer is d. The [Root] partition is the default partition created at installation time. There is no ROOT partition; it always appears with the brackets. Therefore, answer a is incorrect and the reason this is a trick question. The top-level partition that is created is considered a partition root object, but that's not the name of the default partition. Therefore, answer b is incorrect. A child partition must be created within a partition root object, so it cannot be [Root]. Therefore, answer c is incorrect.

Question 4

You are a newly hired network administrator for a large multinational company. The company has a large number of departments with many users. Its current NDS tree has 5,000 objects that consist of two Organizational Units and numerous users, groups, printers, and servers, which are all in a single NDS partition. The NetWare 5 servers are 100MHz Pentium class machines with 64MB of RAM. What can you do to optimize the company's NDS tree? [Choose the two best answers]

- ❑ a. Do nothing. It's optimal to have 5,000 objects in a single NDS partition.
- ❑ b. Create a child partition from one of the Organizational Units and place about half of the objects in it.
- ❑ c. Upgrade the server RAM to at least 128MB.
- ❑ d. Move all the NetWare 5 servers to a single geographic location for centralization of security and the NDS database.

The correct answers are b and c. First, there are too many objects (5,000 in a single partition). One of the guidelines states that there should be from 1,500 through 3,500 objects in a single NDS partition. Second, NetWare 5 servers require 64MB of RAM, so the machines meet the acceptable minimum. However, it would be optimal to increase the amount of RAM on the servers to 128MB. The more RAM, the better. Answer a is incorrect, because this is not an optimal NDS design and you should change something. Answer d is incorrect, because placing all the servers in one central location is not a technique used to optimize an NDS tree.

Question 5

> A child partition is one level higher than a partition root object.
>
> ○ a. True
>
> ○ b. False

The correct answer is b; the statement is false. The child partition is not one level higher than its parent. On the contrary, the child partition is one level lower than its parent object.

Question 6

> You work as a network consultant. You're hired as a contractor to assist a small company in designing its NDS tree. This company has sites in two cities that are 32 miles apart. It uses 56Kbps modem lines to connect its offices and only one city has a server. What would you suggest to optimize partitioning over a WAN link? [Choose the three best answers]
>
> ❏ a. Partition over the WAN link with the existing 56Kbps lines.
>
> ❏ b. Don't partition over the WAN link with the existing 56Kbps lines.
>
> ❏ c. Place an additional server in the other city and partition locally on that server.
>
> ❏ d. Upgrade the WAN link to T1 lines.

The correct answers are b, c, and d. The general rule is not to span partition boundaries across slow WAN links. Therefore, answer b is correct. Adding another server at the other location and partitioning locally on that server would optimize the network. You could then add an Organizational Unit and place all the local resources (in the city with the new server) under that Organizational Unit. Replication would occur locally and be an optimal situation. Therefore, answer c is also correct. By upgrading your 56Kbps lines to a T1 line, you enhance network throughput. This could lead to a decision to partition over the WAN link if necessary. Therefore, answer d is also correct. It's not optimal to partition over a 56Kbps WAN link. Therefore, answer a is incorrect.

Question 7

What are the repair operations that can be performed within NDS Manager?
[Choose the four best answers]

❑ a. Repair Volume Object

❑ b. Repair Local Database

❑ c. Repair Replica Database

❑ d. Repair Network Address

❑ e. Repair Replica

The correct answers are a, b, d, and e. The repair operations that can be performed in NDS Manager are Repair Volume Object, Repair Local Database, Repair Network Address, and Repair Replica. Repair Replica Database is not a valid option. Therefore, answer c is incorrect.

Question 8

Zachary is a network engineer who is about to perform a merge partition operation. What should he do prior to executing the merge partition operation?

○ a. He should delete all the objects in the [Root] partition.

○ b. He should check the synchronization status on both the parent and child partitions.

○ c. He must run DSREPAIR on the server console.

○ d. He must create a separate partition to hold the merged container.

The correct answer is b. Zachary should check the status of synchronization on the parent and child partitions. He does not need to delete the objects in the [Root] partition. Therefore, answer a is incorrect. He does not need to run DSREPAIR on the server. Therefore, answer c is incorrect. He cannot create a separate partition to hold the merged container. The child partition will be merged with the parent partition and the parent partition already exists. It will hold the objects that were in the child partition. Therefore, answer d is incorrect.

Question 9

> Jessie is a network engineer who is about to perform a move partition operation. What rules must she abide by when moving a partition? [Choose the three best answers]
>
> ❏ a. She must make sure the destination container has been created.
>
> ❏ b. She must make sure the container object being moved is a partition.
>
> ❏ c. She must make sure the container object being moved has no child partitions.
>
> ❏ d. She must make sure she deletes the source partition.

The correct answers are a, b, and c. Jessie must make sure all three statements are complied with. She does not need to delete the source partition. Therefore, answer d is incorrect.

Question 10

> Which commands are used to run the repair operation at the server console? [Choose the two best answers]
>
> ❏ a. **LOAD DSREPAIR**
>
> ❏ b. **DSREPAIR**
>
> ❏ c. **DSFIXIT**
>
> ❏ d. **DSCHKDSK**

The correct answers are a and b. You can run repair operations with either **LOAD DSREPAIR** or just **DSREPAIR**. The commands **DSFIXIT** and **DSCHKDSK** do not exist. Therefore, answers c and d are incorrect.

Need To Know More?

 Craft, Melissa, Justin Grant, and Dan Cheung. *CNE NetWare 5 Study Guide*. Osborne McGraw-Hill, Berkeley, CA, 1999. ISBN 0-07-211923-3. Chapter 24 and Chapter 34 provide good information about partitions.

 Hughes, Jeffrey F. and Blair W. Thomas. *Novell's Four Principles of NDS Design*. Novell Press, San Jose, CA, 1996. ISBN 0-7645-4522-1. Chapter 4 provides useful information about NDS partitioning.

 For additional information on partitioning and NDS Manager, review the NetWare 5 online documentation. Use the keywords "partition" and "NDS Manager."

NDS Replica Techniques

Terms you'll need to understand:

√ Replication

√ Synchronization

√ Master replica

√ Read/write replica

√ Read-only replica

√ Subordinate reference replica

√ Replica list

√ Schema

√ Transitive synchronization

√ Heartbeat

√ Limber

√ Connection Management

√ Backlink

√ Server Status Check

Techniques you'll need to master:

√ Determining the need to replicate

√ Understanding default replication values

√ Understanding key replication terms

√ Learning the advantages of replication

√ Understanding replication guidelines

√ Utilizing Novell Directory Services (NDS) Manager to replicate

√ Using WAN Traffic Manager to control wide area network (WAN) synchronization

√ Understanding WAN traffic policies

√ Understanding replicating the audit files

After partitioning your Novell Directory Services (NDS) Directory database, you can then *replicate* it to servers. Replication is done to provide fault tolerance and reliability and to enhance quick access to server resources by client computers. In Chapter 5, you learned how to implement partitioning. In this chapter, you'll learn how to replicate NDS to create an optimal network.

 Remember that *partitions* are logical divisions of the NDS database and *replicas* are the actual data that constitutes the NDS objects within a partition boundary.

NDS Replication Overview

In this section, you'll learn how to determine whether you need to replicate. In addition, we'll discuss the default values, basic terms, and advantages of replication.

Determining The Need To Replicate

Before you replicate your NDS tree to all your servers, you should consider some criteria. After all, if your network is small, there might not be a need to change how replication occurs, because NDS is self-tuning. Therefore, you should understand how the following criteria can affect your decision to alter the default replication strategy:

➤ Number of NDS objects

➤ Number of geographic locations

➤ Number of servers

If your organization meets the following criteria, you might want to accept the defaults and not concern yourself with implementing a replication strategy:

➤ You have a low number of NDS objects—from 1,500 to 3,500 User and resource objects

➤ All your servers are connected by stable LAN connections

➤ Your organization has a need for between 1 and 15 replicated servers (this might be necessary, for example, to support bindery services)

Figure 6.1 provides a flowchart that can help you decide if you need to replicate your NDS tree.

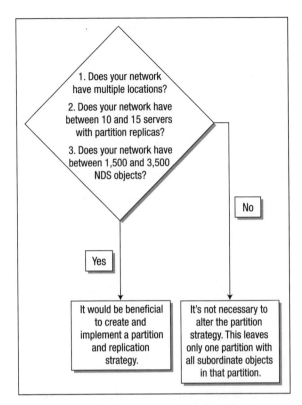

Figure 6.1 Replication decision flowchart.

 If your network has WAN links, you should consider implementing a replication strategy.

Based on your input in the decision flowchart, you'll come up with one of two choices: Accept the replication default values or implement a replication strategy starting with the default values.

Replication Default Values

If you have a small network without remote sites connected via WAN links, NDS provides the default values, and you don't need to change them. The following are the default values Novell considers to be optimal for a small LAN (*small* meaning a network that does not exceed the criteria listed in the previous section):

➤ NDS maintains only one partition, the [Root] partition, and does not split it into other partitions.

➤ Only one NDS tree object is created.

➤ Only one Organization (O=*name)* is created. Many times, this is your company or organization name. For example, O=DEKALB_TECH, where DEKALB_TECH is the name of a technical school.

➤ The administrator User object (typically ADMIN) along with the Server and Volume objects are housed in the Organization container.

➤ NDS will replicate the NDS Directory database to the first two servers installed on the network. Therefore, by default, you'll end up with three copies of the NDS database: The original replica on the first server to go into the tree, plus two other copies, one on each of the next two servers that are inserted into the tree. The replicas, or copies, of the database on the servers are kept up-to-date, or synchronized, automatically by NetWare.

Note: *The NetWare 5 Server install process creates many of the defaults based on the answers you provide during installation.*

If you have a large enough network to change the default replication strategy, this chapter will be valuable to you. It's devoted to modifying the Novell default replication strategy.

Key Replication Terms And Concepts

Before you implement a new strategy, you need to understand the following key replication terms and concepts:

➤ Partition

➤ Replication

➤ Synchronization

➤ Replica types

➤ Replica list

➤ Schema

➤ Transitive synchronization

➤ NDS traffic

The preceding key terms and concepts are discussed in the following sections.

Partition

A *partition* is a logical division of an NDS tree. After a partition is created, either manually or during the install process by accepting the defaults, the partition root object will maintain a list of all servers that receive a copy (replica) of this portion of the NDS Directory.

 When you create partitions, you're logically splitting your NDS Directory database into manageable pieces. These pieces can then be replicated to other servers. NetWare servers hold the replicas of partitions.

Replication

Replication is the process of copying an NDS database to other servers in the tree. The first three installed servers maintain accurate copies of the NDS Directory database through a process called *synchronization*. The first server installed holds the master copy of the NDS Directory. It then sends updates to two other servers by default. The server replicas might not be exactly consistent at any given instant. However, at some point, the replicas will be equal, because synchronization occurs on a continual basis, as discussed in the following section. Novell refers to the partitioned and replicated NDS database as being distributed and "loosely consistent."

Synchronization

Synchronization is the process of automatically keeping the partition replicas consistent. Any changes made to the NDS Directory are automatically replicated to all servers that have a copy of the partition where changes have occurred. This is similar to a DOS **COPY** or **XCOPY** command in that you have a source item and a destination item. In NDS, the items are replicas instead of folders, directories, and files—like in DOS. Synchronization is also an automatic process. There are two types of synchronization that occur among replicas:

➤ **Immediate synchronization** This type of synchronization occurs after an NDS object has changed. For example, deleting or creating a User object in the NDS tree triggers immediate synchronization. This type of change needs to be propagated to the other servers immediately. By default, an immediate synchronization executes 10 seconds after a change is committed to the NDS Directory database.

➤ **Slow synchronization** A slow synchronization triggers when less essential changes that may be common to several NDS objects are made. Login properties, such as network address and login time, are examples of these.

By default, a slow synchronization is executed 22 minutes after an NDS change of this nature. This way, synchronization traffic across the network is minimized.

If replicas are not equal or are considered out of sync, you can manually synchronize them using NDS Manager. For synchronization to occur, the servers must be online.

Replica Types

Now, let's discuss the types of replicas that can exist. A server can hold any one of the following four replica types:

➤ **Master replica** The first server installed on a network has a copy of the NDS Directory, and that copy is called the master replica. There can be only one master replica for any partition. Other servers that are installed hold read/write replicas by default. However, you can manually add additional read/write or read-only replicas. It's mandatory to have the server that has the master replica up and running; its job is to control partition boundary issues, such as creating, merging, moving, deleting, and repairing partitions. The master replica is also needed to create a new replica. It sends and receives updates to the other replica types. If the master replica needs to be down for any length of time, you need to make another replica the master replica.

There can be only one master replica for each partition at one time.

➤ **Read/write replica** A read/write replica can send and receive updates from other replicas. NDS can read and write object data on this type of replica. The changes are then sent to all replicas in the partition. These replicas provide a high degree of fault tolerance. If your users are in remote sites and connected to your main network by a slow WAN link, such as a 56Kbps line, or across very busy routers, then you might consider putting a read/write replica on a server near the users who use it. This way, the **GET NEAREST SERVER** and **GIVE NEAREST SERVER** negotiations will cause the closest physical server to validate the user's login, and the user will gain quick access. It also gives the user quick access to local resources and displays the browse list in Network Neighborhood. It's possible to create as many read/write replicas as you have servers; however, the downside is that for each replica, NDS attempts to synchronize the instances of each server's replica, which can cause excessive network traffic.

Note: Whereas read/write replicas offer a degree of fault tolerance, NDS does not provide fault tolerance on the file system. It only replicates NDS Directory data. An example of NDS data that is replicated is a User object. If a user's address, city, or state information changes, it will be replicated.

➤ **Read-only replica** A read-only replica can only get NDS synchronization updates from either a master replica or a read/write replica; it cannot get changes from a client computer. A network administrator sitting at a client computer can make a change, such as deleting or adding a user in NetWare Administrator; however, the change will be sent to a master or read/write replica, which will, in turn, synchronize its NDS database to the read-only replica. Be careful about placing a read-only replica at a remote site across a slow WAN link. Any changes made by an administrator at the remote site are sent "across the wire" to the master or read/write replica at the home office and then back down the wire to the read-only replica. In this case, you have fault tolerance, but you increase network traffic.

The read-only replica types have been created by Novell for some future implementation of NDS. Read-only replicas must be manually created using NDS Manager. They only get synchronized when the partition replicas synchronize.

➤ **Subordinate reference replica** These replicas cannot be created manually. NDS automatically creates subordinate reference replicas to maintain parent/child relationships across partition boundaries. Subordinate reference replicas allow parent partitions to locate servers that contain the data representing their child partitions. NDS automatically deletes subordinate references when they become unnecessary. If a replica of a child partition is copied to a server that has the parent partition, the subordinate reference is removed by NDS (for example, when a partition merge operation occurs). Subordinate references are really indexes or pointers that contain only enough information to get a child partition's name across the partition boundary for the parent partition. Subordinate reference replicas are generated on servers that contain a parent partition's replica, but not the child partition's replica. Subordinate reference replicas produce very little network traffic.

 Subordinate reference replicas do not provide any NDS fault tolerance. Master, read/write, and read-only replicas do provide fault tolerance. You cannot create subordinate reference replicas.

Unlike the other replica types, subordinate reference replicas exchange date and time information between servers and update only the partition root object at the top of the partition. Although they yield very little synchronization traffic, they are generated by the system, and a poorly designed NDS tree could create a large number of subordinate reference replicas. The cumulative effect of a large quantity of them could hamper network utilization by resulting in additional synchronization traffic. Remember that all replicas participate in synchronization. You have control over the number of other replica types that exist, because there's a one-to-one correspondence between the other replica types and servers— they are physical. Because NetWare creates subordinate reference replicas and they are not physical in nature like servers, many of them could be built dynamically.

 The rule to remember that governs the creation of subordinate references is as follows: Any server that receives an instance of a parent partition (master, read/write, or read-only replica), but does not have a copy of any child partitions to that parent, will receive a subordinate reference to that child partition. In other words, subordinate references are created on servers, "where the parent is, but the child is not."

Figure 6.2 shows a few of the replica types. To see this view, open NDS Manager, and click on View|Partitions And Servers.

Note: Read-only replicas are not able to support user authentications. Only the master and read/write replicas can support the necessary NDS updates that occur during the login process.

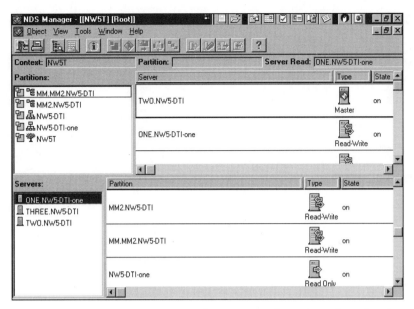

Figure 6.2   NDS Manager view of master, read/write, and read-only replica types.

Replica List

The *replica list* is the list of servers that are to send and/or receive the NDS Directory information for a given partition. In NDS Manager, select a partition and on the right-hand side, you'll see the server name and replica type. Figure 6.3 shows that master, read/write, and read-only replicas exist for a partition named NW5-DTI-one. You can check the integrity of the replicas on each server in the replica list by running a continuity check. This is known as "walking the replica ring."

> *Note:*   *The replica list is also called the replica ring.*

Schema

The *schema* is a set of rules that determines object classes, containment rules, and what type of information you can store about an object, such as what is required and what is optional. Every single object is called an object class, and each object class has properties associated with it. For example, a user is an object class and each User object has certain properties, such as first name, last name, department, and so on. Each property has a set of values. For example,

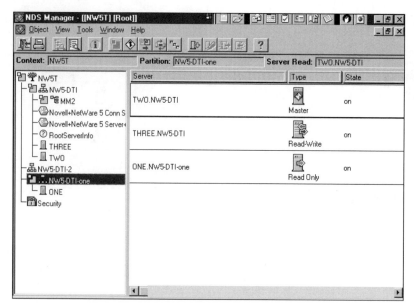

Figure 6.3   The replica list for a partition.

Todd is a value for the first name property, and Meadors is a value for the last name property. All the objects of a certain NDS tree comprise the schema for that tree. There are two types of schema in NetWare 5:

➤ **Base schema**   This is the schema that ships straight out of the box with NetWare 5.

➤ **Extended schema**   This is the schema that reflects the changes you make to the base schema to fit the needs of your organization.

You can access a User object's schema by opening NDS Manager, clicking on Object|Schema Manager, and double-clicking on User. The base schema for a User object is shown in Figure 6.4.

How do schemas relate to partitions and replicas? Well, NetWare 5 replicates to other servers, and those servers will replicate only the objects and properties that are in the default base schema or in the schema you modify, called the extended schema.

   Think of a schema as a framework for what goes into an NDS database.

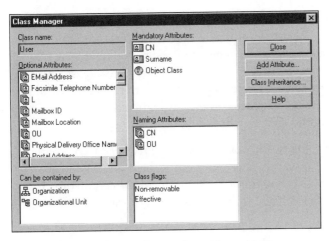

Figure 6.4   The base schema for a User object.

Transitive Synchronization

Transitive synchronization is the process in which servers with differing protocols can synchronize their replicas. In NetWare 5, you can have servers that
run the following protocols:

➤ **IP only** The Internet Protocol (IP) is part of the Transmission Control
Protocol/Internet Protocol (TCP/IP) suite of protocols used to access
hosts on the Internet.

➤ **IPX only** Internetwork Packet Exchange (IPX) is Novell's proprietary
protocol. It's not used over the Internet.

➤ **Both IPX and IP** Although this causes more traffic because of the
multiple protocols, you can run both protocols on a NetWare 5 server.

*Note: You can select the protocols for the server during installation, or
you can add them afterwards.*

With a multiprotocol arrangement, you can have different servers with different protocols in your network. You can have an IP-only server as your Web
server for your point of entry into the Internet, and you can have IPX-only
servers on your local intranet. These two protocols are not compatible; however, the replicas on each server need to be synchronized. This cannot be
accomplished if each server is using a different communications protocol.

This is where transitive synchronization comes in. Transitive synchronization
stems from the mathematical principle called the transitive property of equal-
ity. Basically, for the two servers to synchronize their replica partitions, there

must be a liaison server that runs both protocols. When an NDS change is made, a source server determines if the destination servers can communicate. If they can, the update occurs. If the source and destination servers are running different protocols, a server that runs both protocols (called a transitive server) intervenes. The source server sends the updates to the transitive server, and the transitive server forwards the updates to the destination servers. Several benefits are derived from this situation, including the following:

➤ In a multiprotocol network, not all servers are required to run both IP and IPX. This eliminates unnecessary traffic, because you don't have both protocols generating traffic. Each protocol has certain broadcast characteristics that will add traffic to the network wire.

➤ Only one server is needed to have a transitive server. Although this places a large burden on that server, in a large organization, this could be a dedicated server chartered with the task of performing transitive synchronization.

NDS Traffic

Other than replica and transitive synchronization, several other types of traffic are created on the network. They are as follows:

➤ **Schema synchronization** This occurs once every four hours, and it's performed to make sure the schema is the same across all partitions. It also ensures that all schema changes are consistent.

➤ **Heartbeat** Heartbeat executes every half hour, by default, and it runs as a background process to make the NDS Directory objects the same across all replicas in the replica list.

➤ **Limber** This runs five minutes after the server is booted and then once every three hours thereafter. Limber makes sure a server's index pointer table is updated to reflect changes in the server's name and address among the replicas. It also verifies that the NDS tree name is consistent among servers in the replica list or replica ring.

➤ **Connection Management** This process ensures a highly secure virtual connection for servers in the replica list to communicate across.

➤ **Backlink** This process runs 2 hours after the NDS Directory is open and then every 13 hours (780 minutes). It ensures that pointers to NDS objects that are not stored on a server's replica are consistent. These pointers are called *external references*; they are local identifiers assigned to a process when the process needs to access resources on other servers. You can change this process's settings with a server console **SET** command. For example, to change the interval to 5 hours (300 minutes) on a server named NW5, use the following command:

```
NW5: SET NDS BACKLINK INTERVAL = 300
```

➤ **Server Status Check** The Server Status Check process is initiated on a server that does not have a replica. It connects to either a master or read/write replica, and the process runs every six minutes.

As you can see, there's a lot of traffic generated on a NetWare network. Now that you're familiar with most of the NDS replication key terms, let's take a look at some of the advantages of NDS replication.

Advantages Of NDS Replication

The following advantages can be achieved by NDS replication:

➤ **Network fault tolerance** This is the main goal of NDS replication. By replicating the NDS partitioned database, you can increase network resource availability. The database will be replicated automatically to other servers, and, if one goes down, the other servers will be able to provide access to NDS resources. Users can be authenticated on the server that is still up as long as it has a replica of the partition that existed on the server that went down. Replication is transparent to the users.

➤ **Reduced network synchronization traffic** With organizations becoming more global, there's a big emphasis on enterprise management. To minimize synchronization traffic flow, you need to determine the best way to implement replication.

➤ **Enhanced user response time to resources** Another benefit provided by replication is enhanced response time for users. With replication, a copy of a database is placed on multiple servers. By placing servers in strategic locations, you can enhance access to resources, decrease the amount of time it takes to perform searches, improve the speed of displaying the browse list, and improve login access.

➤ **Access to bindery services** By creating a replica on a server, pre-NetWare 4.x clients can use bindery emulation to access NDS objects stored in the partition. Users can then log on to a server in the partition with a bindery connection. However, you must enter the **SET BINDERY CONTEXT** command at the server console. For example:

```
NW5: SET BINDERY CONTEXT = "OU=NIGHT.O=DEKALBTECH"
```

Now, let's take a look at some NDS replication guidelines.

NDS Replication Guidelines

The following guidelines can be used to help you create an optimal network. Whether you have one site or many sites, you need to appraise you organizational needs periodically. These factors relate to the following:

➤ Number of replicas

➤ Location of replicas

Number Of Replicas

Novell recommends that you have at least three replicas for meeting fault-tolerance goals, which is why NetWare automatically creates replicas (one master and two read/write replicas) on the first three servers installed. If you want more replicas, you have to create them. It's also suggested that you never exceed 10 replicas of a single partition on one network. Doing so causes excess synchronization traffic that can slow network performance.

One server can store multiple replicas as long as the replicas represent different partitions. However, you should not have more than 15 to 20 replicas on one server. Having too many replicas can cause excessive synchronization traffic on a server—which can become a network bottleneck. Also, note that other factors affect replication synchronization traffic in terms of replica location, including:

➤ Speed of the network boards, routers, hubs, and bridges

➤ Quantity and speed of the servers holding replicas

➤ Volume of LAN/WAN traffic flow

The guidelines we're using are for servers with a bare minimum of 64MB of RAM on a Pentium class computer. NetWare 5 requires 64MB just to install and run; therefore, you should add additional RAM on the servers—more is better.

Location Of Replicas

The location of replicas should be centered around a department or project team. In other words, the data should be close to the users that need to access it. Place a read/write replica on a server physically close to users for speedy login. If you have a large number of users at remote sites, consider placing a replica on a server at that site. This reduces overall synchronization traffic across a slow WAN link. However, you must weigh the tradeoff of the server's administrative costs at that location.

The location of replicas must strike a balance between synchronization cost and network performance. Additional replicas may be beneficial for speed of fulfilling users' requests for NDS resources. However, the larger the number of servers involved in a replica ring, the greater the synchronization traffic. Synchronization costs are particularly important to consider if the physical layout of the network dictates that replicas of the same partition must exist on servers in different physical locations connected via WAN links. This would be the case if a remote site had only one server. For fault tolerance, it would be necessary to place a copy of this particular partition on an off-site server.

 Make sure you replicate the [Root] partition—all other objects stem from it.

Replication Using NDS Manager

As discussed in Chapter 5, NDS Manager is the software utility you use to both partition and replicate an NDS tree. The tool is NDSMGR32.EXE, and it's located in SYS:\PUBLIC\WIN32. Just as a reminder, you can execute NDS Manager by double-clicking on NDSMGR32.EXE or by opening the Tools menu in NetWare Administrator. (See Chapter 5 for more detail on NDS Manager.) Let's take a look at what you can do with NDS Manager in regards to replication:

➤ Add replicas

➤ Delete replicas

➤ Change replica types

➤ Check partition continuity

➤ Synchronize partitions immediately

➤ Send and receive updates

➤ View synchronization errors

➤ View transitive synchronization

➤ Repair replicas

Adding A Replica

The Add Replica option allows you to add a replica of a partition. When you hear the word *replica*, think "the server on which the partition is stored." Follow these steps to add a replica of a partition to a particular server:

1. Open NDS Manager.

2. Make sure the Tree View is selected (View|Tree).

3. Click on an existing partition to highlight it, then choose Object|Add Replica. (Alternatively, you can right-click on the partition and choose Add Replica, or choose the Add Replica icon on the toolbar.)

4. The Add Replica screen (shown in Figure 6.5) appears. You can add either a read/write or read-only replica. Choose one.

5. Click on the browse button to the right of the Server Name row.

6. Browse to find the server to which you want to add the replica, and highlight it to select it. Click on OK.

7. Click on OK again to confirm your request and begin the process.

 You cannot add a subordinate reference replica or a master replica.

Deleting A Replica

To delete a replica, follow these steps:

1. Open NDS Manager.

2. Make sure you can see your replica list on the right-hand side of the screen. (The partitions will be on the left.) Click on the replica you want to delete on the right side of the screen.

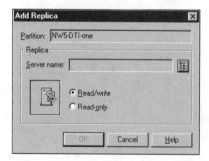

Figure 6.5 The Add Replica dialog box.

3. Click on Object|Delete. (Alternatively, right-click on the replica and choose Delete.)

4. Confirm your request to begin the process.

You can only delete read/write and read-only replicas. To delete a master replica, you have to make a new master replica on another partition. If the server is being completely removed, then you need to delete the Server object in NDS Manager.

> *Note: Deleting a replica can speed up your WAN/LAN because it results in less synchronization traffic; however, it might slow user access to resources.*

Changing A Replica Type

To change the type of replica held on a server, you need to do the following:

1. Open NDS Manager.

2. Click on the replica you want to change in the right-hand side of the screen.

3. Click on Object|Replica|Change Type. The Change Replica Type dialog box appears (see Figure 6.6).

4. Select Master, Read/write, or Read-only.

You cannot change the replica type for a master replica or create a subordinate reference replica using the Change Replica command.

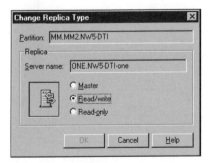

Figure 6.6 The Change Replica Type dialog box.

Checking Partition Continuity

Do the following to check the integrity of replica rings:

1. Open NDS Manager.

2. Click on the partition you want to check, and select Object|Partition Continuity.

3. After the Partition Continuity screen displays, select View|Replica List Table. This is also called "walking the replica ring." Figure 6.7 shows the list of replicas in partition continuity.

Synchronizing A Partition Immediately

NetWare synchronizes automatically; however, if you want to manually activate synchronization, you can. Use the following steps to synchronize immediately:

1. Open NDS Manager.

2. Click on the partition you want to synchronize in the left side of the screen.

3. Click on Object|Partition Continuity. (Alternatively, right-click on the partition and select Partition Continuity.)

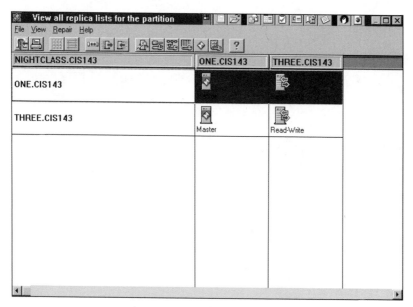

Figure 6.7 The View All Replica Lists For The Partition screen.

4. Highlight the replica you want to synchronize, and click Repair|
   Synchronize Immediately.

5. Confirm the statement about generating extra network traffic by clicking
   on Yes.

6. Confirm again to process by clicking on OK.

You can perform the preceding steps on an NDS object you recently changed
to have those changes take effect immediately.

Sending And Receiving Updates

Use the following steps to receive updates from the master replica:

1. Open NDS Manager.

2. Click on a partition on the left side of the screen.

3. Click on Object|Partition Continuity. (Alternatively, right-click on the
   partition and select Partition Continuity.)

4. Highlight the replica you want to start receiving updates about, and
   click on Repair|Receive Updates or Repair|Send Updates. Note that you
   cannot receive updates to a master replica.

5. Confirm by clicking on OK to begin the process.

Viewing Synchronization Errors

You can view any replica synchronization errors in the Partition Continuity
screen. Any errors will result in an exclamation point next to the server replica.
Figure 6.8 shows server replicas with synchronization errors. You can double-
click on a replica with an error, and click on the question mark beside it to find
out what the error is. Network administrators should be familiar with this
feature of NDS Manager, because the help screens offer some useful actions to
help resolve any Directory errors.

Viewing Transitive Synchronization

You can view transitive synchronization on the Partition Continuity screen.
Click on View|Transitive Synchronization Table. A screen similar to the one
shown in Figure 6.9 appears.

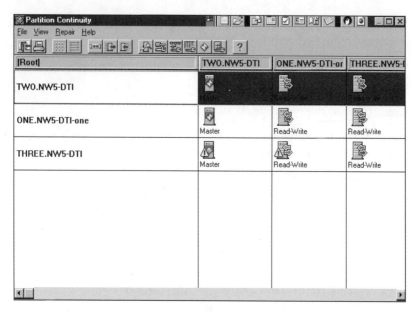

Figure 6.8 Viewing synchronization errors.

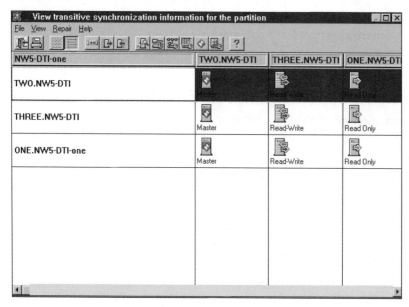

Figure 6.9 Viewing transitive synchronization.

Repairing A Replica

If the partition on a replica becomes corrupt, you might need to run a repair replica operation:

1. In the Partition Continuity screen, highlight a partition, and click on Repair|Repair Replica.

2. Confirm that you want to repair the replica on the server shown by clicking on Yes.

3. Another screen appears asking if you want to continue with the operation. Click on Yes again. A log similar to the one shown in Figure 6.10 appears and shows if there were any errors.

We'll now turn our attention to a few synchronization commands you can use at the server console.

Synchronization-Related Server Commands

In previous versions of NetWare (for example, NetWare 4.x), DSTRACE referred to a group of SET commands available at the server console. Now, in

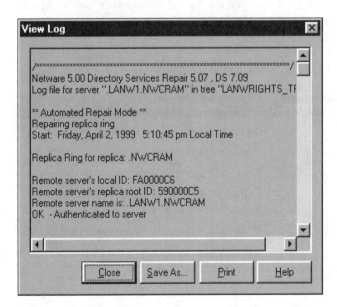

Figure 6.10   The View Log for a repair replica action.

NetWare 5, DSTRACE is a utility (a NetWare Loadable Module, or NLM) that provides monitoring capabilities for NDS events. DSTRACE can be used to determine and track the health of NDS as it communicates with other NetWare 5 servers in the tree.

Table 6.1 presents a partial list of DSTRACE commands related to synchronization. There are other synchronization commands that can be executed on the server, and we'll discuss them in a bit more detail than the commands shown in Table 6.1.

You can use a command to specify the interval of time that synchronization has not occurred because of the inactivity of the servers. (This is called the heartbeat, as mentioned earlier in this chapter.) The default is 30 minutes, but it can range from 2 to 1,440 minutes. If you have replicas in the replica list that cross a WAN, you should set this interval high. It will cause synchronization to wait for the specified inactivity interval and thereby reduce WAN traffic. The following example sets the inactivity command to five hours (300 minutes):

```
SET NDS INACTIVITY SYNCHRONIZATION INTERVAL = 300
```

The next command specifies that only certain version of NDS will be synchronized. The default value is **OFF**, meaning all versions of DS.NLM can synchronize. To restrict synchronization to only version 4.21 of DS.NLM, issue the following command:

```
SET NDS SERVER SYNCHRONIZATION RESTRICTIONS = ON,421
```

Table 6.1 Synchronization commands for the server console.	
Command	**Description**
DSTRACE SCREEN = ON	Enables NDS events to be sent to the screen.
DSTRACE SCREEN = OFF	Disables NDS events to be sent to the screen.
DSTRACE FILE = ON	Enables NDS events to be sent to the default file—SYS:\SYSTEM\DSTRACE.LOG.
DSTRACE FILE = OFF	Disables NDS events to be sent to the default file.
HELP DSTRACE	Provides help on the use of the DSTRACE NLM.

Use the **MODULES** command at the server console to determine the version of DS.NLM.

To specify that all servers are up in NDS, run the following command:

```
SET NDS SERVER STATUS = UP
```

You might issue the preceding command if a server is really up, but NDS does not see it as up.

Now, let's look at a tool to help you manage WAN traffic.

WAN Traffic Manager

WAN Traffic Manager is a tool in NetWare 5 that allows you to manage NDS synchronization traffic across WAN and LAN links. It's used to optimize traffic on your network and reduce operational costs. WAN Traffic Manager allows you to do the following:

➤ Restrict synchronization traffic based on:

  ➤ The type of traffic you want to allow or disallow

  ➤ The associated cost of traffic that you can set

  ➤ The time of day you want to allow or disallow traffic

➤ Manage NDS traffic among all servers

➤ Handle replica synchronization

WAN Traffic Manager Components

There are several components of WAN Traffic Manager:

➤ **WTM.NLM** WAN Traffic Manager is an NLM that is executed on a Novell server. Prior to sending NDS traffic on the network, WTM.NLM checks for a WAN traffic policy to determine what traffic can be sent. If you have servers in a replica list across a WAN link, it's best to run WTM.NLM on all the servers in the list. You can either load this NLM at the server console or add it to the server's AUTOEXEC.NCF file for automatic execution at server startup. To execute WTM.NLM on a server named NW5, you would enter the following command:

```
NW5: LOAD WTM
```

➤ **NetWare Administrator snap-in** This WAN Traffic Manager interface allows you to create LAN Area objects and WAN traffic policies, and then allows you to associate the two. After WAN Traffic Manager is installed, you can create a LAN Area object in NetWare Administrator.

Note: WAN Traffic Manager is installed from the NetWare 5 Server Installation CD. Under Additional Products and Services, select "WAN Traffic Manager Services".

➤ **WAN traffic policies** These policies are the rules that govern what type of traffic can be transmitted across the network and when it can go. WAN traffic policies can be applied to an NDS Server object, or you can create a LAN Area object with policies applied to a group of servers. You can create traffic policies and associated costs for LAN Area objects or Server objects. WAN traffic policies are discussed in the following section.

WAN Traffic Policies

There are a number of WAN traffic policies that come with NetWare 5. In addition, you can create your own. Note that each of these policies is really made up of two subpolicies: One policy exists for synchronization traffic, such as external references, limber, schema synchronization, backlink, and login restrictions, and the other policy exists for all other traffic. The policies are as follows:

➤ **1-3AM** This policy limits the time traffic can be sent to between 1:00 and 3:00 in the morning.

➤ **7AM-6PM** This policy limits the time traffic can be sent to between 7:00 in the morning and 6:00 in the evening.

➤ **COSTLT20** The Cost Less Than 20 policy prevents traffic unless the cost is less than 20.

➤ **IPX** This policy only allows IPX traffic to be generated.

➤ **NDSTTYPS** There are a number of sample policies here that contain variable parameters NDS passes to a request.

➤ **ONOSPOOF** The Already Open, No Spoofing policy only allows traffic to be distributed on existing WAN sessions. It assumes all other sessions are being spoofed, or captured. *Spoofing* is when someone posing as an authorized user captures data.

➤ **OPNSPOOF** The Already Open, Spoofing policy only allows existing traffic to be sent, but, if a session has not been used (open) for 15 minutes, NetWare assumes such connections are spoofed, or captured, and does not use those connections.

➤ **SAMEAREA** This policy only allows traffic to be sent in the same network area. For TCP/IP traffic, the area is the network ID of the IP address or address class. For IPX/SPX traffic, this policy is determined by the **NET=** parameter specified on the **BIND** statement in the AUTOEXEC.NCF file on the server.

WAN Traffic Manager can be used as a software firewall to filter out packets of data.

Using WAN Policies

Question

To use a WAN policy, follow these steps:

1. Open NetWare Administrator.

2. Open the properties pages of the Server object or the LAN Area object by double-clicking on it. (Alternatively, right-click on the object and select Details, or highlight the object and select Object|Details.)

3. In the right side of the dialog box, there is a WAN Policies tab. Click on it.

4. Click on the Predefined Policy Groups drop-down list, and pick the policy of your choice.

5. Click on Load Group. After the policy group is loaded, it will indicate if errors exist. If no errors exist, click on OK.

6. Confirm to apply your policy.

If you want to apply a policy to a group of servers, create a LAN Area object.

WAN Traffic Manager SET Commands

After you've loaded WTM.NLM, you can use a variety of **SET** commands to help you manage the WAN Traffic Manager. Table 6.2 lists the WAN Traffic Manager **SET** commands that are designed for use on the server console.

 One word of caution about replicating partitions where auditing is turned on. Servers with audit files that participate in replication will replicate their audit files automatically to all servers in the replica ring. If your audit files take up 32MB on one server and replication occurs to five other servers, then 32MB of space is needed on each server for a grand total of 160MB on your network.

Sample Company Scenario

In Chapter 5, we partitioned the sample company into MB Enterprises. In Figure 6.11, you can see an overview of the new company with respect to replication.

Table 6.2 WAN Traffic Manager SET commands.	
Command	**Description**
WANMAN = ON	Turns on WAN Traffic Manager.
WANMAN = OFF	Turns off WAN Traffic Manager.
WANMAN REFRESH IMMEDIATE	Starts WAN Traffic Manager software.
WANMAN POLICY ENABLE = policy_name	Enables or loads a policy.
WANMAN POLICY DISABLE = policy_name	Disables or unloads a policy.
WANMAN LOGFILE = ON	Turns on logging of WAN Traffic Manager activities. The file is SYS:\SYSTEM\ WANMAN.LOG.
WANMAN LOGFILE = OFF	Turns off logging of WAN Traffic Manager activities.
WANMAN LOGFILE MAX SIZE = size_in_KB	Specifies the default log size maximum, which is set at 512K, but it can range from 10K through 10MB. If the maximum is reached, WANMAN.LOG is renamed to WANMAN.OLD, and new data is written to WANMAN.LOG.

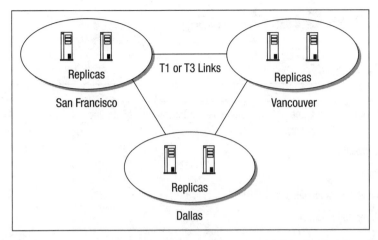

Figure 6.11   The sample company's tree hierarchy showing replicas.

Other suggestions include:

➤ **Reduce the number of departments that overlap.** You could delete over-lapping objects in the newly merged NDS tree. For example, you could consolidate the Marketing functions that existed in both companies into one.

➤ **Reduce the number of Server objects in the NDS tree with overlapping roles if they cause excessive synchronization traffic.** You could delete the Server objects to avoid unnecessary replication.

➤ **Add T1 or T3 lines between all the offices.** This would enhance WAN traffic throughput in case you want to replicate across the WAN.

➤ **Implement transitive synchronization where possible.** For example, if you could determine that all clients could get by with just one protocol, say IPX, then they could run only IPX. If other clients need Internet access, they could run IP only. Then, a server that has both IP and IPX loaded could act as the transitive synchronization server.

➤ **Implement a WAN traffic policy to reduce network flow during peak times.** You might be able to limit certain synchronization traffic, such as backlink, Connection Management, and Server Status Check, to non-peak hours. For example, you could use the 1-3AM WAN traffic policy.

There are a number of ways to implement an efficient network for the new company. The options offered in this section are only possible suggestions.

Practice Questions

Question 1

> Which of the following types of NDS traffic ensures the server's name and address are consistent among replicas?
>
> ○ a. Heartbeat
>
> ○ b. Limber
>
> ○ c. Connection Management
>
> ○ d. Server Status Check

The correct answer is b. Limber is the background process that is run to ensure a server's name and address. Heartbeat ensures consistency among NDS Directory objects. Therefore, answer a is incorrect. Connection Management traffic ensures a highly secure virtual link among servers in a replica ring. Therefore, answer c is incorrect. Server Status Check is initiated by a server with no replica. Therefore, answer d is incorrect.

Question 2

> Which tools allow you to replicate the NDS Directory tree? [Choose the two best answers]
>
> ❏ a. NDSMGR32.EXE
>
> ❏ b. NDSMGR32.BAT
>
> ❏ c. NMSNAP32.DLL
>
> ❏ d. NWADMIN32.EXE

The correct answers are a and d. You can replicate the NDS Directory tree with NDSMGR32.EXE (NDS Manager) and NWADMIN32.EXE (NetWare Administrator). However, to accomplish this in NetWare Administrator, you have to copy NMSNAP.DLL to the folder SYS:\PUBLIC\WIN32\SNAPINS. Then, you'll see it on the Tools menu in NetWare Administrator. NDSMGR32.BAT has an incorrect .BAT extension. Therefore, answer b is incorrect. NMSNAP32.DLL is the DLL file needed to see NDS Manager on NetWare Administrator's Tools menu. Therefore, answer c is incorrect.

Question 3

Which of the following replica types are created by the system? [Choose the three best answers]

❑ a. Master replica

❑ b. Read/write replica

❑ c. Read-only replica

❑ d. Subordinate reference replica

The correct answers are a, b, and d. The master replica is created at install time by the system; the second and third servers installed after the master replica is created will automatically receive read/write replicas; and subordinate reference replicas are pointers to parent partitions where there is a replica with no parent. A read-only replica must be created by an administrator. Therefore, answer c is incorrect.

Question 4

Which type of synchronization occurs 10 seconds after an NDS change?

○ a. Extended synchronization

○ b. Transitive synchronization

○ c. Immediate synchronization

○ d. Slow synchronization

The correct answer is c. Immediate synchronization occurs 10 seconds after an NDS update. There is no such thing as extended synchronization. Therefore, answer a is incorrect. Transitive synchronization uses a "middle-man" server that is running both IP and IPX to synchronize the changes on IP-only and IPX-only servers. Therefore, answer b is incorrect. Slow synchronization occurs with a group of changes and occurs every 22 minutes. Therefore, answer d is incorrect.

Question 5

> The type of schema that comes straight out of the NetWare 5 box is called the base schema.
>
> ○ a. True
>
> ○ b. False

The correct answer is a; the statement is true. The base schema is a set of procedures that govern what properties are required or optional for an object class in NDS.

Question 6

> Which type of network traffic is generated to ensure that NDS objects are consistent in the replica list?
>
> ○ a. Limber
>
> ○ b. Heartbeat
>
> ○ c. Extended schema
>
> ○ d. Server Status Check

The correct answer is b. Heartbeat ensures integrity of the objects in NDS across replicas. Limber makes sure a server's name and internal address are consistent. Therefore, answer a is incorrect. The extended schema has nothing to do with network traffic. Therefore, answer c is incorrect. Server Status Check is started by a server with no replica. Therefore, answer d is incorrect.

Question 7

> What are the replication operations that can be performed within NDS Manager? [Choose the best answers]
>
> ❏ a. Add a replica
>
> ❏ b. Change a replica type
>
> ❏ c. Repair a replica
>
> ❏ d. Run a partition continuity check

Answers a, b, c, and d are correct. All of these operations can be performed within NDS Manager. Note that running the partition continuity check is also called "walking the replica ring."

Question 8

Zachary is a network engineer who is about to change a replica type. Which types of replicas can he change the replica to? [Choose the three best answers]

❑ a. Subordinate reference replica

❑ b. Master replica

❑ c. Read/write replica

❑ d. Read-only replica

The correct answers are b, c, and d. He can change the current replica to a master, read/write, or read-only replica. Zachary cannot change the current replica type to a subordinate reference replica. Therefore, answer a is incorrect.

Question 9

Jessie is a network engineer and makes a change to a user's password. The user must have the change seen right away on his or her remote server. What can Jessie do to make the change occur to meet the user's demands?

○ a. She should do nothing. The change will occur within 22 minutes and that should meet the user's needs.

○ b. She can go into NDS Manager and change the replica type to a subordinate reference replica.

○ c. She can go into NDS Manager and delete the server the replica is on. Then, the system will see a problem has occurred and will propagate the update right then.

○ d. She can go into NDS Manager and synchronize the partition immediately.

The correct answer is d. Jessie can go into NDS Manager and synchronize the partition immediately. Answer a is incorrect, because 22 minutes will not meet the user's needs. Answers b and c are incorrect, because the answers given in these options will not trigger the update to the user's server immediately.

Question 10

Micki works as a network manager for a large firm with headquarters in Atlanta, Georgia, and three remote offices in Florida and Alabama. The firm has 15 NetWare servers that handle billing, customer service, and payroll functions. There are five Windows NT Servers that run Structured Query Language (SQL) servers in Alabama and two Windows NT Servers in Florida. All these servers communicate over a 100BaseT LAN running on 450MHz Pentium class CPUs with 256MB of RAM each. Atlanta has 150 workstations, and all the computers at this site only run Novell's native protocol (IPX). However, one of the NetWare servers is a dedicated Web server connected to the Internet; they also have a backup Web server. These two servers only run the protocol to allow them Internet connectivity (TCP/IP). What can Micki do to have all the NetWare servers synchronize their replicas?

○ a. She must make one of the servers a read-only replica.

○ b. She should upgrade the LAN connection and the server's CPUs, and add more RAM to each server.

○ c. She needs to set up a server that runs both IP and IPX for transitive synchronization to occur.

○ d. She must replicate the replicas on all servers.

The correct answer is c. This question is tricky, because there is a lot of detail to get through. However, that is how problems come to you in business. Micki should have one server running both the IP and IPX protocols. As mentioned, 13 of the 15 NetWare servers are only running Novell's proprietary protocol, IPX. The two Web servers are only running IP for Internet connectivity. For them to synchronize their replica information, they must use a transitive server that acts as a go-between for each of the other servers running dissimilar protocols. When a source server using one protocol wants to replicate with a destination server using a different protocol, the change will be sent to the transitive server. Because the transitive server runs both protocols, it will forward the change to the destination server based on the protocol the destination understands. The other options will not synchronize the NetWare servers' replicas. Therefore, answers a, b, and d are incorrect.

Question 11

You make a change to your current schema. What is this schema now known as?

○ a. Base schema

○ b. Limber schema

○ c. Heartbeat

○ d. Extended schema

The correct answer is d. After you make a change to the schema, it is known as the extended schema. The base schema comes with NetWare 5 with no custom modifications. Therefore, answer a is incorrect. There is no limber schema, and heartbeat deals with synchronization. Therefore, answers b and c are incorrect.

Question 12

For fault tolerance, how many read/write replicas will Novell NetWare 5 automatically set up for you?

○ a. 0

○ b. 1

○ c. 2

○ d. Unlimited

The correct answer is c. Besides the master replica, NetWare will create up to two additional replicas for you to meet the fault-tolerance needs of the partition. These are created on the next two servers that are installed into a particular partition as read/write replicas. Because answer c is correct, answers a and b are incorrect. You can have an unlimited number, but you must add these additional replicas. Therefore, answer d is incorrect. Keep in mind that it is possible to have too many replicas, because that can increase synchronization traffic.

Question 13

For this question, you'll need to refer to the following two screenshots. In this scenario, Todd is a LAN administrator for a small college. He's attempting to set up NDS partitioning and replication for a class he teaches called CIS143. He has set up an Organization Unit called DAYCLASS and one called Eveningclass. Eveningclass has been created as a partition. In the first figure, Todd has created an NDS partition for the [Root] partition called CIS143. This partition resides on server ONE. In the second figure, what would cause server ONE to receive a subordinate reference of partition Eveningclass?

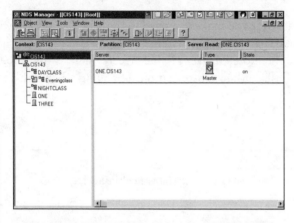

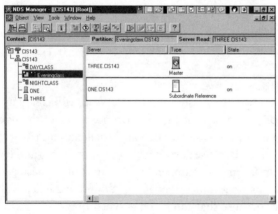

(continued)

Question 13 (continued)

○ a. Todd is placing the replica across a WAN link, which automatically makes a server a subordinate reference on server ONE.

○ b. The subordinate reference is automatically created on server ONE, because the server has a replica of both the parent, CIS143, and the child, Eveningclass.

○ c. The subordinate reference is automatically created on server ONE, because it has a replica of the parent, CIS143, but not a replica of the child partition, Eveningclass.

○ d. The subordinate reference is automatically created on server ONE, because it has a replica of the child, Eveningclass, but not a replica of the parent partition, CIS143.

The correct answer is c. A subordinate reference is automatically created on a NetWare server when the server has a replica of a parent partition but not a replica of the child partition. In this scenario, the parent partition, CIS143 (the [Root] partition), has been replicated to server ONE. You can see from the first figure that server ONE has the Master of [Root]. However, in the second figure, you can see that CIS143's child partition, Eveningclass, has server THREE as its master replica. Because server ONE has no NDS data corresponding to the Eveningclass partition (neither a read/write, nor a read-only replica), NDS automatically created a subordinate reference of Eveningclass on server ONE. This is to link the child partition Eveningclass to its parent, CIS143. All other answers represent incorrect scenarios. Therefore, answers a, b, and d are incorrect.

Need To Know More?

 Craft, Melissa, Justin Grant, and Dan Cheung. *CNE NetWare 5 Study Guide*. Osborne McGraw-Hill, Berkeley, CA, 1999. ISBN 0-07-211923-3. Chapter 24 and Chapter 34 provide good information about replication.

 Hughes, Jeffrey F. and Blair W. Thomas. *Novell's Four Principles of NDS Design*. Novell Press, San Jose, CA, 1996. ISBN 0-7645-4522-1. Chapter 5 provides useful information about NDS replication techniques.

 For additional information on partitioning and NDS Manager, review the NetWare 5 online documentation. Use the keywords "replication" and "NDS Manager".

Time-Synchronization Techniques

7

. . . .

Terms you'll need to understand:

√ Time synchronization

√ Universal Time Coordinated (UTC)

√ Time radius

√ Time provider and time consumer

√ Polling and polling interval

√ TIMESYNC.NLM and TIMESYNC.CFG

√ Single reference time server

√ Primary and secondary time servers

√ Reference time server

√ Time provider group

√ Service Advertising Protocol (SAP)

√ Network Time Protocol (NTP)

Techniques you'll need to master:

√ Knowing the role of time synchronization

√ Understanding the time-stamping process and the components of a time stamp

√ Recognizing the benefits of time stamping

√ Understanding time synchronization in Internetwork Packet Exchange (IPX)-only, Internet Protocol (IP)-only, and IP/IPX mixed networks

√ Learning time-negotiation methods

√ Understanding SAP and configured lists

√ Working with the Network Time Protocol (NTP)

√ Determining the need to modify the time-synchronization strategy

Novell *time synchronization* is the process of ensuring that changes made to an object in the Novell Directory Services (NDS) database tree are accurate and consistent across all replicas in partitions. In this chapter, you'll learn when and how to implement time synchronization, the role time synchronization plays in a Novell environment, how servers negotiate time, how different protocols affect time synchronization, and the types of time servers.

Overview Of Time Synchronization

Whenever multiple changes occur to a single piece of data, time synchronization makes sure the changes are made in the correct order. This is done to prevent data from being written inconsistently and causing problems with the Directory. Remember that the NDS database can be dispersed to other replicas in a Novell network. Because changes can occur to NDS objects in different replicas at different times by different administrators, NDS must track these changes to ensure they're consistent.

A change to an object first occurs in a server replica. After the replica receives the change, it replicates the change to the other servers in the replica ring or replica list. If one object is changed in several different replicas or if the object is modified several times in the same replica, the order of the changes must be in the correct time sequence. Novell accomplishes this through a process known as *time stamping*, which is covered in the following section. Other time synchronization techniques covered in the following sections include:

➤ Time radius

➤ Polling

➤ Time sources

➤ NDS time stamp fields

➤ TIMESYNC.NLM

Time Stamping

Every NDS change has a current date and time attached to it—this is called the time stamp. Servers read the time stamps and process them in date/time order. This keeps multiple changes to a single object in an NDS database consistent. Time synchronization ensures the time on each server is consistent with all servers in the replica list or ring; this does not necessarily mean the time of day is correct on the servers. The time stamp uses a formula to get the server's time based on Greenwich Mean Time (GMT), which is 0 degrees longitude on a map. This is called the Universal Time Coordinated (UTC) and is made up of three variables: the local time, the time zone in which the server is located, and whether daylight saving time (DST) is in effect. UTC is based on the following formula:

```
UTC = local time + or - (time zone) - (DST)
```

> *Note:* *You might also see UTC abbreviated as UCT, which stands for Universal Coordinated Time.*

For example, Atlanta, Georgia, is five hours behind GMT. Atlanta uses eastern standard time (EST) for part of the year (the fall and winter months) and eastern daylight time (EDT) during the spring and summer months. Therefore, if it's 10 A.M. on a server in Atlanta on EST, the formula is as follows:

```
UTC = 10 + 5 - 0 = 15
```

The formula for UTC time for the same server based on EDT is:

```
UTC = 10 + 5 - 1 = 14
```

Novell servers adjust for time zone and daylight saving time changes. Servers synchronize their time based on the UTC time.

Time Synchronization Radius

The internal clock of a server adjusts and is synchronized within a certain time period called a *time radius*. A time radius is the amount of time that a server can be different than its time provider and still be considered synchronized. A *time provider* is a server that gives the time to either a workstation or a server, called the *time consumer*, and it is the official timekeeper on the network. If the time on a server is within the time radius, the server's time is synchronized and should provide consistent time stamps when a file is created, deleted, or modified. The default value for the time radius is 2,000 milliseconds or 2 seconds; it can be altered with the following **SET** command or in the MONITOR utility. The following example changes the time radius value to 4,000 milliseconds, or 4 seconds:

```
SET TIMESYNC SYNCHRONIZATION RADIUS = 4000
```

You can increase the time radius variable to provide greater latitude for errors between time-synchronized servers, and you can decrease the value to minimize the margin of error.

 You should not set the time radius to less than 2 seconds. Just as house clocks and wristwatches gain and lose time, servers have a certain degree of randomness in their clocks that cause slight time errors. By setting the radius too low, time synchronization might not be established because of this randomness.

 If time provider servers are separated by a wide area network (WAN) link or a satellite link, consider raising the synchronization radius. This will allow for delays in data transmission that occur because of the distance. Satellites are particularly prone to *propagation delay*, which is signal delay caused by the distance from earth to the satellite and back again.

Polling

A time consumer checks with a time provider to determine if its time is accurate—this is called *polling*. The polling process occurs every 10 minutes, or 600 seconds. When a server's time becomes out of sync, the polling process narrows to 10 seconds until the time is synchronized. The polling interval then returns to 10 minutes. The range of the polling interval is from 10 seconds to 31 days. You can change the polling interval with a server console **SET** command. In the following example, the polling interval is set to 20 minutes, which is represented as 1,200 seconds:

```
SET TIMESYNC POLLING INTERVAL = 1200
```

 All servers in the same NDS tree are required to use the same polling interval.

Time Sources

Servers can get their time from various sources, either internal or external:

➤ **Internal** Servers on the network receive their time from a time source provider, which is a computer on a local network.

➤ **External** Servers receive their time from an external source, such as the following:

> ➤ **Internet time** Time received from an Internet Service Provider (ISP).

> ➤ **Atomic clocks** A highly accurate time mechanism that calibrates its time based on the vibration of atomic molecules.

> ➤ **Radio clocks** A method whereby you check the server's time against an accurate radio clock. The server's time is adjusted according to a time signal that is broadcast on a frequency that can be received by a suitable network board.

Note: A list of third-party time sources was compiled by Novell and published on the NetWire NOVLIB forum. The file is called TIMESG.TXT and can be referenced from the following Web site: http://consulting.novell.com/toolkit/docs/timesg.html.

 To correctly set the server's time, use the **DOWN** command to bring the server down, and set the correct date and time in the DOS Complementary Metal Oxide Semiconductor (CMOS). When you boot the server, the NetWare clock is set to the DOS clock.

NDS Time Stamp Fields

An NDS time stamp record is made up of a total of 64 bytes and is highlighted in Figure 7.1. The various time stamp fields are described as follows:

➤ **Seconds** This value stores the UTC time in seconds since the *epoch*. (The epoch is the starting point for NDS time as of January 1, 1970.) This field holds the actual time an event takes place. An event includes creating, renaming, modifying, or deleting an object. By retaining the value to the second, it's guaranteed that each time stamp is unique for

Seconds since 1/1/1970 epoch (32 bits)	Replica Number (16 bits)	Event Identifier (16 bits)

Figure 7.1 The NDS time stamp fields.

events that are just a second apart. This causes a rename event to be executed before a delete event if the rename event was issued first.

➤ **Replica Number** This field holds the number of the replica where the event occurred. When replicas are created they are given a replica number, which is unique. Having a replica number field ensures a unique time stamp across replica partitions in your network. Therefore, if administrators modify a single object on different server partitions (replicas) at the same second, the Replica Number field would be unique on the servers.

➤ **Event Identifier** The Event Identifier field ranges from 1 to 64. Because numerous events can occur in any given second, the Event Identifier generates a time stamp to keep track of the separate events. For example, let's say five create events occur in the same second. Although the Seconds field might be the same, the Event Identifier field assigns each event a unique number. In this case, the first create event would have an Event Identifier field of 1, the second create event would have a 2, and so on.

The TIMESYNC.NLM Utility

Time synchronization is handled by TIME-SYNC.NLM, which is a NetWare Loadable Module (NLM) that only runs at the server and is automatically started when the server boots up. TIMESYNC.NLM reads the server's AUTOEXEC.NCF file for time zone and DST information. The following console commands are examples of statements from a server s AUTOEXEC.NCF file. In this example, the server s time zone is Eastern Standard Time five hours from GMT , and DST is in effect:

```
SET TIME ZONE = EST5EDT
SET DAYLIGHTS TIME OFFSET = 1:00:00
SET START OF DAYLIGHT SAVINGS TIME = (APRIL SUNDAY FIRST 2:00:00 AM)
SET END OF DAYLIGHT SAVINGS TIME = (OCTOBER SUNDAY FIRST 2:00:00 AM)
```

 Don't unload TIMESYNC.NLM from the server. If you do, time synchronization will not occur, and this could cause problems with NDS and application data on servers in the replica list.

You can also change the other parameters in the TIMESYNC.NLM utility by modifying the TIMESYNC.CFG file, running server **SET** commands, or using the MONITOR utility. For example, other commands that you can enter in the TIMESYNC.CFG file are as follows:

```
# TIMESYNC.CFG is updated automatically
# when changes are made to the server console
# TIMESYNC configuration parameters.
Configured Sources = OFF
Synchronization Radius = 2000
Type = SINGLE
```

 If you place **SET** time-synchronization commands in the server's STARTUP.NCF file, your **SET** commands will never get read and executed by the TIMESYNC.NLM utility—the TIMESYNC.NLM utility will use the default values. This is because the TIMESYNC.CFG file is read after the server's STARTUP.NCF file.

Now that you've seen an overview of time synchronization, let's look at some of the time-synchronization benefits provided for various applications.

Time-Synchronization Benefits For NDS And Applications

Time synchronization provides for consistent changes for the following types of data, which are discussed in detail in the following sections:

➤ NDS objects

➤ File systems

➤ Network applications

➤ Workstations running local applications

➤ Email applications

NDS Objects

The best way to demonstrate the effects of time synchronization on NDS objects is by example. Suppose a network administrator made a change to an NDS object while another network administrator made a different change to that same object. If the first administrator changed the name of an NDS User object and the second administrator moved the same User object to another NDS context, time synchronization would ensure the changes are done in proper time sequence. In other words, time synchronization ensures that the first request is done first and the second request done next—in correct time-sequence order.

If time synchronization wasn't available to order the events, the following scenario might occur: If the second administrator's move request was done first, the User object would be moved to another NDS context before the first administrator's rename request was done. Therefore, the first administrator's rename request would fail, because the User object would be in a different location or context.

> *Note:* *Time synchronization ensures requests are handled in first-in first-out (FIFO) order.*

File Systems

Just as time synchronization can maintain consistency among NDS objects, it also maintains consistency among files and folders in the file system. For example, let's say you have a folder called PAYDATA on a shared network file server. If a user logs into the Novell server and issues an operation to delete the folder and another user tries to copy a file to PAYDATA, time synchronization would cause the operations to be done in sequential order. You might wonder why the users can't just coordinate the events themselves. Although it's possible in a large organization with a multitude of users, it's not probable. With the lack of communication that exists in organizations, you can't assume users will check with each other. Therefore, the network maintains data integrity by enforcing time synchronization.

Network Applications

Time synchronization is probably the most critical in network applications where users are at individual client computers, and they access and update data from a centralized database stored on a server. For example, let's look at an airline flight reservation database application that is accessed by users (the travel agents) from their workstations. Time synchronization is extremely critical here because there are only so many seats on an airplane. Assume that one travel agent inputs a customer request for the last seat on a plane. Seconds later, a second travel agent receives a customer request for a seat on the same plane. The second travel agent is still showing there's one seat left. Time synchronization ensures the first customer gets the last seat and the second customer does not. Time synchronization keeps a logical order to the events recorded.

Workstations Running Local Applications

Workstations can get their time from servers and thereby maintain consistency of their locally executed application's time with a Novell server. To configure a workstation to get its time from a server, insert the following command in the client workstation's login script:

```
SET_TIME ON
```

> *Note:*   *The default value for this parameter is based on Novell's Client32 advanced property setting for station time and is set to **ON**.*

To have a client workstation not receive its time from a server, place the following command in the same login script:

```
SET_TIME OFF
```

Email Applications

Time synchronization is important with respect to email, because it puts the email messages in order according to time. Time synchronization sorts multiple email messages from users in correct time order, again FIFO, in your email's inbox. (This is usually the default setting, but the sort order can be changed.) Time synchronization ensures that the messages get sent to you with the correct date and time on them. They will have the correct date and time even if your mail server cannot send them right away. For example, your boss sends you an email message requesting your presence at a certain meeting. A few minutes later your boss changes his or her mind and sends another email canceling the meeting. Time synchronization ensures that you receive these messages in the proper order. Think of the confusion if time synchronization did not occur. You might get the second email message first and wonder what meeting had been canceled.

Now that you've seen an overview of the benefits of time synchronization, let's look at using time servers in an IPX-only environment.

Time Servers In IPX-Only Environments

The time synchronization utility, TIMESYNC.NLM, provides support for the following protocol environments:

➤ **IPX-only** IPX-only environments are Novell networks running the proprietary Internetwork Packet Exchange/Sequenced Packet Exchange (IPX/SPX) protocol only. IPX provides speed, and SPX provides reliability. IPX is easily routable, like IP, but it cannot be used to interface with the Internet.

➤ **IP-only** Novell provides a Transmission Control Protocol/Internet Protocol (TCP/IP) protocol stack environment in which you can run only IP. This environment is called IP-only, rather than TCP/IP-only, because it provides the same functionality as the IPX protocol stack. This protocol is used if you want to connect your network to the Internet.

➤ **Mixed IP/IPX** Sometimes, you might want to run an IP/IPX mixed network. You could run IP on your Web server to access the Internet, and you could run IPX on your internal network. This provides a type of firewall that prevents hackers, who might be able to intrude onto your Web server over TCP/IP, from gaining access to your servers running IPX-only. Because TCP/IP and IPX/SPX are not compatible, the intruder cannot get to the IPX-only servers. Consider placing your in-house applications that don't need Internet access on those servers.

In this section, we'll discuss the IPX-only environment, and, in the following section, we'll discuss IP-only and mixed environments.

Novell time servers, running IPX-only, perform the following basic tasks:

➤ Act as time providers to server utilities (NLMs) that require time synchronization.

➤ Provide time synchronization to client workstations with **SET_TIME ON** in their login scripts or client configuration properties.

➤ Give status information about time synchronization.

➤ Maintain synchronization by either acting as a time provider or time consumer.

Novell provides for the following types of IPX-only time servers:

➤ Single reference

➤ Primary

➤ Secondary

➤ Reference

We'll discuss each of these in more detail in the following sections, as well as how to configure time servers, the processes of server time negotiation, and how servers locate each other.

Single Reference Time Server

The single reference time server is Novell's default type of time server, and it's generally used in smaller networks—it's typically not used on WANs. The single reference time server is the server that maintains the master time and propagates the time to secondary time servers and client workstations.

 A single reference time server does not synchronize its time with other servers; its time is considered accurate. It gets its time from the DOS CMOS clock or from an external source and does not adjust its clock.

Because the single reference time server is considered the master time keeper, all other servers must be up and able to connect to it. A single reference time server does not participate in polling. When you install the first server in an NDS tree, it's considered to be the single reference time server.

 There can be only one single reference time server on a local area network (LAN).

Primary Time Server

A primary time server synchronizes its time with either another primary time server or a reference time server. Primary time servers poll other primary time servers and reference time servers and vote with these time servers to determine the correct network time. After the servers agree, the time on the primary time server is adjusted accordingly. The time on a primary time server is corrected 50 percent per polling interval. The polling time interval is then reduced to make polling occur much more frequently. For each interval, the primary time server's time is adjusted to half the difference, until eventually the times are synchronized. The time is then passed to secondary time servers and workstations. Primary time servers offer a high degree of fault tolerance compared to single reference time servers. If one server fails, then another server can be used as the time provider.

You're required to have either a second primary time server or a reference time server for the voting process to occur. Each server polls the others, so the servers must be up and running.

It's advisable to place a primary time server at local geographic sites when on a WAN. This allows for faster delivery of time to the workstations and other local servers. At the same time, if the local server fails, a remote server across the WAN can act as a time provider.

Primary time servers are best used when you have remote sites connected via a WAN link. By placing the primary time servers at each site, time synchronization is faster, and fault tolerance is provided.

As you have probably recognized by now, it's important that time is not set backwards in the NetWare 5 environment. NDS gets very confused when it receives time-stamped events that happened in the past. When primary time servers adjust their clocks, they never adjust backwards. The primary time servers that are slow increase the speed of their internal clocks, and the servers that are fast decrease the rate of advancement of their internal clocks. In this way, after some number of polling loops, the servers will converge to the same time.

Secondary Time Server

Secondary time servers are considered time consumers that get their time from single reference, primary, or reference time servers. Secondary time servers act as time providers to client workstations and can be configured to act as time providers to other secondary servers. This is the default time server type for servers installed after the initial server. Unlike primary time servers, secondary time servers do not participate in the voting process. Secondary time servers adjust their clock 100 percent, if necessary, for each polling interval.

Secondary time servers will not attempt to synchronize their time with other time providers when determining the correct network time.

For optimizing network traffic, consider these suggestions for secondary time servers:

➤ Place secondary time servers physically close to primary or reference time servers. This reduces network traffic when time synchronization occurs, because the server won't have to span a WAN link.

➤ Reduce the number of routers between secondary time servers and their corresponding time providers. This reduces the number of routers, known as hops, that time synchronization traffic must travel.

➤ If you have a single reference time server, make sure the other servers are configured as secondary time servers. This helps the single reference time server synchronize its time with workstations.

➤ If you have several primary or reference time servers, make the other time servers secondary servers. Again, the secondary time servers can help the primary or reference time servers distribute the time to the workstations.

Note: Most of your NetWare servers will be secondary time servers.

Reference Time Server

The reference time server gets its time from an external time source and is a time provider to primary and secondary time servers. It can also provide time to client workstations. The differences between a reference time server and a primary time server are as follows:

➤ Whereas the primary time server adjusts its internal clock, the reference time server does not.

➤ The reference time server has a higher weighting in the time arbitration process, which is described later in this chapter.

The reference time server provides consistent time with an external resource and is a central point of time for the entire WAN or LAN. You would use this in an environment where time accuracy is critical. Many organizations, such as banks, use reference time servers to get their time from an atomic clock or an Internet site. Think of the interest a bank could lose if the time on its network servers was inaccurate.

If you have more than one reference time server, the servers must all use the same external time resource. Otherwise, they will propagate different times to your primary and secondary time servers and clients, and the NDS time stamp will be inconsistent.

Because a reference time server can distribute its time to primary time servers, consider having at least two primary time servers for your reference time server. That way, if one of the primary time servers fails, the other primary time server can distribute the time to other time consumers; this provides a higher degree of fault tolerance. (Note that for time to be synchronized on the network, the reference time server must have at least one primary time server available as its voting partner.)

 When using a reference time server, fault tolerance is maintained by having several primary time servers that can synchronize the time to secondary servers and clients.

Configuring Time Servers

To create a certain type of time server, you can use the **SET** command at the server console or the MONITOR utility. Enter the following **SET** command at the server console to create a reference time server:

```
SET TIMESYNC TYPE = REFERENCE
```

To specify the time server type using the MONITOR utility, perform the following steps:

1. Open the server console and type "MONITOR".

2. Choose Server Parameters|Time|Timesync Type.

3. Choose the time server type you want.

 You can also set a server's type in the TIMESYNC.CFG file using the **TYPE** statement. For example, to set a server to be a reference time server in the TIMESYNC.CFG file, enter the following:

```
TYPE = REFERENCE
```

Server Time Negotiation

There are two distinct methods of server time negotiation, which are dependent on the types of time servers you have in your organization. You can either use the default single reference time server or you can use a time provider group.

Single Reference

In a single reference time server environment, you have one single reference time server. All other servers are secondary time servers. The secondary time servers receive their time from the single reference time server. This is the default configuration for a NetWare 5 environment. The time is negotiated from a central point—the single reference time server. The term *negotiation* may be a misnomer here because there's very little to negotiate. The secondary time servers *will* adjust their time to the single reference time server. The time might be inaccurate, but the times are consistent for NDS time stamps. For every polling interval, there is a 100 percent adjustment in the secondary server's time if the secondary time server's time is outside the single reference time server's time-synchronization radius.

 A secondary time server is time synchronized on the first polling interval because it closes the time gap by 100 percent.

Time Provider Group

In a time provider group, you have at least one server acting as the reference time server and you have two or more servers acting as primary time servers. The reference time server gets the correct time from an external source and provides it to the primary time servers. The primary time servers, in turn, provide the time to secondary time servers and client workstations. The reference time server polls the primary time servers and then the voting process occurs. The result is a weighted average of the time on the reference and primary time servers. However, the reference time server has a higher weighting because it's considered most accurate. It's weighted with a factor of 16, whereas the primary time servers are weighted with a factor of 1 each. The following formula results in the time provider group time:

```
time provider group time = ((reference time * 16) +
(primary 1's time * 1) + (primary 2's time * 1)) / 18
```

Table 7.1   Time servers and sampled times.

Server Type	Time In HH:MM:SS	Fractional Value
Reference	4:20:00	4.33
Primary 1	4:10:00	4.17
Primary 2	4:15:00	4.25

Using Table 7.1, the group time in the preceding example would be ((4.33 * 16) + 4.17 + 4.25) / 18 = about 4:19:30. To get the fractional part of 4.33, which is .33, take the minutes portion of 4:20, which is 20, and divide it by 60. You'll get .33, or 1/3. Therefore, the group time is roughly 4:19:30. Now, each primary server will adjust its time 50 percent of the difference between its time and the group time. Primary server 2 will adjust its time to be 4:17:15, which is halfway between 4:15:00 (its current time) and 4:19:30 (the voted time, which is based on the weighted average). You can see that because of the higher weighting assigned to the reference server, time will more quickly converge to the correct time (the accurate time maintained by the reference server).

The primary time servers will adjust their time differences by 50 percent for every polling interval; the reference time server *will not* change its time at all.

Remember the polling interval is now changed to 10 seconds instead of 10 minutes, because the servers are out of time sync. This occurs very rapidly and within a few polling intervals, the reference and the two primary time servers' times are all synchronized. Then, the polling interval is reset to 10 minutes.

In sum, servers negotiate their time to generate an accurate NDS time stamp. An accurate NDS time stamp is necessary to order the events that occur in a Novell network.

Now that you've had a look at how servers negotiate their time, let's investigate how servers find each other to synchronize their time in an IPX-only environment.

Methods Servers Use To Locate Each Other

Novell NetWare servers running the IPX/SPX protocol must locate each other so they can correctly exchange time information. The polling process and the subsequent voting process assume the servers are available and they can see each another. The methods servers use to locate each other are the Service Advertising Protocol (SAP) and a configured list.

Using The Service Advertising Protocol (SAP)

NetWare servers automatically advertise themselves using SAP. By default, as a server boots up, it uses SAP to advertise its network address over the physical connection. SAP is used by servers as they are brought down to advertise that their services are no longer in use.

> SAP generates additional network traffic, but it's necessary for servers to broadcast their presence.

The following time servers use SAP, by default, to announce themselves:

➤ Primary

➤ Single reference

➤ Reference

Reference and primary time servers use SAP to discover who they should poll to negotiate their time. Secondary time servers act as time consumers and use SAP only to locate the time providers. By default, SAP is on but it can be turned off very easily by issuing the following server command:

```
SET TIMESYNC SERVICE ADVERTISING = OFF
```

One benefit of SAP is that there's very little administrative maintenance. After a server is installed, it's automatically configured to use SAP. Now, you'll learn about using configured lists for servers to discover their time source or voting partners.

Using Configured Lists

With a configured list, you list the particular time servers that a given server should attempt to contact for time synchronization. Normally, using SAP is appropriate; however, you might consider using a configured list if your needs meet any of the following conditions:

➤ You want to disallow servers from getting time from particular time sources.

➤ You change your network configuration by adding and removing test servers in your network frequently.

➤ Your network has at least two reference time servers.

➤ Your network has multiple primary time servers.

The configured list is held in the file TIMESYNC.CFG and can be changed to accommodate a configured list using the following steps:

1. At the server console, type "EDIT".

2. Enter the desired file name, which is SYS:\SYSTEM\TIMESYNC.CFG by default.

3. Place the following entry in the file after it appears:

```
TYPE = time_server_type
SERVICE ADVERTISING = OFF
CONFIGURED SOURCES = ON
TIME SOURCES = s1;s2;s3;s4;
```

In the previous code, *time_server_type* is one of the following: single, reference, secondary, or primary. And, *s1* through *s4* are the names of NetWare servers.

The servers listed in the **TIME SOURCES** statement are considered the *configured list*. Servers in the list are separated by semicolons (;), and they are arranged in priority order for providing time on the network. The last semicolon in the list is required. To save the changes, press Esc.

4. Confirm by clicking on Yes.

You might be wondering why there are so many servers in the configured list. To understand this, you have to understand how the configured list works. It depends on the time server type. If we consider a secondary time server, the list provides an ordered sequence of which server(s) should be contacted for the network time. The first server listed is contacted first. If available, it provides the network time, and no other servers in the list are contacted. If the first server in the list is unavailable, the second server in the list is contacted. If the second server is available, it provides the time, and no other servers in the list are contacted; otherwise, NetWare continues searching the list until the list is exhausted. Now let's consider a time provider—a reference or primary time server. In this case the configured list provides the names of servers that will be contacted for the voting process. The list defines the voting group, which contains the servers that will negotiate time as described previously.

If none of the servers can be contacted, you can use a combination SAP and configured list approach, which we cover in the following section.

Using A Combination Of SAP And Configured List

You can use the SAP and configured list methods concurrently on the same network. However, the servers listed in the configured list are contacted first, and SAP is used *only* if none of the servers in the list is available. This setup is fault tolerant, because time providers using SAP to advertise their presence can still be contacted to provide network time in case all the servers in the list are down.

In NetWare 5, you can run an IP-only environment. It's fairly straightforward to set up, and you can do this during server installation or with ConsoleOne afterwards. In the following section, you'll learn how to configure time synchronization in IP-only and IP/IPX mixed environments.

Time Synchronization In IP-Only And Mixed IP/IPX Environments

In the previous section, you learned that TIMESYNC.NLM is needed in an IPX-only environment; it's also needed if you're running IP on a network. However, an additional NLM is required, and you must manually load it—it's called the Network Time Protocol (NTP), or NTP.NLM. NTP.NLM creates and uses a file on the server called NTP.CFG, which has the IP addresses of time providers. NTP.CFG acts much the same way as the **TIME SOURCES** list in the TIMESYNC.CFG file in an IPX-only environment.

NTP.NLM is found in the SYS volume in the ETC directory.

After you've loaded NTP.NLM on your NetWare server running IP, NTP becomes the master time keeper for both IP and IPX environments. The servers running the TIMESYNC.NLM will then act as time consumers, receiving their time from NTP. Next, you need to set your IPX servers to be secondary time servers. The IPX secondary time servers receive their time from the IP server running NTP.NLM. The secondary time servers refer to NTP via the Novell Migration Agent.

For IPX and IP servers to communicate, you must load the Compatibility Mode Driver (CMD), SCMD.NLM, with the Migration Agent option on a server. Once loaded on any server, IPX workstations can communicate in IP-only environments.

There are two types of time servers in IP-only and mixed IP/IPX environments: server and peer, as discussed in the following sections.

Server

Server-type time servers receive their time from an Internet source. These servers look in the NTP.CFG file to find an external time source and adjust their clocks accordingly. The local server can adjust its own time to the remote server, but the remote server does not adjust its time to the local server. These servers also act as time providers to secondary time servers. The server type uses the **SERVER** command in the NTP.CFG file. The command can have either an IP address or a hostname as the parameter. For example, to get the time from MIT using an IP address, the following command would be placed in the NTP.CFG file:

```
SERVER 129.7.1.6
```

To get the time from the NASA Ames Research Center using a hostname, the following command would be used:

```
SERVER ntp.nasa.com
```

 If you're running TCP/IP, but your LAN is not connected to the Internet, the local server will not be able to synchronize its time to an external time source. In this case, it can refer to its own hardware clock to get the network time. To specify the local clock timer, use the IP address 127.127.1.0.

Peer

A peer-type time server provides for the following scenarios:

➤ A local server can synchronize its time with a remote server.

➤ A remote server can synchronize its time with a local server.

A peer-type time server acts as a time provider to other peers and to secondary time servers. The peer time server uses the **PEER** command in the NTP.CFG file. To create a peer time server environment with two IP-only servers on your network, you could add a peer command in each server's NTP.CFG file that points to the other server. For example, one server has the IP address 165.100.100.1, and the other server has the IP address 165.100.100.2. The NTP.CFG entry for 165.100.100.1 would be as follows:

```
PEER 165.100.100.2
```

The NTP.CFG entry for the other server, 165.100.100.2, would be:

```
PEER 165.100.100.1
```

Each server would be able to adjust its time to its peer depending on the reliability of the servers.

Using NTP.CFG

To run NTP.NLM, go to your server console and type "NTP". The server will load NTP and display console messages, indicating it's synchronizing the local clock with a remote time source. If you have multiple entries, NTP will load the different time servers in reverse order of appearance. The following output is the default NTP.CFG file that is used when NTP.NLM gets loaded:

```
#The syntax is SERVER IP ADDRESS or server HOSTNAME
#server bitsy.mit.edu
#or
#server 18.72.0.3
#This is the local clock timer.
#Only turn it on for the primary time source or in an
#isolated network.
#The primary time source is the server which acts as a
#time source
#for all internal servers (or the server that has the
#connection to the Internet or remote time source).
#Local clock timer will kick in when all outside sources
#become unavailable.
server 127.127.1.0
#Uncomment line below to point to time server at
#Lawrence Livermore National Laboratory
#serverclock.llnl.gov
#Uncomment line below to point to time server at
#NASA Ames Research Center
#server ntp.nasa.com
#Uncomment line below to point to time server at
#U.S. Naval Observatory
#server ntp2.usno.navy.mil
#MIT
```

```
server 129.7.1.66
#NIST Central Computer Facility
server 129.6.16.36
#Sony
server 198.93.3.1
```

You've had a chance to look at how time is synchronized in IPX-only and IP-only or IP/IPX mixed environments. Now, let's explore the need to implement a time-synchronization strategy that differs from the default strategy.

Determining Which Time-Synchronization Strategy To Implement

As discussed previously, there are two general strategies for implementing time synchronization on your network:

➤ Single reference time server (this is the default)

➤ Time provider group

We'll discuss the advantages and disadvantages of each later in this section, but first we'll discuss the criteria used to decide which time-synchronization strategy to use.

Criteria Used To Determine A Time-Synchronization Strategy

Consider the following characteristics of your network when deciding whether to use the default strategy or to implement a time provider group strategy:

➤ **Number of NetWare servers** If you have more than 30 Novell NetWare servers, you should consider veering from the default strategy.

➤ **Multiple sites connected via WAN links** If you have multiple geographic sites separated by a WAN link, such as a T1 or T3 connection, you might want to implement a time provider group strategy.

➤ **Type of protocol in use** If you're using the IP protocol on any of your servers, change the default time-synchronization strategy.

➤ **Number of time zones** If you have multiple sites dispersed over different time zones, modify the default time-synchronization strategy.

Single Reference Time Server

If your network does not meet any of the characteristics in the previous section, using the single reference time server is your best bet. The server should be located centrally and its clock must be accurate. By default, the initial server installed in an NDS tree is a single reference time server. You should check the time on the servers periodically to ensure accuracy. Let's look at some advantages and disadvantages of a single reference time server.

Advantages Of A Single Reference Time Server

A single reference time server provides the following benefits:

➤ It's the default and there's no configuration file, such as TIMESYNC.CFG or NTP.CFG, to maintain.

➤ If you add more servers to the network, you don't need to set up anything on them. NetWare automatically creates secondary time servers after the first server is installed. Single reference time servers automatically provide the time to secondary time servers.

Disadvantages Of A Single Reference Time Server

There are some drawbacks to a single reference time server, including the following:

➤ You have no fault tolerance. If the single time server is down, it will not act as a time provider. If you have a secondary time server, you can use the SET command at the console to make it a single reference time server.

➤ An incorrectly configured server could cause the incorrect time to be dispersed, thereby yielding an inaccurate NDS time stamp. This could cause events, such as creating, deleting, renaming, or updating files, to be performed out of sequence.

➤ The single reference time server must be available to all secondary time servers.

Time Provider Groups

Time provider groups are used in case you need to implement a time-synchronization strategy other than the default. With a time provider group, there's a reference time server that provides the time to primary servers. Reference time servers and primary time servers vote on the time, and then the time on the primary servers is adjusted, if needed. The primary time servers provide time to the secondary time servers. Primary and secondary time servers can provide the time to client workstations. You should keep the number of time servers to a minimum to reduce time-synchronization traffic. Novell recommends a ratio of no more than seven primary servers per reference server. If you want to have more servers that are time servers, consider creating another time provider group. To provide fault tolerance, consider placing time providers on multiple network routes. If one route fails, time synchronization is still maintained.

Advantages Of Time Provider Groups

A time provider group gives your network several advantages, including the following:

➤ Provides fault tolerance in case of server failure. If a reference time server fails, the time can be provided to secondary time servers and clients by the primary time servers. Or, if one of the primary time servers fails, the time can be provided by other primary time servers.

➤ Gives you, as a network administrator, complete control over the time-synchronization strategy. Nothing is automatic, in contrast to the single reference time server method.

However, time provider groups are not without disadvantages, which are discussed next.

Disadvantages Of Time Provider Groups

Time provider groups pose the following disadvantages:

➤ Because nothing is automatic, you have to administer each of the TIMESYNC.CFG and NTP.CFG files on each of the servers.

➤ Excessive time-synchronization traffic might be created because of the number of time providers. Additional activity is seen because of the polling and voting processes.

You've seen ramifications of using the default time-synchronization strategy or using a time provider group. In the following section, we explore the role of time synchronization in our sample company scenario.

Sample Company Scenario

In this section, we examine time synchronization in relation to our sample company—MB Enterprises. Let's recap the needs of MB Enterprises with respect to time synchronization. MB Enterprises has the following characteristics:

➤ The company spans three cities separated by wide geographic distances via a WAN link.

➤ There are a total of 44 servers in the new company. There are 12 servers in San Francisco, 10 servers in Dallas, and 22 servers in Vancouver.

➤ Vancouver has an Internet department; therefore, the servers must be running IP.

➤ The cities span various time zones.

Based on this scenario, the following suggestions are given to manage time synchronization for MB Enterprises:

➤ **Set up a time provider group for each city** Because MB Enterprises has 44 servers, it meets the criteria of using a time provider group. However, because there are more than seven servers in each city location, it's best to make each city a time provider group. There needs to be a reference time server and then multiple primary time servers. The primary time servers will get their time synchronized from the reference time server. The reference time server will get its time from an external source. Fault tolerance is met because the primary time servers can provide time synchronization in case the reference time server goes down.

➤ **Use an IP/IPX mixed environment** Because there's an Internet requirement, there must be a server running IP, which requires the configuration of an NTP.CFG file that points to an Internet server as its external time source. This will be a server-type time server. If it's discovered that the network can use IP-only, that would be the optimal approach because it would reduce protocol traffic. If some IPX applications need an IPX server, an IP/IPX mixed environment is suggested.

You need to know that this is only one possible answer. As an organization changes, the time-synchronization strategy will need to be reevaluated. Management might decide to collapse and combine functions, causing a whole site to be removed. On the other hand, MB Enterprises might acquire other companies in other remote cities as well, which could cause new sites to be added.

Practice Questions

Question 1

A single reference time server is the default method used by Novell.

○ a. True

○ b. False

The correct answer is a; the statement is true. The first server that is installed is the single reference time server, and this is the Novell default. Subsequently installed time servers are secondary time servers.

Question 2

Which types of update activities benefit from NDS time synchronization? [Choose the best answers]

❑ a. NDS objects and properties

❑ b. Network applications

❑ c. File system activities

❑ d. Email applications

The correct answers are a, b, c, and d. NDS objects and properties and network applications, such as database applications, changes to the file system, and email applications, all benefit from time synchronization.

Question 3

Secondary time servers will act as time providers to reference time servers, primary time servers, and client workstations.

○ a. True

○ b. False

The correct answer is b; the statement is false. Secondary time servers will only provide the time to client computers by default. They do not provide time to reference or primary time servers.

Question 4

Which type of time server participates in the polling and voting processes with respect to deciding on the network time? [Choose the two best answers]

- ❑ a. Secondary time servers
- ❑ b. Primary time servers
- ❑ c. Single reference time servers
- ❑ d. Reference time servers

The correct answers are b and d. Primary time servers and reference time servers participate in the polling and voting processes and then announce a time they want to vote. The time among the reference and primary time servers is calculated based on a weighted average. The primary time servers then adjust their time to 50 percent of the difference between their time and the averaged time. Secondary time servers and single reference time servers don't participate in any voting activities. Therefore, answers a and c are incorrect.

Question 5

Jessie works as a network administrator, and she's attempting to implement a configured list method for the servers to receive their network time from. She wants to make sure the reference time server, named MEADORS-A, is attempted first, and a primary server, named MEADORS-B, is referenced next. How should she configure her **TIME SOURCES** statement in the TIMESYNC.CFG file?

- ○ a. **TIME SOURCES = MEADORS-B, MEADORS-A,**
- ○ b. **TIME SOURCES = MEADORS-A; MEADORS-B;**
- ○ c. **TIME SOURCES = MEADORS-B; MEADORS-A;**
- ○ d. **TIME SOURCES = MEADORS-A;MEADORS-B**

The correct answer is b. For the reference time server, MEADORS-A, to be accessed first and MEADORS-B next (in the event MEADORS-A is down), Jessie should make her entry appear as shown in answer b. Note that a semicolon is required at the end of the list to terminate the configured list. Answers a and d contain syntax errors and are incorrect, because they use commas and lack a terminating semicolon, respectively. Answer c is incorrect, because it places the reference time server last in the configured list. In that case, it will only be contacted if MEADORS-B is down.

Question 6

> Jessie has a server that functions as an Internet Web server. It has a large number of hits a day from outside the network. She wants to have the server get its time from an external source. She does not want to have her local server provide time to the external source. What should Jessie do?
>
> O a. She needs to configure the AUTOEXEC.BAT file with the server command to point to the IPX address or hostname of the external source.
>
> O b. Jessie must implement a single reference time server network by altering the defaults.
>
> O c. She should configure the NTP.CFG file with the server command. It should point to the IP address or the hostname of the external time source.
>
> O d. She should configure the NTP.CFG file with the peer command.

The correct answer is c. Jessie must set up the NTP.CFG file with the server command to point to the external source. The AUTOEXEC.BAT file is the improper place to put the server command, and the server command should point to the IP address, not the IPX address. Therefore, answer a is incorrect. A single reference time server is the default. Therefore, answer b is incorrect. Because Jessie does not want the local server to update the remote source, she must use the server command instead of the peer command in the NTP.CFG file. Therefore, answer d is incorrect.

Question 7

> What is the default polling interval used when reference and primary time servers negotiate the time?
>
> O a. 10 seconds
>
> O b. 2,000 milliseconds (2 seconds)
>
> O c. 2 hours
>
> O d. 10 minutes

The correct answer is d. By default, reference and primary time servers will poll each other in 10 minute intervals. If the time is different, this interval will be reduced to 10 seconds until the primary time servers are in sync with the reference time server. Therefore, answer a is incorrect. 2,000 milliseconds (2 seconds) and 2 hours do not represent the default polling interval used by reference and primary time servers. Therefore, answers b and c are incorrect.

Question 8

Zachary is a LAN administrator and he wants to set the time on one of his users' workstations so it will be received from the server. To accomplish this using a login script statement, which command would be correct?

○ a. **SET TIME ON**

○ b. **SET_TIME OFF**

○ c. **SET_TIME = SERVER TIME**

○ d. **SET_TIME ON**

The correct answer is d. Zachary must set the user's login script to have the statement **SET_TIME ON**. Answers a and c have incorrect syntax, and answer b turns off the feature. Therefore, answers a, b, and c are incorrect.

Question 9

Zachary is a network manager working for a medium-sized company. There are two sites connected by a T1 WAN link with 12 servers on one end and 15 on the other. His goal is to maintain an optimal network, and he needs to decide how many reference time servers he should maintain. What is the optimal number?

○ a. 1

○ b. 2

○ c. 27

○ d. 15

The correct answer is b. Zachary only needs to have two reference time servers. There needs to be one at each end of the WAN link. He could get away with maintaining only one reference time server, but then he'd have to decide at which site to place it. Then, the other site would have to get its time from the site with the reference time server. This would cause excess WAN traffic. Therefore, answer a is incorrect. Answer c is just a sum of the servers in both sites and Zachary does not need that many time servers. Therefore, answer c is incorrect. Answer d is the number of servers at one end of the WAN link. Therefore, answer d is incorrect.

Question 10

> What is the factor given to the reference time server when calculating the time
> for the time provider group?
>
> ○ a. 1
>
> ○ b. 4
>
> ○ c. 16
>
> ○ d. 32

The correct answer is c. The factor used for the reference time server is 16. The
reference time server is weighted more heavily, because it's considered more
accurate than the time on the primary time servers. After all, it can access an
external time source. The factor for the primary time servers is 1. Therefore,
answer a is incorrect. Answers b and d do not represent the factor given to the
reference time server when calculating the time for the time provider group.
Therefore, answers b and d are incorrect.

Need To Know More?

 Craft, Melissa, Justin Grant, and Dan Cheung. *CNE NetWare 5 Study Guide.* Osborne McGraw-Hill, Berkeley, CA, 1999. ISBN 0-07-211923-3. Chapter 24 and Chapter 34 provide good information about time-synchronization issues.

 Hughes, Jeffrey F. and Blair W. Thomas. *Novell's Four Principles of NDS Design.* Novell Press, San Jose, CA, 1996. ISBN 0-7645-4522-1. Chapter 8 of this book provides useful information about NDS time-synchronization techniques.

 For additional information on partitioning and NDS Manager, review the NetWare 5 online documentation. Use the keyword "synchronization".

Creating Accessibility And Administration Plans

8

Terms you'll need to understand:

√ Needs analysis

√ Legacy device

√ Remote user

√ Mobile user

√ Enterprise-wide Admin

√ Server Admin

√ Password Admin

√ Special Use Admin

Techniques you'll need to master:

√ Analyzing your network and user needs with regard to NDS tree design

√ Developing an accessibility plan for your network

√ Creating an administrative plan for your network

The last step in the design phase of the project—the *needs analysis* process—is necessary regardless of the layout of the network. Throughout this chapter, we'll examine the steps involved in analyzing your network and establish guidelines for implementing the Novell Directory Services (NDS) design. Finally, we'll examine MB Enterprises (which was created from the merger of Munson Media and Burmeister Publishing) and discuss how the needs analysis process might proceed as the project continues.

Analyzing Your Network's NDS Needs (Needs Analysis)

Perhaps the single most important function of NDS is to provide easy access to network resources. You can do this with NDS because it can be designed to provide a logical map of network resources, a single login for each user, and a single point of administration through the use of client software, login scripts, and various NDS objects that represent physical network resources. The client software is used to connect clients to the network, whereas the login scripts and NDS objects are used to establish the user environment. Throughout this portion of the chapter, we'll examine establishing the user environment by specifying how users will access network resources. As we continue, it's imperative to keep two principles in mind: the user environment must be centrally managed, and applications and services must be easy to administer.

By the time you finish this chapter, you should be able to create a plan for your user environment that outlines how the client software, login scripts, and NDS objects will be used to establish your NDS environment and provide access to network resources. There are three steps in creating the user environment plan, which are discussed in the following sections. First, you must review the users' needs, including access to physical network resources, applications, and legacy network services (if they exist on your network). Second, you must establish guidelines for each section of the user environment. Finally, you must design accessibility plans to implement the guidelines.

Resource Needs

As mentioned, the first step in developing your NDS accessibility plan is to determine your users' needs for physical network resources, including printers, networked peripherals such as scanners, and network storage space. During this evaluation, you must interview your network users and, in addition, find out the status of several situations related to resource access. For example, if all users in a particular container will utilize a particular resource in the same way, you can provide all users similar access to the resource (that is, all users in the Indianapolis container can have access to all printers in the Indianapolis office).

Along these same lines, you should determine if there are resources in a container that only a select group of users needs to access. For example, a color plotter in an engineering department should probably not be accessible to all users because of the costs involved in operating that type of equipment.

You should also determine if there are resources that need to be shared across container lines or over different LANs. This type of access requires a different implementation than resources that are shared within a container. Other considerations are the network operating systems and workstation operating systems in use on your network. Finally, remembering the principle of keeping administration easy, you must consider how you'll make changes to the way users access resources in the system.

Legacy Interactivity Needs

Many companies will choose not to completely scrap the existing network and migrate to NetWare 5 immediately. Few companies have the resources or funding to migrate all systems in one fell swoop. In fact, there are many circumstances in which all systems cannot be upgraded. Because of this, you must consider the requirements for including legacy devices in your NDS tree.

> *Note: A legacy device is defined as one that is not NDS aware. Any NetWare 3 resource (or even NetWare 2) is a legacy resource because it only recognizes the NetWare bindery and not NDS.*

By this token, if there are NetWare 3 (or NetWare 2) devices on your network, you must consider including guidelines for setting the bindery context in your accessibility plan. The NetWare server bindery context is able to include up to 16 containers, making it easy to place bindery-based devices in the NDS tree. But before jumping right into creating a bindery context, we must consider which applications and resources (such as printers) are bindery-based and which users can access them. After determining the number of applications and resources that require bindery context access, organize your users into groups and include specific accessibility guidelines for these groups in your plan.

 Remember that PCs running DOS or Windows are not the only workstations that can attach to NetWare networks. Macintosh users can log in to the NDS tree and operate as typical users. OS/2 clients can log in to the NDS tree, but they can only execute their personal login scripts or default OS/2 login scripts, not container or profile scripts. Unix users connecting to the tree using UnixWare can log in as bindery-based clients, but they do not run any login scripts at all.

Application Needs

The final consideration during the review process is examining the types of applications and data files the users will need to access. The first question you need to ask yourself is which of these applications or files will need to be available to all users. You can manage access to these files and applications for the tree as a whole, rather than for individual Group or User objects. You also need to determine which applications are shared within containers and across WAN links—physical resources, applications, and files that require this type of access warrant specialized implementations. You must also find out if there are applications that should be launched automatically for users and if there are applications that should be automatically added to users' desktops. (These applications can be managed through various utilities available with NetWare 5.) Finally, you must consider which groups of users require access to which files and applications and whether they are accessed from within a container or across container boundaries.

Creating An Accessibility Plan

After you've completed the process of gathering pertinent user data, you should be ready to create your accessibility guidelines. The guidelines you create will determine how NDS objects are used to create the user environment. Remember to make sure that your services and applications are easy to manage, and that you're able to manage the users' environments from a central location. In addition, the guidelines you establish must outline which objects you'll use to establish the user environment and how you'll secure that environment. You must specify how you'll administer user access by manipulating object placement within the NDS tree and identifying security rights to particular resources. In the following sections, we'll examine guideline recommendations for many types of NDS objects and situations.

Alias Objects

An Alias object represents, or points to, another object in the Directory tree. Because Alias objects can be overused, you need to establish guidelines for them that define when they can be used and which objects cannot be used with Alias objects. Remember to only create Alias objects for resources outside of a user's existing container.

Application Objects

Application objects need to be placed close to the users that will access them. If your network connects multiple locations via WAN links, like the MB Enterprises network, you should create Application objects in the containers that represent each physical location. In the event that you have multiple application servers at each location, you must create Application objects that correspond to each application on each server.

Drive And Directory Mapping

Data directories and drive mappings that are used company-wide should be accessed using an established standard. For example, many email programs require the email database to be located on the M: drive. In this case, you should establish a company-wide mapping so the M: drive always directs the system to the correct location for the database. If you're using multiple servers for email, you should use the same directory for all servers to ensure compatibility and standardization. By doing this, you ensure easy network administration and training when new people are added to the team.

You use the Directory Map object to simplify drive mapping. Directory Map object placement should be considered on a case-by-case basis. You must identify the names of the objects and the data they represent before implementing them.

Group Objects

You should only use NDS Group objects to group together individuals from the same physical location. In addition, group size should be limited to 1,500 members and should not span partition boundaries.

Login Scripts

Profile objects should be used to create login scripts for users in more than one container needing the same access to the network. If you use multiple login scripts per container (through the use of Profile objects or **INCLUDE** statements), strict rules must be defined as to how they are used. For example, a container might include both Marketing and Sales users—both of which require different login scripts.

Although profile login scripts are more difficult to manage than container login scripts, they are nonetheless easier to maintain than individual user login scripts. Also, remember that, although group login scripts do not exist, you can use the container login script to establish specific group settings using the **IF MEMBER OF...** command.

As mentioned, user login scripts are more difficult to manage and maintain than container or profile login scripts. However, there are instances when only a user login script can be used to establish the user environment. Your accessibility plan must include guidelines that depict when to use personal login scripts to provide access to specific applications and data files.

Organizational Role Objects

As you know, Organizational Role objects can be used to help ease administration of the network. These objects should be placed in the tree according to the function of the role. Novell recommends at least two Organizational Role objects: network administrator and backup administrator. Creating these roles enables you to delegate some responsibilities without granting blanket access to all resources. Trustee assignments can be made easily to the Organizational Role object that will provide administrative rights in a single container or branch of the tree.

Policy Packages

User, Workstation, and Container Policy Packages are the three types of Policy Packages with which you need to be concerned regarding your accessibility plan. User and Workstation Policy Packages should be placed in the same container as the users that utilize them. When considering the placement of Container Policy Package objects in your NDS tree, there are two constant rules: Place Container Policy Package objects as high in the tree as possible without spanning a WAN link and have one per geographic location.

Security

Whether to use Inherited Rights Filters (IRFs) and how they are implemented should also be included in your accessibility plan. Remember that IRFs affect how all users (even administrators) access directories and NDS objects. If IRFs are used, it's important to carefully plan their implementation. It's important to recall that the Supervisor NDS object right can be blocked with an IRF. You should also keep special security considerations in mind as you finalize your accessibility plan.

One of the main concepts to remember is that you should not grant the Supervisor NDS right to Server objects. This right is inherited by the file system and can pose a rather large threat to your security structure.

Many of the considerations we've outlined in the accessibility guideline sections may or may not be necessary, depending on the structure of your network. For example, many WAN link and partition issues do not exist on small networks. However, each point is important to remember when you develop your plan.

Creating The Administration Plan

After you've determined your users' needs and created your accessibility plan, it's time to develop the administration plan. This strategy document must include client configurations (including mobile user configurations), common login script settings, a standard for the structure of the file system on all servers, guidelines for including legacy resources, security guidelines, and Z.E.N.works object configurations. When developing this document, you must remember the two key design principles: the user environment must be centrally managed, and applications and services must be easy to administer.

Client Configurations: Standard And Mobile Users

The configuration options for most users are very straightforward and easy to consider. The operating system has very little effect on the configuration options available (save those that can only access Bindery objects). The first consideration is the name context for the client computers. Which server should be utilized as the preferred server and which tree is the preferred tree are also important. Finally, you must determine which network drive letter should act as the first network drive (this is often the F: drive).

Mobile users have a separate set of considerations. Before discussing these considerations, however, we must make a distinction between remote users and mobile users. A *remote user* is someone who uses a dial-up connection to access the network and resources within his or her home container. For example, a remote user could be an account representative who travels to various customer sites and accesses the network only for email and file access within his or her container. On the other hand, a *mobile user* is a person who travels outside of his or her normal physical location and accesses information, applications, and network resources in a local container. A mobile user also needs access to the home container where his or her User object resides. Prime examples of mobile users are IS technicians who travel to various company sites. They need access to the local resources for their site's container, but they also require access to their files in their home containers and, perhaps, applications in both containers. In summary, there are really two types of mobile users to be considered: those who carry notebook computers with them and those who use existing workstations at various locations.

As with all users, you must assess the needs of the mobile users on your network. The first thing to consider is where mobile users attach to the network. If there's a single point of access, such as a modem pool, it's easier to administer mobile users' access than if they were each connecting to a modem attached to their regular desktop machine. You should also consider whether the traveling user needs to access resources at the local office or only at his or her home office while on the road (that is, are they a remote user or a mobile user). Two more very important considerations are how often a user visits a particular location and how long the user stays at each location. If a user is very mobile and visits one location per month for three days, it might not be necessary to make special accommodations. However, if the user stays at each location he or she visits for three weeks, it's worthwhile to ensure the user has access to all necessary resources. Finally, if the user carries his or her own notebook computer or uses an existing workstation, this will have an effect on the user environment configuration.

Novell has a number of suggestions and solutions for managing mobile users. For example, you can use contextless logins for mobile users. When you configure the Novell client to use contextless logins, users don't have to provide an NDS context when they log in. To configure a client to use contextless login, you must be running NDS Catalog Services on the NetWare 5 server. In this type of configuration, NDS Catalog Services retrieves the context information for the user when he or she attempts to connect to the network. When the user specifies a tree and username during the login process, the correct username and context are located in the catalog, and the context is automatically added to the login. If the specified username exists in more than one context, Catalog Services allows wildcards and provides the user a list of valid username and context pairs from which to select.

Another method of accomplishing the same task is to educate users on their complete names and contexts. This way, when users log in, they can manually enter their distinguished names and access the appropriate resources. This method usually works best for IS personnel traveling to other sites, but might not work for a mobile sales force. Another option is the use of Alias objects in the tree. If there's a small number of mobile users, you can create an Alias object for each user below the top Organization object in the tree. These Alias objects should then be configured to point to the appropriate User objects in the appropriate containers in the tree. In this way, the mobile users have a very simple distinguished login name to remember (for example, .JBoyes.MB).

In addition, you can use unique login scripts for mobile users that provide the users access to network resources regardless of the location from which they log in. However, as we've mentioned, this is not a preferable method, because individual login scripts are more difficult to manage than container or profile login scripts. Finally, you can utilize the client configuration software itself to set the users' preferred servers and name contexts. This is done either through the Client Properties configuration screen for Windows 95/98 and Windows NT clients or through the NET.CFG file for Windows 3.1 or DOS users.

The method of managing mobile users on your network depends, at least in some part, on the number of mobile users and the means by which they access the network. For example, any number of mobile users can utilize contextless logins. However, it would be very difficult to manage client configurations or individual login scripts if you have 200 mobile users. Alias objects are best suited for users that split their time between offices and when there are less than 20 users. When planning your administration document, you must consider the number of mobile users and the type of access they require.

Common Login Scripts

Login scripts are used as an additional method to access network resources. Four types of NDS objects have the login script property: Organization, Organizational Unit, User, and Profile. These login scripts are executed in a specific order, from container to profile, to user, to default. The profile login script is only executed if the User object is associated with a specific profile; the default login script is run if a user login script does not exist. In addition, User objects in a subcontainer cannot automatically execute a parent container login script. In the example shown in Figure 8.1, users in the Texas container will not execute the U.S. container login script.

You should use the information gathered from the needs assessment and the accessibility guidelines to create the administration plan for your login scripts. You must first consider whether you want to create a common working environment for all users in a container. If so, you should create a container login script. The second step in this section of the process is to evaluate the needs of the users across groups of users and/or containers. If you need to set up common user environments for specific groups of personnel, use a Profile object and create a login script for the profile. Then, assign the users to the Profile object. Lastly, you must look at the individual user requirements. If there are specific users that require special access to network resources, user login scripts should be created.

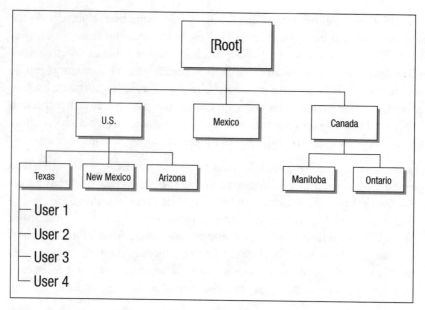

Figure 8.1   A sample container configuration.

 User login scripts should only be used when absolutely necessary. They are more difficult to maintain and manage than profile or container login scripts, and they increase the complexity of network administration.

File System Structure

To ensure ease of administration, you should establish a standard file system structure. In doing so, you must decide how many volumes you're going to have on each server and if those volumes will be dedicated to specific functions. For example, a standard volume configuration for a server might be three volumes: one for the NetWare operating files (the SYS volume), one for user data called DATA, and one for applications called APPS. You must consider the user and application storage requirements and whether specific applications necessitate standard drive mappings. As mentioned earlier, for example, some email packages may require mapping the mail database to the M: drive.

Legacy Resources

NetWare 5 uses bindery services to provide compatibility with earlier versions of NetWare client software. You issue the **SET BINDERY CONTEXT** command on a NetWare server to enable bindery services. When you do this, you can set the server's bindery context to one or more containers in the NDS tree. A legacy client uses bindery calls to search for a Bindery object. The client also searches the available containers in the order in which they appear in the context list. As part of the administration plan, you must determine where bindery-based resources will be located in the NDS tree and which containers, groups, and users require access to those resources.

Security

In regard to your administration plan, the focus on security should be on the roles of network administrators and the security defaults for user accounts, as we'll discuss in the following sections.

Container Admin Organizational Role Object

One of the most frequently created administration roles in large networks is the Container Admin Organizational Role object, which is used to divide NDS management tasks among network administrators to ease overall administration. This Organizational Role object should be granted rights to manage the container in which it's currently located. After this object has been created, you can easily assign one or more administrators to the role. This is also an efficient design in the event that one administrator leaves and another person takes his or her place. Rather than completely re-creating the original user's access, you can assign the rights to the Organizational Role object and simply assign the new User object to that role.

Enterprise-Wide Admin Organizational Role Object

It's also a good idea to create an Enterprise-wide Admin Organizational Role object to manage the entire tree. This object should be granted full access to the [Root] object, and you can use an Organizational Role object in a hidden NDS tree security area to control access to the Enterprise-wide Admin role.

Backup Admin Organizational Role Object

You should create a Backup Admin role to perform backups and other administrative functions. You use other Organizational Role objects in various containers throughout the NDS tree to control the Backup Admin role. You should avoid assigning it the object rights to change the members of the role, the partitions on the servers, and other objects in the container. This Organizational Role object should be granted full file system rights to all servers and volumes in its container. In addition, this object should be given the rights needed to install servers.

Server Admin Organizational Role Object

The Server Admin role is created for managing a specific server and is also controlled by Organizational Role objects in various containers throughout the NDS tree. The Server Admin role is often granted all object rights within the container where it resides—except Create and Rename, which prevent the user from adding new objects to the tree, and partitioning and installing servers. However, the person assigned the Server Admin role can modify such things as login scripts and passwords. The Server Admin role is granted full file system rights only to those directories that are required for managing the server, such as APPS, PUBLIC, and USERS.

Password Admin Organizational Role Object

The Password Admin role has some of the most restrictive rights for administrators, such as severely limited property rights to Group and User objects, passwords, and login scripts. An Organizational Role object in the container where its management is needed controls the Password Admin role. The Password Admin role is not assigned the Create or Rename object right to any object, nor is it given the rights required to install and partition servers. In addition, this role is not granted any special file system rights.

Special Use Admin Organizational Role Object

Novell also recommends creating a Special Use Admin Organizational Role object, which is used on servers that the IS department doesn't control—for example, a server in a software engineering or Q/A testing environment. The Special Use Admin role is controlled by an Organizational Role object in a container not controlled by IS. The Special Use Admin role is granted minimal access rights to the NDS tree and can only modify login scripts, assign group membership rights, and change passwords. This role is not granted the ability to create objects, modify the membership of the role, install servers, or manage partitions. However, it is granted complete file system rights to the managed servers.

User Account Defaults

The final portion of your administrative plan involves establishing the security defaults for the user accounts on your network. Novell recommends a number of defaults, but these should be determined on a case-by-case basis. The following list discusses the available security options and recommended settings:

➤ **Expiration dates** By default, most accounts should not have an expiration date. There are many cases in which this is a good idea—such as temporary workers who will leave the company after a specific project—but it's generally not a good idea to set an expiration date.

➤ **Connections** You should limit the number of concurrent connections to two. This actually involves setting two options: Limit Concurrent Connections (Yes) and Maximum Connections (2).

➤ **Passwords** It's always a good idea to require a password for all users on your network, and this should be the default setting. The default minimum password length for your users should be set to six. This decreases the chances that someone will guess a particular user's password, but it's not too long as to make passwords difficult for users to come up with or remember. We also recommend forcing periodic password changes every 30 to 45 days and requiring unique passwords. This ensures that users change their password, do not use the same passwords over and over, and don't have to pick new passwords too frequently. In addition, you should limit the number of grace logins after a user's password has expired to three. This also requires two settings: Limit Grace Logins (Yes) and Grace Logins Allowed (3).

➤ **Intruder detection** It's recommended that you enable intruder detection lockout to prevent unauthorized users from guessing passwords. The intruder detection setting allows a user to enter the wrong password a certain number of times, then locks the account for a specific amount of time when the correct password is not entered. We recommend setting the incorrect login attempts to three to allow forgetful users a reasonable number of tries without giving the unauthorized users too many chances. The bad login count retention time should be set to at least 15 minutes.

It's also recommended that once detection has been made, the account be locked for at least 30 minutes. If a user forgets his or her password while on vacation and locks his or her account, the user can easily call the administrator while the account is locked and have it reset to gain access. However, if the lockout is actually caused by an intruder, chances are the administrator won't hear from him or her. There are many companies that set the length of lockout to days or even weeks to ensure that the legitimate user calls the administration team to reset his or her account.

Z.E.N.works Objects

NetWare 5's new Z.E.N.works objects are the primary tools used to configure the user environment. Using the information gathered from your users and the accessibility plan you developed, you can develop an administrative plan for Application objects and Container, User, and Workstation Policy Package objects—all of which are part of Z.E.N.works.

When developing the administration plan for Application objects in the NDS tree, you must first determine which applications will be run from which servers and which, if any, will be run from local hard drives. After you determine which applications will be run from servers, you must decide which servers will host which applications and where the Application objects should be placed in the NDS tree. Application objects can be associated with other NDS objects, and you should determine this association at this point in the process. Because different applications have different requirements, you must ensure that users have sufficient hardware and operating system power to run the applications. Along the same lines, you must determine whether specific applications require mapped drives or printer ports, and make the appropriate accommodations in your administration plan. The plan must also consider whether all applications will be made available to all users or whether restrictions will be implemented. Finally, consideration should be given regarding whether application load balancing and/or fault tolerance will be used and, if so, in what way they will be implemented.

In terms of your Container Policy Package administration plan, you must consider where the Policy Package objects will be placed in the NDS tree. In addition, it must be decided with which containers each Policy Package object should be associated. Finally, you must decide the search level and search order for the container policy.

The first consideration when dealing with User and Workstation Policy Package objects is which operating systems will be supported. Along the same lines, consideration must be given as to which NDS objects will be associated with the Policy Packages. Z.E.N.works has the ability to control the operating system on Windows-based clients. Knowing this, you must determine whether desktop preferences will be controlled by the User Policy Package. If you decide that this type of control is needed, you must also decide which Control Panel settings will be used for the Windows Accessibility Options, Display, Keyboard, Mouse, and Sounds. By the same token, Z.E.N.works can also control the Windows system policies. If you determine that these settings will be controlled through the User Policy Package, you must determine the settings for the Control Panel, Desktop, Network, Shell, System, and Windows 95 Shell. Finally, you must determine which types of schedules will be used for the User Policy Packages. Workstation Policy Packages allow the administrator to control such things as forcing applications to run, configuring a logon banner, and so on.

Note: For more information on Z.E.N.works and the various types of Policy Packages, see the Z.E.N.works online documentation at www.novell.com/documentation/lg/zen/docui/index.html.

Sample Company Scenario

As we've discussed throughout this chapter, this phase of the design process consists of three steps: gathering information, creating an accessibility plan, and creating an administration plan. In this section, we'll examine MB Enterprises and how the structure of the company and network affects this project step.

Gather Information

As you went about interviewing users to determine the needs for the design of the NDS tree at MB Enterprises, you learned quite a few interesting bits of information. In the Burmeister Publishing house in San Francisco, the vast majority of users are limited to accessing resources within their container. Because the company is divided across three separate buildings with many networks, the design is very straightforward in this respect. There is, however, one printer (a high-speed laser named HP-SF-12) that is located in the Production department's container that must be accessed by users in many different departments. In addition, there's a color printer in the Marketing department that should be shared with the Munson Media Marketing and Advertising departments after the merge. Because all equipment currently on the network can be easily configured to support NDS, it has been decided that all servers on the Burmeister Publishing side of the house will be upgraded to NetWare 5.

Munson Media, on the other hand, has slightly different requirements. There are a number of printers that are used in the magazine publishing house that cannot be upgraded to support NetWare 5 and NDS. For this reason, we must enable bindery contexts on the publishing servers in Dallas. The executive staff at the Dallas office also has two printers that should only be accessed by members of the executive staff. Other than these exceptions, the Dallas office of Munson Media has a very straightforward configuration. However, the Vancouver office has a more intricate design. Because it's the home of the IS, Call Center, and Internet departments, it has some very specific requirements. The Call Center has its own IS staff to handle all issues that arise within the 200 member call team. The Call Center staff is strictly limited to accessing their local container, and the Call Center IS staff only manages those accounts and resources. The Online Production department is inaccessible to internal users except the course and container administrators. The same holds true for the Test and Q/A department in that it's a mirror of the production network, including security restrictions.

The majority of the workstations at both sites are Dell PCs running Windows 95 and Windows 98. There are a few Windows NT Workstation systems, but they are used exclusively in the IS departments. Of course, no marketing or advertising department would be complete without a contingent of Macintosh systems. There's a total of 23 Macs at both companies, and they must share information with the PCs via the NetWare servers.

As happens during all merges, similar departments in both companies will have to share information during and after the merge. For this reason, shared volumes on the Executive/Administration, Marketing, Editing/Acquisition, Publishing, and IS servers must be created. In addition, the Microsoft Office suite, including Outlook (for email access), will be run from various servers throughout the company. There's a centralized database of customer information that is being developed and will reside in the Vancouver office. The customer database will need to be accessed by users in every department after it is completed.

Therefore, the question remains, "How does this apply to the NDS design process?" Well, first we've identified access requirements for both companies. There are resources (both devices and applications) in both companies that must be accessed across container lines as well as across network and partition boundaries. Finally, there are a number of devices on the Munson Media network that must access the NetWare servers via the bindery; therefore, bindery contexts must be created.

Create An Accessibility Plan

Using the information that we've gathered about the MB Enterprises network and organization, we can make some determinations regarding which NDS objects we will use to establish the user environment. Policy Package objects are an option that we can use on the network; however, they are not a necessity. If it's decided that Container Policy Packages will be used, remember that one Policy Package object should exist for each geographic location. Although the San Francisco office is a complex of three buildings, it can be treated as a single geographic location. Alias objects are similar in this configuration in that they aren't necessary, but can be added if desired.

Because there are shared applications that must be accessed by all users, it's probably a good idea to create Application objects. Many of these applications require standard drive mappings, so these should be established using Directory Map objects or through container login scripts. There are also large numbers of people, such as the Call Center staff, that require similar access. As with most networks, the use of groups is an effective management strategy. Along the same lines, Profile objects should be used to easily establish the users' environment through login scripts. Because there are many departments (and therefore many containers) that have dedicated administrators, Organizational Role objects should be created.

Because they are more difficult to administer and there are a large number of users, we won't utilize user login scripts except in rare circumstances. By the same token, IRFs can be difficult to manage and won't be used in this configuration. Further, we must consider the special security measures that must be put in place. As mentioned, the Call Center staff should not be granted access outside its container. In addition, there are a number of container administrators that will be performing various tasks on the NDS tree.

Create An Administration Plan

As we discussed earlier in this chapter, the administration plan sets the standards for implementing the design. Because Policy Packages and Alias objects are not necessary, we won't discuss them here. We've also determined that the management required for IRFs and user login scripts is prohibitive, so they will not be discussed either.

An Application object should be created for the Microsoft Office suite and the shared database that will be used. There may also be a need for additional Application objects for accounting or publishing packages. Each server should follow the same file system structure, and the same drive mappings should be used for all applications and users by implementing Directory Map objects. Each site's container login script should be configured to provide general access for all users in the container. The subcontainers for each department can be designed to provide more specific access, with the profile login scripts serving the remaining configuration needs. Remember that because user login scripts will not be used, the default login script will execute automatically. This behavior can be modified by including the **NO_DEFAULT** login script statement in the container script.

Because there are many different client configurations, including Macs and PCs, a number of variations are available. Remember that in the NetWare 5 NDS environment, Macintosh computers are able to connect as fully functional clients. For each type of client computer on the network, you must determine the preferred tree and context. Contextless login is an option, but it's not necessary here. There are a number of members of the IS staff that must access resources in various containers, but they are familiar with context functionality and are properly trained in accessing remote resources. Other than these users, there are no mobile users on this network.

Remember that there are printers in the Dallas office that require access to the bindery on the NetWare servers. For this reason, bindery context settings must be established for all affected servers. The various container administrators should be granted sufficient access to manage their containers, but not excessive access that allows them to affect users outside their containers. Because the IS departments are so large, particularly in Vancouver, it's a very good idea to develop special administrative roles for the various network functions. A Backup Admin and Server Admin are minimum requirements. It has been decided that the senior network administrator at the Vancouver site will oversee the entire network and should therefore be granted the access rights of an Enterprise-wide Admin.

Finally, we must determine the default settings for the user accounts. By default, no account will have an expiration date, and temporary employees in the Call Center department will only be granted access for a predetermined amount of time. We'll limit the number of concurrent connections to three, because many users use at least two stations at a time (for example, many users in the Advertising department use PCs and Macs logged in at the same time). Of course, we will require a password, and the default minimum password length will be six characters. We'll also require periodic password changes every 60 days, but will not require unique passwords for most users. Grace logins will be limited to six. We will not, by default, lock a user's account if an intruder is detected. However, in certain containers we might be more concerned about security issues and unauthorized access. For those containers, we'll enable intruder detection, limit the invalid login attempts to 4 every 45 minutes, and, in the event that the account is locked, it will remain locked for at least 4 hours.

Practice Questions

Question 1

Which of the following is the correct order for login script processing?

- a. Container, user, profile, and default
- b. Container, default, user, and profile
- c. Container, profile, default, and user
- d. Container, profile, user, and default

The correct answer is d. Login scripts are executed in a specific order: container, profile, user, and default. The profile login script is only executed if the User object is associated with a specific profile, and the default login script is run only if a user login script does not exist. Answers a, b, and c contain the incorrect order and are therefore incorrect.

Question 2

Which of the following commands is used at the console to enable access for legacy resources?

- a. **SET NAMING CONTEXT**
- b. **SET LEGACY ACCESS**
- c. **SET BINDERY CONTEXT**
- d. **SET BINDERY ACCESS**

The correct answer is c. To provide access to the server for legacy resources, the server's bindery context must be set with the **SET BINDERY CONTEXT** command. Whereas the answers in the other options sound plausible, they do not exist in the NetWare 5 environment. Therefore, answers a, b, and d are incorrect.

Question 3

Which of the following are examples of a remote user? [Choose the two best answers]

❑ a. A home-based telecommuter

❑ b. A traveling IS professional who visits each site for two weeks

❑ c. A consultant who is at a specific site for the full length of a project (two years)

❑ d. A sales representative who accesses email from hotels while on the road

The correct answers are a and d. Although not specifically spelled-out in the text, telecommuters access their home containers in the same manner that traveling sales reps would. A traveling IS professional is actually a mobile user who requires access to different containers while on the road. Therefore, answer b is incorrect. A consultant who is at a site for two years is a local user, regardless of whether he or she is actually employed by the company. Therefore, answer c is incorrect.

Question 4

Which of the following administrators is granted the lowest level of access?

○ a. Password Admin

○ b. Server Admin

○ c. Special Use Admin

○ d. Backup Admin

The correct answer is a. Password Admins are granted severely limited property rights to Group and User objects, passwords, and login scripts. They are not able to create or rename objects, nor are they able to manage partitions or install servers. They are granted no file system rights. The Server Admin role is granted a fairly high level of access to perform actions such as install servers and manage partitions. Therefore, answer b is incorrect. The Special Use Admin role is used to grant some level of administrative access for containers not controlled by IS, which requires a higher level of access than Password Admins. Therefore, answer c is incorrect. The Backup Admin is granted full access to the file systems to ensure that reliable backups are made. This is a fairly high level of access. Therefore, answer d is incorrect.

Question 5

Which of the following are recommended group restrictions? [Choose the two best answers]

❑ a. Should not include less than 1,500 users

❑ b. Should not span partition boundaries

❑ c. Should not include more than 1,500 users

❑ d. Should not be used to assign similar access to a number of users

The correct answers are b and c. As discussed in the accessibility plan section of this chapter, groups should not include more than 1,500 users, and members should not be located on different sides of a partition boundary. Answer a is the inverse of answer c and is therefore incorrect. By their very nature, groups are created to assign similar access to a number of users. Therefore, answer d is incorrect.

Question 6

Which of the following principles must always be considered when designing accessibility and administrative plans? [Choose the two best answers]

❑ a. The user environment must be centrally managed.

❑ b. All users must have unfettered access to network resources.

❑ c. Applications and services must be easy to administer.

❑ d. The user security plan must be as restrictive as possible.

The correct answers are a and c. The two principles that must be remembered throughout the design process are that the user environment must be centrally managed, and the applications and services must be easy to administer. Unfettered access to network resources is never a good idea on a network, because it implies an open security structure. Therefore, answer b is incorrect. By the same token, a fully restrictive security plan does not adequately serve the users' needs. Therefore, answer d is incorrect.

Question 7

Which of the following login scripts should be used only in exceptional situations?

○ a. Profile

○ b. User

○ c. Default

○ d. Container

The correct answer is b. User login scripts should only be used as an exception, because they are more difficult to manage than profile and container login scripts. Therefore, answers a and d are incorrect. The default login script runs if there is no user login script present. Therefore, answer c is incorrect.

Need To Know More?

 Clarke, David James, IV. *CNE Study Guide for Core Technologies.* Novell Press, San Jose, CA, 1996. ISBN 0-7645-4501-9. Amongst other topics, Chapter 4 covers creating an accessibility document.

 For additional information about the various NDS objects discussed throughout this chapter, review the NetWare 5 online documentation using object names (such as User object, Application object, Group object, and so on) as keywords.

Implementing
The Design

9

Terms you'll need to understand:

√ DSMERGE

√ Schema

√ WAN Traffic Manager

√ Novell Directory Services (NDS) Manager

Techniques you'll need to master:

√ Understanding the steps required to merge two NDS trees

√ Knowing how to use NDS Manager

√ Understanding the use of WAN Traffic Manager

Throughout this book, we've covered the various design phases related to Novell Directory Services (NDS). Now, it's time to actually implement your design. The implementation process varies from network to network, depending on the requirements. The first step, on networks that require it, is merging the NDS trees. From there, we'll move to managing the new tree using WAN Traffic Manager and NDS Manager. Then, we'll examine modifying the newly developed NDS tree for efficient operation. Finally, you'll learn how to implement the user environment developed in Chapter 8.

Using DSMERGE

There are many NDS designs that do not require merging existing NDS trees. For example, the current structure can be easily adjusted to accommodate the new design, or the new NDS structure can be designed from scratch. However, there are many times, as in the case of MB Enterprises, that a new design requires two trees to be combined. The actual merge process is very straightforward—you simply run a single NetWare Loadable Module (NLM) at the server console. However, there are actually four major tasks that must be completed to ensure a successful merge: preparation, execution, confirmation, and cleanup.

Task 1: Preparation

In preparation for an NDS merge, you need to verify the following:

➤ Your system is functioning properly.

➤ Time synchronization is working between the various servers in the two trees.

➤ Both trees are using the same schema.

➤ Top-level containers (immediately below [Root]) are uniquely named.

➤ You have a good backup of both NDS trees.

➤ The existing trees are thoroughly documented.

When getting ready for the merge, you must ensure that you have a reliable backup utility. In addition, you should be familiar with many of the NetWare management utilities, including TIMESYNC, Schema Manager, DSMERGE, NDS Manager, DSREPAIR, and NetWare Administrator. For more information on each of these utilities, refer to the online documentation.

As mentioned, part of the preparation process is verifying that time synchronization is established between all the servers and working properly. If time is not in sync, the merge will fail. To verify that time synchronization is operating on servers and that the servers are synchronized, issue the **TIME** command at the server console. The sixth and seventh lines of the displayed information tell you whether time synchronization is active and whether time is synchronized to the network.

In addition, both trees must be using the same schema. The NDS schema defines containment rules, valid NDS objects, and the information that is required when creating the objects. The *base schema* is the schema that ships with NetWare. NetWare 5 provides the ability to modify the schema using the Schema Manager, but it's generally not necessary. Once the schema has been modified, it is considered *extended*. Extending the schema should only be considered if you want to associate information with particular objects that is not covered in the existing fields for the object. For example, you might want to track each user's access badge number. Using the Schema Manager, you can create a new attribute called Badge Number and associate it with the User object class.

Note: Be aware that installing additional products such as Z.E.N.works, GroupWise, Border Manager, and so on results in schema extensions.

You must also have a good backup of both NDS trees before starting the merge. Although the merge process itself is protected by the transaction-tracking process, you should make a backup of the trees. Doing this will ensure that you have the tools necessary for recovery if something goes wrong during the merge process.

Finally, you must make sure that the existing trees are thoroughly documented. After the merge is complete, you'll perform a cleanup process. For this process, you need accurate information regarding existing login scripts, users that have access to the [Root] objects of both trees, and the bindery services commands in the AUTOEXEC.NCF files on the servers in both trees. By obtaining this documentation before the merge, you're ensuring that the process goes smoothly.

Task 2: Execution

After preparing your servers for the merge, you're ready to use the DSMERGE NLM to combine the two existing NDS trees. To do this, follow these steps:

1. Type "DSMERGE" at the source server console.

2. After the application loads, select Check Time Synchronization to verify that the servers are in sync.

3. Press Esc to return to the main menu, then select the Merge Two Trees option.

4. Enter the administrator name and password for the source and target trees, then press F10 to merge the trees.

Task 3: Confirmation

After the merge is complete, you should confirm that the new NDS tree is stable. This task is particularly necessary if you're creating partitions, adding another tree to the combined tree immediately, or moving containers within the tree. Performing additional high-level NDS actions, such as adding another tree, while the tree is unstable can corrupt the target NDS tree. The easiest way to confirm that a tree is stable after a merge is to verify the replica status is On for all replicas on the source and target servers. This is done through the DSREPAIR utility, which is run on the server console. Under the Advanced Options menu, select Replica And Partition Operations. The Replica State field, which is located on the right, should be recorded as On.

Task 4: Cleanup

The cleanup portion of the merge involves establishing NDS administration rights, correcting bindery service commands and login scripts, finalizing the structure of the tree, and updating the NDS settings on the workstations on the network. By default, the source User object that was used to perform the merge has Supervisor object rights to the [Root] of the new NDS tree. Users who previously had access to the [Root] of the source tree no longer have the same level of access. For this reason, if you note the resource access of the trustees of the [Root] of the source tree before the merge, you can easily restore the trustee assignments to the new [Root] after the merge is complete. If your network uses a distributed administration style, you can also grant trustees of the source tree's [Root] rights to all container objects immediately below the [Root] before performing the merge. By doing this before the merge, the users will be granted the requisite access when the merge is complete.

You also need to make sure that all bindery services commands found in the AUTOEXEC.NCF files on the servers indicate the correct name for the NDS tree and context. Login scripts also need to be updated with the new information, because resources might not be in the same position in the tree. To make the necessary adjustments to these commands and login scripts, refer to the information you gathered before the merge process. This is also the time you adjust the structure of the new tree by moving, creating, deleting, and renaming containers as necessary. Finally, you must adjust the NDS settings on all workstations on the network to address the new NDS tree and the appropriate context. Because it could take some time to change the settings on every workstation on the network, it's a good idea to create Alias objects for any container objects that are moved from their original context to more easily direct work-stations to the new tree and context.

Tree Management With WAN Traffic Manager And NDS Manager

After your tree has stabilized, you might find it necessary to manage its structure and function using either WAN Traffic Manager or NDS Manager. In addition, you may find it necessary to modify the NDS tree. All of these topics are covered in the following sections.

WAN Traffic Manager

WAN Traffic Manager is designed to control server-to-server traffic over WAN links (specifically, only periodic NDS events such as replica synchronization and the Janitor process). However, it does not control, administer, or initiate user events or other server-to-server traffic, such as time synchronization. WAN Traffic Manager exists because WAN links are generally significantly slower than LAN links, and bandwidth is required for use by network users and resources (and should not be consumed by server maintenance functions). Although specifically designed for WAN links, WAN Traffic Manager can be used to control server-to-server communication between any servers on the network. By removing this extraneous traffic from a network that is stretched to its limit because it's handling user traffic, users are provided with improved response time to network resources.

WAN Traffic Manager is actually run on the server as the WTM.NLM (WAN Traffic Manager NLM). The function of the Traffic Manager is controlled by WAN policies that are established through NetWare Administrator. The policies are stored as NDS property values in a NetWare Server object or a LAN Area object. These policies control what times of the day server-to-server traffic is transmitted.

Two predefined policies are included as part of WAN Traffic Manager installation and can easily be adjusted to fit your network. To enable or change the policies for a particular server, follow these steps:

1. Start NetWare Administrator and select the appropriate server.

2. Right-click on the Server object and select Details.

3. Choose the WAN Policies option and click on the Predefined Policy Groups.

4. Select the group to apply and click on Load Group.

NDS Manager

NDS Manager is used to manage and maintain partitions and replicas in the NDS tree. It allows you to view, create, and merge partitions and replicas; view server information; and move container objects within the tree. After launching NDS Manager, select View|Tree, then select the partition you want to view. Information such as the names of replicas stored on each server, the types and state of the replicas, and the last successful partition synchronization is displayed in the dialog box. Creating a partition is as simple as selecting Create Partition from the Object menu in NDS Manager after you've selected the Organizational Unit object.

NDS Manager is also used to move container objects in an NDS tree, as follows:

1. After starting NDS Manager, locate and select the container you want to move.

2. Select Partition from the Object menu, then select Move. (Alternatively, right-click on the container and select Move.)

3. Choose Select Object and select the Organizational Unit to which you want to move the container from the Available Objects list. Initiate the move and refresh the window to ensure the move was executed.

Because moving a container changes the context of all objects in the container—and thereby their distinguished names—preparations should be made similar to those made before merging trees. The context information for each user's workstation must be changed to reflect the new tree structure. Alias objects can be used to point to the new structure until the name context settings can be changed on all workstations.

> *Note:* *Before a container can be moved, it must be a partition root object. For more information on using NDS Manager, see Chapter 5.*

NDS Tree Modification

After the initial merge is complete, you should modify your NDS tree to follow the design principles we've discussed throughout this book. Changes should be made from the top down, and the new tree should reflect the structure of your network and organization. After the upper layers have been appropriately adjusted, modify the lower layers of the tree to optimize administration. Also, consider how login scripts and bindery services are used on the network and container sizes. This is also the point at which you should apply any naming standards you've developed.

A good NDS design should look similar to a pyramid, descending logically from the [Root] to the larger Organizational Units, to departments, to resources. Naming standards should be implemented to provide consistency across your network to allow users easy access to all resources.

User Environment Implementation

The final step in the NDS design and implementation process is putting your user environment plan in place. Use the information in the accessibility and administration plans created in Chapter 8 to establish and control the user environment. Remember that the plan you put in place should allow the user environment to be controlled centrally, and application and service management should be as simple as possible. You should settle on and implement a standard file system structure to ensure ease of use and security. Mobile users and their needs must be identified, and your plan must provide access for both standard and mobile users. Utilize Z.E.N.works Policy Packages and Application objects to provide users with a standard operating environment, regardless of the operating systems being used.

All user environment implementation steps take place through NetWare Administrator. For example, login scripts can be configured by opening the appropriate container, Profile, or User object. Remember that user login scripts should only be used as exceptions, rather than rules. Application objects require you to supply the path to the application and associate the object to a User, Group, or container object. The client configuration parameters differ from operating system to operating system. For example, to set the preferred tree and name context for a Windows 95/98 client, open Control Panel|Network, select the Novell NetWare Client software, then click on Properties. In the end, the Z.E.N.works objects you use depend on the structure of your network and the environment you wish to provide your users.

Sample Company Scenario

As you can imagine, one of the final steps in our sample company network plan is to merge the two separate NDS trees to form MB Enterprises. Before starting the merge, we need to make a backup of both trees and ensure that time synchronization is active. MB Enterprises has settled on an enterprise backup solution that provides easy backups of NDS. At the console of the source and target servers, we'll use the **TIME** command to verify that the servers are synchronized with the network. Neither Burmeister Publishing nor Munson Media has modified their schema, so there should be no problems on this front.

Also, before we proceed, we must document the administrative rights of the [Root] trustees of both trees and determine if these rights are still needed by all users after the merge. While reviewing this information, we find that there are seven users at Burmeister Publishing that have administrative access to the [Root] and only two at Munson Media. Because IS management resides at the Vancouver office, one of the Munson Media employees will actually perform the merge. This leaves eight users for which a determination must be made. After careful review, you decide to grant administrative access to the new [Root] only to three additional staff: the remaining Munson Media administrator and two Burmeister Publishing administrators. The other Burmeister Publishing employees who currently have administrative access to their [Root] object will be assigned as Enterprise-wide Admins, but removed from the highest access level.

To actually accomplish the merge, we'll need to use the DSMERGE NLM at the source server console. The two trees are called the *source* and *target* trees. The merge function is similar to a copy or move command in MS-DOS. In our case, the source tree—Burmeister Publishing—is merged with the target tree—Munson Media—to form a new tree. The new NDS tree will look like the sample shown in Figure 9.1.

As mentioned, the administrator account performing the merge, generally the Admin User object in the source tree, will be made a trustee of the new [Root]; the user will also have NDS Supervisor rights. Also, any user that has the Supervisor NDS rights on the source [Root] tree will not have those rights on the new

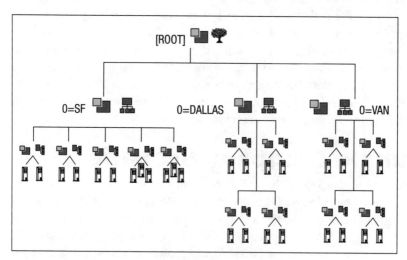

Figure 9.1 The merged MB Enterprises tree.

tree—the rights are deleted. Therefore, these rights must be assigned after the merge is complete. Another point regarding a merge operation is that the top-level containers on the source [Root] will become partition root objects after the merge.

After the merge is complete, we'll load DSREPAIR on the servers to verify the replica status. We'll also need to adjust the login scripts and bindery service commands in the AUTOEXEC.NCF files on all servers on the network. The structure of the NDS tree will also need to be adjusted to reflect the structure of the network. The similar departments in all divisions should be combined into containers, while retaining the geographic separateness. For example, the Editing and Acquisitions containers can be combined into one container called E/A, but there should be subcontainers for San Francisco and Dallas.

Because of the large number of workstations on the network, a plan must be invoked to adjust the preferred tree and name context settings. Alias objects can be used to point to the new containers and locations of the resources. The users should also be educated, before the merge takes place, that they may need to use a slightly different method for logging in after the change takes place. For this type of situation, it might also be a good idea to enable contextless logins for a short period of time to allow all workstations to be properly adjusted.

Because there are three T1 lines connecting the three sites and there's a lot of data that will be transmitted between the sites, we'll use WAN Traffic Manager. Remember that each server will need to be adjusted individually. Because the company generally operates during normal business hours, we can use the predefined profiles to limit server-initiated traffic to the middle of the night.

We must also look at implementing the user environment based on the administration plan developed in Chapter 8. In that chapter, we determined that there are a number of objects that will be used in the new tree. For example, Application objects will be used to facilitate access to the Microsoft Office suite and the customer database. Each of these objects is easily added through NetWare Administrator. You must provide the path to the applications when creating the objects. Because it's not a good idea to share applications across WAN links, there are application servers at each site and the Application objects should point to the application servers within each container.

Organizational Role and Profile objects will also be used on the tree and must be implemented at this time. All these functions are available through NetWare Administrator. Aside from the configuration changes that must take place on each workstation, the majority of the implementation process is handled through NetWare Administrator. Before implementing the user environment, you must decide whether the new default user settings that were established will be assigned to existing users or only to new users as they are added. If the new default settings will be applied to all users, a plan must be put in place to adjust the user settings after the merge is complete. Generally, a container-by-container migration is the best option. Using this method, you can educate the users to the new requirements before changing their settings. To ensure a consistent user environment, we advise setting all users' configurations the same, and we will do so in the MB Enterprises tree.

The steps outlined throughout this book describe how the MB Enterprises NDS tree can be developed, planned, and implemented. MB Enterprises' NDS tree utilizes partitions and replicas and spans many servers in many geographic locations. Although many of the NDS objects and features discussed in this text might not be necessary on your network today, all networks change with time, and the information we've provided gives you the background you need to tackle challenges as they arise.

Practice Questions

Question 1

Why do client workstation configurations have to be changed after a successful merge?

○ a. Alias objects will be put in place to direct users to the new context.

○ b. The User object will be deleted and must be re-created during the merge.

○ c. The Server object context will change as a result of the merge.

○ d. The User object's distinguished name will change as a result of the merge.

The correct answer is d. Because the distinguished name represents the full path to the User object, it will change during the merge process. The client workstation configuration must be changed to reflect the new preferred tree and name context of the user. Alias objects can be used to assist the users in connecting to the NDS tree before their workstations are configured with the new name context information. This will aid the merge process, but does not affect the workstation configurations themselves. Therefore, answer a is incorrect. The merge process automatically deletes and re-creates User and other objects, but this also has no bearing on the workstation configuration. Therefore, answer b is incorrect. Whereas the server context may change during the merge, one of the benefits of NDS is that the actual server location does not affect client accessibility. The user logs into the tree, not to a particular server. Therefore, answer c is incorrect.

Question 2

> Which of the following NLMs is used to limit server-to-server communication
> to off-peak hours?
>
> ○ a. DSREPAIR
>
> ○ b. WTM
>
> ○ c. DSMERGE
>
> ○ d. NETADMIN

The correct answer is b. WTM.NLM is used to manage server-to-server communication and limits server-initiated traffic to off-peak hours. DSREPAIR
and DSMERGE are utilities that are used to manage and maintain the NDS
Directory. Therefore, answers a and c are incorrect. NETADMIN is a character-
based version of NetWare Administrator found in earlier versions of NetWare,
but it does not actually control server communications. Therefore, answer d is
incorrect.

Question 3

> Which of the following statements describes considerations before merging
> two NDS trees? [Choose the two best answers]
>
> ❑ a. Both trees must be using the same naming convention.
>
> ❑ b. Time synchronization must be functioning between the servers in
> the NDS tree, and the trees must be in sync.
>
> ❑ c. Both trees must be using the same schema.
>
> ❑ d. DSREPAIR should be running on both trees before the merge.

The correct answers are b and c. The time on both trees must be in sync, which
is accomplished through time synchronization, and both trees must be using
the same schema before the merge takes place. The naming convention used
on your network should be standard, but the trees to be merged do not have to
share a naming convention before the merge. Therefore, answer a is incorrect.
Although it's a good idea to make sure the directories are in good shape before
performing the merge, a good backup is more important than running a repair
on the trees. Therefore, answer d is incorrect.

Question 4

> What's the easiest way to confirm that the NDS structure has stabilized after a merge?
>
> ○ a. Verify the partition status
>
> ○ b. Verify the time-synchronization status
>
> ○ c. Verify the replica status
>
> ○ d. Continue with another merge

The correct answer is c. If all replicas indicate a status of On through DSREPAIR, the merge process is complete and stable. Neither the partition status nor the time synchronization status provides a good indication of the stability of the NDS tree. Therefore, answers a and b are incorrect. Continuing with another merge if the tree is not stable will cause the new merge to fail and the target server's directory to be damaged. Therefore, answer d is incorrect.

Question 5

> Which of the following users is automatically granted Supervisor access to the [Root] of the new tree after a merge?
>
> ○ a. The user that ran the merge
>
> ○ b. The Enterprise-wide Admin
>
> ○ c. Admin
>
> ○ d. All users who had Supervisor access to the [Root] of the old trees

The correct answer is a. By default, the source User object that was used to perform the merge has Supervisor object rights to the [Root] of the new NDS tree. None of the other users listed, including the users who previously had Supervisor [Root] access to the source tree, is granted this type of access to the new [Root]. For this reason, it's important to document which users have Supervisor access before performing the merge. Also for this reason, answers b, c, and d are incorrect.

Need To Know More?

 Clarke, David James, IV. *CNE Study Guide for Core Technologies.* Novell Press, San Jose, CA, 1996. ISBN 0-7645-4501-9. The various objects and applications are covered throughout the book.

 For additional information on the various NDS objects and utilities discussed throughout the chapter, review the NetWare 5 online documentation using the object or application names as keywords. For example, a search for "Schema Manager" provides an extensive list of matches, including an overview of the Schema Manager and a document titled "Understanding Schema Manager."

Sample Test

In this chapter, we provide pointers to help you develop a successful test-taking strategy, including how to choose proper answers, decode ambiguity, work within the Novell testing framework, decide what you need to memorize, and prepare for the test. At the end of the chapter, we include 68 questions on subject matter pertinent to Novell Test 050-634: "NDS Design and Implementation." Good luck!

Questions, Questions, Questions

There should be no doubt in your mind that you're facing a test full of specific and pointed questions. NDS Design and Implementation is a form exam that consists of 68 questions that you can take up to 105 minutes to complete. This means you must study hard so you can answer as many questions as possible correctly, without resorting to guesses.

Note: We expect Novell to change this test to an adaptive format eventually. See Chapter 1 for more information on adaptive testing.

For this exam, questions belong to one of six basic types:

➤ Multiple-choice questions with a single answer

➤ Multiple-choice questions with multiple answers

➤ Multipart questions with a single answer

➤ Multipart questions with multiple answers

➤ Questions requiring you to operate simulated NetWare console or utility interfaces

➤ Questions using graphics with clickable hotspots

Always take the time to read each question at least twice before selecting an answer, and always look for an Exhibit button as you examine each question. Exhibits include graphics information related to a question. An exhibit is usually a screen capture of program output or GUI information that you must examine to analyze the question's contents and formulate an answer. The Exhibit button brings up graphics and charts used to help explain a question, provide additional data, or illustrate page layout or program behavior.

Not every question has only one answer; many questions require multiple answers. Therefore, it's important to read each question carefully to determine how many answers are necessary or possible, and to look for additional hints or instructions when selecting answers. Such instructions often occur in brackets, immediately following the question itself (as they do for all multiple-choice, multiple-answer questions).

Simulation questions can be a mixed blessing. These task-oriented questions allow you to demonstrate your abilities to complete a certain task or to apply some analysis or management technique. The NetWare Administrator utility appears often in NetWare 5 simulation questions because it's the nerve center for NetWare administration. In addition, the NDS Manager simulation appears commonly with questions regarding partitioning and replication. This means it's essential for you to spend some time familiarizing yourself with the key administration and management tools in NetWare 5, so you'll be ready when simulations show up in test questions.

Picking Proper Answers

Obviously, the only way to pass any exam is to select enough of the right answers to obtain a passing score. However, Novell's exams are not standardized like the SAT and GRE exams, and they can sometimes be quite a bit more challenging. In some cases, questions can be hard to follow or filled with technical vocabulary, and deciphering them can be difficult. In those cases, you may need to rely on answer-elimination skills. Almost always, at least one answer out of the possible choices for a question can be eliminated immediately because it matches one of these conditions:

➤ The answer does not apply to the situation.

➤ The answer describes a nonexistent issue, an invalid option, or an imaginary state.

➤ The answer can be eliminated because of the question itself.

After you eliminate all answers that are obviously wrong, you can apply your retained knowledge to eliminate further answers. Look for items that sound correct, but refer to actions, commands, or features that are not present or not available in the situation that the question describes.

If you're still faced with a blind guess among two or more potentially correct answers, reread the question. Try to picture how each of the possible remaining answers would alter the situation. Be especially sensitive to terminology; sometimes, the choice of words (*remove* instead of *disable*) can make the difference between a right answer and a wrong one.

Only when you've exhausted your ability to eliminate answers, and you're still unclear about which of the remaining possibilities is correct, should you guess at an answer (or answers). Guessing gives you at least some chance of getting a question right; just don't be too hasty when making a blind guess.

Decoding Ambiguity

Novell exams have a reputation for including straightforward questions. You won't have to worry much about deliberate ambiguity, but you will need a good grasp of the technical vocabulary involved with NetWare and related products to understand what some questions are trying to ask. In our experience with numerous Novell tests, we've learned that mastering the lexicon of Novell's technical terms pays off on every exam. The Novell tests are tough, but fair, and they're deliberately made that way.

However, you need to brace yourself for one special case. Novell tests are notorious for their use of double negatives and similar circumlocutions, such as, "What item is not used when creating a <insert your favorite task here>?" Our guess is that Novell includes such Byzantine language in its questions because it wants to make sure examinees can follow instructions to the letter, no matter how strangely worded those instructions might be. Although this may seem like a form of torture, it's actually good preparation for those circumstances where you have to follow instructions from technical manuals or training materials, which are themselves not quite in the same ballpark as "great literature" or even "plain English." Even though we've been coached repeatedly to be on the lookout for this kind of stuff, it still fools us anyway from time to time. Therefore, you need to be on the lookout and try to learn from our mistakes.

The only way to beat Novell at this game is to be prepared. You'll discover that many exam questions test your knowledge of topics that are not directly related to the issue raised by a question. This means that the answers from which you must choose, even incorrect ones, are just as much a part of the skill assessment as the question itself. If you don't know something about most aspects of administering NetWare 5, you may not be able to eliminate obviously wrong answers because they relate to a different area of the operating system than the one that's addressed by the question at hand. In other words, the more you know about administering NetWare in general, the easier it will be for you to tell a right answer from a wrong one.

Questions often give away their answers, but you have to read carefully to see the clues that point to those answers. Often, subtle hints appear in the question text in such a way that they seem almost irrelevant to the situation. You must realize that each question is a test unto itself and that you need to inspect and successfully navigate each question to pass the exam. Look for small clues, such as the mention of utilities, services, and configuration settings. Little things like these can point to the right answer if properly understood; if missed, they can leave you facing a blind guess.

Because mastering the technical vocabulary is so important to testing well for Novell, be sure to brush up on the key terms presented at the beginning of each chapter. You may also want to read through the Glossary at the end of this book the day before you take the test.

Working Within The Framework

The test questions appear in random order, and many elements or issues that receive mention in one question may also crop up in other questions. It's not uncommon to find that an incorrect answer to one question is the correct answer to another question, and vice versa. Take the time to read every answer to each question, even if you recognize the correct answer to a question immediately. That extra reading may spark a memory or remind you about a networking feature or function that helps you on another question later in the exam.

Review each question carefully; test developers love to throw in a few tricky questions. Often, important clues are hidden in the wording or special instructions. Do your best to decode ambiguous questions; just be aware that some questions will be open to interpretation.

You might also want to jot some notes on the piece of paper or plastic sheet you are provided about questions that contain key information.

 Don't be afraid to take notes on what you see in various questions. Sometimes, what you record from one question—especially if it isn't as familiar as it should be or reminds you of the name or use of some utility or interface details—can help you with other questions later in the test.

Deciding What To Memorize

The amount of memorization you must undertake for an exam depends on how well you remember what you've read and how well you know the software by heart. If you're a visual thinker and can see drop-down menus and dialog boxes in your head, you won't need to memorize as much as someone who's less visually oriented. The tests will stretch your recollection of NetWare 5 concepts, tools, and technologies.

At a minimum, you'll want to memorize the following types of information:

➤ The organization of an NDS design project, including its phases and procedures, its members, and their responsibilities.

➤ The reasons for having naming standards, and when they should be defined.

➤ How NDS object naming works, including relative and distinguished names, and typeful and typeless names.

➤ The concepts of NDS tree design, including how to design the upper and lower layers of the tree.

➤ Time synchronization, including when custom design is necessary, what the server types are and how they work together, and how the provision of network time changes when IP-only or mixed IP/IPX networks are in use.

➤ Partitions and replicas, including when custom design is necessary, the types of replicas, when subordinate references are created, and the default partitioning and replication rules.

➤ The components of an administrative strategies document.

➤ The requirements for planning and performing tree merges.

If you work your way through this book and try to exercise the various capabilities of NetWare 5 that are covered throughout, you should have little or no difficulty mastering this material. Also, don't forget that The Cram Sheet at the front of the book is designed to capture the material that's most important to memorize; use this to guide your studies as well. Finally, don't forget to obtain and use Novell's Test Objectives for Course 575 as part of your planning and preparation process.

Preparing For The Test

The best way to prepare for the test—after you've studied—is to take at least one practice exam. We've included one here in this chapter for that reason; the test questions are located in the pages that follow. (Unlike the preceding chapters in this book, the answers don't follow the questions immediately; you'll have to flip to Chapter 11 to review the answers separately.)

Give yourself no more than 105 minutes to take the exam, keep yourself on the honor system, and don't look at earlier text in the book or jump ahead to the answer key. When your time is up or you've finished the questions, you can check your work in Chapter 11. Pay special attention to the explanations for the incorrect answers; these can also help to reinforce your knowledge of the material. Knowing how to recognize correct answers is good, but understanding why incorrect answers are wrong can be equally valuable.

Taking The Test

Relax. Once you're sitting in front of the testing computer, there's nothing more you can do to increase your knowledge or preparation. Take a deep breath, stretch, and start reading that first question.

There's no need to rush—you have plenty of time. If you can't figure out the answer to a question after a few minutes, though, you may want to guess and move on to leave more time for remaining unanswered questions. Remember that both easy and difficult questions are intermixed throughout the test in random order. Because you're taking a form test, you should watch your time carefully. Try to be one-quarter of the way done (17 questions) in at least 26 minutes, halfway done (34 questions) in at least 52 minutes, and three-quarters done (51 questions) in 78 minutes.

Set a maximum time limit for questions and watch your time on long or complex questions. If you hit your time limit, you need to guess and move on. Don't deprive yourself of the opportunity to see more questions by taking too long to puzzle over answers, unless you think you can figure out the correct answer. Otherwise, you're limiting your opportunities to pass.

That's it for pointers. Here are some questions for you to practice on.

Sample Test

Question 1

In the following figure, server FS2 holds replicas of [Root], Paris, and NYC. For which partitions will NDS place a subordinate reference on FS2? [Choose the two best answers]

❑ a. [Root]

❑ b. Paris

❑ c. Sales

❑ d. NYC

❑ e. Rio

```
                        ╭──────────╮
                        │ [Root]   │
                        │ O=ABC    │
                        ╰──────────╯
        ┌───────────────────┼───────────────────┐
  ╭──────────╮        ╭──────────╮        ╭──────────╮
  │ OU=PARIS │        │ OU=NYC   │        │ OU=RIO   │
  │   └ FS1  │        │   └ FS2  │        │   └ FS3  │
  ╰──────────╯        ╰──────────╯        ╰──────────╯
        │
  ╭──────────╮
  │ OU=SALES │
  ╰──────────╯
```

Question 2

Which tool can be used to move containers to their new location after a tree merge?

○ a. NDS Manager

○ b. PARTMGR.EXE

○ c. NetWare Administrator

○ d. DSMERGE.NLM

Question 3

Which of the following characteristics of a network can be attributed to good NDS design? [Choose the three best answers]

❑ a. Easy access to network resources

❑ b. Low paging rates on workstations

❑ c. A network that hackers cannot easily penetrate

❑ d. A network in which traveling employees can access their data

Question 4

Which of the following statements are true of an effective high-level design process? [Choose the two best answers]

❑ a. Uses innovative design strategies

❑ b. Provides optimum NDS capabilities

❑ c. Is the product of a single individual's experience and work

❑ d. Is based on a thorough analysis of the organization's business

Question 5

An NDS consultant reviewing a NetWare 5 installation notices that there are three Printer objects in one container: Lori'sPostscript, Flash, and HP4ACCTG. Which of the following comments could he make regarding these naming conventions?

○ a. The naming standards are poorly designed.

○ b. These administrators are not following the standards.

○ c. As long as the users know what the printer names mean, these names are OK.

Question 6

Which two approaches should be taken regarding the NDS design process? [Choose the two best answers]

❑ a. Design based on the enterprise's administrative structure

❑ b. Design based on the data flow of the enterprise's major production systems

❑ c. Design based on the enterprise's existing data networks

❑ d. Design based on the enterprise's corporate policies and procedures

Question 7

Which of the following roles is *not* usually found in a small organization's NDS design project?

○ a. Project manager

○ b. Server administrator

○ c. NDS expert

○ d. Connectivity specialist

○ e. Printing specialist

Question 8

Which of the following considerations should be assessed when developing the accessibility needs document? [Choose the three best answers]

❑ a. Requirements for access to printers and network storage

❑ b. Requirements for access to network applications

❑ c. Requirements for partitioning

❑ d. Requirements for access to bindery services

Question 9

Your mobile users are complaining that when they access the network from other company locations, they can't print to the local printers, applications take a long time to load, and their home directories are not available. Which part of the NDS project was not carried out well?

○ a. Designing a partitioning plan

○ b. Implementing the WAN Traffic Manager

○ c. Creating the accessibility needs document

○ d. Creating administrative strategy

Question 10

The responsibilities of the project manager include which of the following? [Choose the four best answers]

❏ a. Software evaluation

❏ b. Documentation of the NDS tree design

❏ c. How the rollout of the new operating system is to be carried out

❏ d. Costs of implementation, software licensing, and operations

❏ e. Training the users and administrators

Question 11

Ensuring that all servers agree on the time is critical to the correct operation of NDS. Whose responsibility is it to implement the time-synchronization strategy?

○ a. Project manager

○ b. Server administrator

○ c. NDS expert

○ d. Connectivity specialist

Question 12

When using the Network Time Protocol (NTP), what are the valid time provider types? [Choose the two best answers]

- ❏ a. Peer
- ❏ b. Secondary
- ❏ c. Primary
- ❏ d. Server

Question 13

Which of the following tasks are the responsibility of the connectivity specialist? [Choose the three best answers]

- ❏ a. Designing coordinated login scripts
- ❏ b. Designing the internetwork for efficient data transfer
- ❏ c. Influencing the design of time synchronization and partitioning strategies from the point of view of network traffic
- ❏ d. Advising the project on WAN routing and protocols with regard to NDS traffic

Question 14

As the NDS expert, you have completed the NDS design. What is the next step in the project?

- ○ a. Coordinating NDS implementation
- ○ b. Planning the user environment
- ○ c. Determining a partition and replica strategy
- ○ d. Planning a time-synchronization strategy

Question 15

In the following figure, server FS2 holds a replica of [Root] and of NYC. For which partitions will NDS place a subordinate reference on FS2? [Choose the two best answers]

❑ a. [Root]

❑ b. Paris

❑ c. Sales

❑ d. NYC

❑ e. Rio

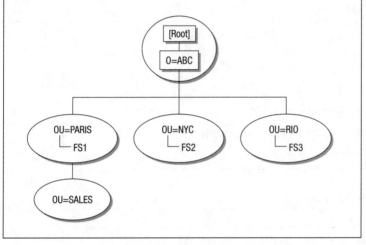

Question 16

What is the name of the phase in the NDS project that follows the project-approach phase?

○ a. The tree-design phase

○ b. The time-synchronization phase

○ c. The design phase

○ d. The user-planning phase

Question 17

A user whose workstation is in the Sales.Paris.ABC context needs to print to the LJ5 Printer object in the CAIRO.ABC container. Which **CAPTURE** command should be used?

○ a. **CAPTURE P=LJ5.**

○ b. **CAPTURE P=CAIRO.LJ5.**

○ c. **CAPTURE P=LJ5.CAIRO.**

○ d. **CAPTURE P=LJ5.CAIRO..**

Question 18

Which procedures of the design phase are conditional? [Choose the two best answers]

❏ a. Tree design

❏ b. Planning time synchronization

❏ c. Setting partition and replication strategy

❏ d. User environment planning

Question 19

Which replica types can be used for login authentication? [Choose the two best answers]

❏ a. Subordinate reference

❏ b. Master

❏ c. Read-only

❏ d. Read/write

❏ e. All of the above

Question 20

Which of the following contains the first three phases of the NDS design process in the correct order?

○ a. Preparing for NDS design, designing an NDS tree, and determining a partition and replication strategy

○ b. Project approach, design, and implementation

○ c. Designing an NDS tree, determining a partition and replication strategy, and planning time-synchronization strategy

○ d. Implementation, design, and project approach

Question 21

Which of the following steps is not part of the first step of the design phase, designing the NDS tree?

○ a. Creating a naming standards document

○ b. Designing the upper layers of the tree

○ c. Designing the lower layers of the tree

○ d. Planning time-synchronization strategy

Question 22

Which program is used to merge two NDS trees?

○ a. NDS Manager

○ b. NetWare Administrator

○ c. DSMERGE.NLM

○ d. DSREPAIR.NLM

Question 23

After a merge is complete, several administrators from the source tree complain that they cannot manage their containers any more. Why has this happened?

○ a. The merge process deleted their User objects.

○ b. Their User objects had rights to the root of the source tree, and those rights were removed by the merge.

○ c. Their container objects have been moved under a new top-level container, so the administrators' container management rights have been lost.

○ d. The person running the merge failed to select the Retain Administrator Rights option in NDS Manager.

Question 24

Which of the following characteristics of a network can be attributed to good NDS design? [Choose the three best answers]

❑ a. Ability to log in even when a workstation's preferred server is down

❑ b. Easy addition of servers and printers to the network

❑ c. Fast response to database queries

❑ d. Predictable naming of network resources

Question 25

Which of the following are benefits of a well-designed naming standard? [Choose the two best answers]

❑ a. Efficient time-synchronization implementation

❑ b. Easy tree browsing for users

❑ c. Fast synchronization of replicas across the WAN links

❑ d. Easy administration of the tree by NDS administrators

Question 26

In an IPX-only network, what is the default time-synchronization configuration?

○ a. A reference server and two or more primary servers voting on the network time

○ b. A single reference server providing time to secondary servers

○ c. A secondary time server providing time to a single reference time server

○ d. A primary server and two or more reference servers voting on the network time

Question 27

How many child partitions can a parent partition have?

○ a. 1

○ b. 16

○ c. 35

○ d. No limit

Question 28

How many parent partitions can a child partition have?

○ a. 1

○ b. 16

○ c. 40

○ d. No limit

Question 29

Which of these tasks is not generally the responsibility of the project manager?

○ a. Organizing meetings with project staff and management

○ b. Acting as a pipeline between the team, user departments, and management for suggestions and concerns

○ c. Ensuring that the servers are configured adequately to support the requirements of NDS

○ d. Explaining the effects that the new system will have on the enterprise

Question 30

Some of the servers in a newly implemented NDS tree are reporting that they are not synchronized to network time and they cannot perform partitioning operations. Which member of the team needs to review this problem?

○ a. Server administrator

○ b. Workstation expert

○ c. Connectivity specialist

○ d. NDS expert

Question 31

Mark is a network engineer who needs to change a replica type. Which type of replica can he *not* change the replica to?

○ a. Master

○ b. Read-only

○ c. Read/write

○ d. Subordinate reference

Question 32

In the following figure, each server holds replicas of the [Root] partition and its own partition. How many subordinate references will NDS create?

○ a. 0

○ b. 2

○ c. 3

○ d. 6

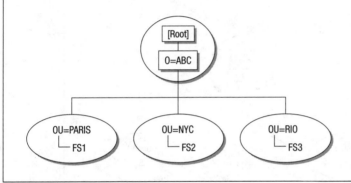

Question 33

Which of the following contains the correct order of the three procedures in planning the user environment phase?

○ a. Create accessibility guidelines, design administrative strategy, and create an accessibility needs document

○ b. Create an accessibility needs document, create accessibility guidelines, and design administrative strategy

○ c. Design administrative strategy, create an accessibility needs document, and create accessibility guidelines

○ d. Design administrative strategy and create accessibility guidelines

Question 34

In the following figure, each server holds replicas of the [Root] partition, its own partition, and one other partition. How many subordinate references will NDS create?

○ a. 0

○ b. 2

○ c. 3

○ d. 6

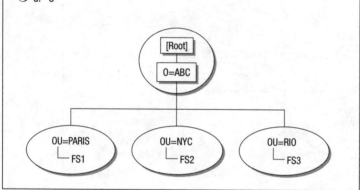

Question 35

In the following figure, what is the total number of replicas that would have to be stored on the servers to provide the recommended level of fault tolerance?

○ a. 3

○ b. 4

○ c. 6

○ d. 12

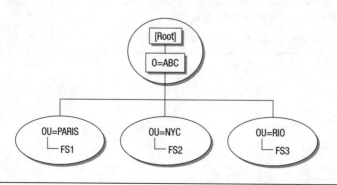

Question 36

Determining a partition and replica strategy is conditional—it's only necessary if certain conditions are true. Which of the following statements, if true, would make a partition and replica strategy necessary? [Choose the three best answers]

- ❑ a. There are 10,000 objects in the tree.
- ❑ b. There are 2,600 objects in the tree.
- ❑ c. There are servers in more than one geographical location.
- ❑ d. There are 10 servers holding replicas.
- ❑ e. There are 22 servers holding replicas.

Question 37

After a merge has completed, several users from the source tree complain that they cannot log in, and therefore cannot access their home directories. Why has this happened?

- ○ a. Their User objects were duplicates of objects in the target tree and NetWare file security stops them from accessing the other users' directories.
- ○ b. The merge process merges NDS trees, not directories. The administrators should have copied the home directories to the target servers.
- ○ c. The name of the top-level object has changed for users in the source tree. The users need to change the login context parameters for their workstations.
- ○ d. It's a time-synchronization problem. When the new tree stops issuing synthetic time, the home directories will be available again.

Question 38

Christine sees that the NetWare 5 Server objects have three pages that are not seen in the default NDS schema: LAN Area Membership, WAN Policies, and Cost. Which of the following facilities has been installed?

- ○ a. WAN Traffic Manager
- ○ b. NetWare 5 Accounting
- ○ c. LAN-WAN Synchronization Services
- ○ d. NetWare Administrator

Question 39

At 3 P.M. local time, a user whose User object is in a partition with replicas stored only on servers in the Adelaide site is attempting to login via a server in the Montevideo site. A WAN Traffic Manager policy called **1-3AM, NA** has been applied for the Montevideo server. Will the user be able to log in?

○ a. Yes

○ b. No

Question 40

An administrator wants to move the container OU=SALES.OU=PARIS.O=ABC to its new location under the container OU=BRUSSELS.O=ABC. Which tool should the user use?

○ a. DSMERGE

○ b. DSREPAIR

○ c. NetWare Administrator

○ d. NDS Manager

Question 41

In the following figure, replicas are distributed as in the following table. Which servers hold subordinate reference replicas? [Choose the three best answers]

	[Root]	Paris	Sales	NYC	Rio
FS1	M	M	M	R/W	
FS2	R/W	R/W		M	R/W
FS3			R/W	R/W	R/W
FS4	R/W		R/W		M

❏ a. FS1

❏ b. FS2

❏ c. FS3 – 1 subordinate reference

❏ d. FS3 – 2 subordinate references

❏ e. FS4 – 1 subordinate reference

❏ f. FS4 – 2 subordinate references

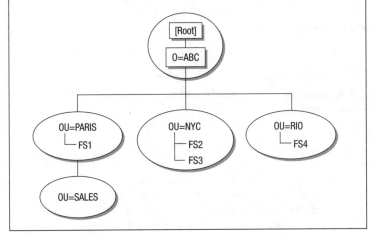

Question 42

Christine is a new NetWare administrator who is concerned about the number of subordinate references in her NDS tree's replica table. What can she do to remove the subordinate references that trouble her? [Choose the two best answers]

❑ a. Delete the subordinate references in NDS Manager.

❑ b. Place a read/write replica of the partitions on the servers where the subordinate references now exist in NDS Manager.

❑ c. Remove the replicas of each parent partition from the servers where the subordinate references exist in NDS Manager.

❑ d. Delete the subordinate references in NetWare Administrator.

Question 43

You're preparing to merge two trees. Which of the following steps should be completed before you can perform the merge? [Choose the four best answers]

❑ a. Synchronize the time on the two trees.

❑ b. Synchronize the schemas on the two trees.

❑ c. Back up the two trees.

❑ d. Ensure the top-level objects in the two trees have different names.

❑ e. Ensure the credentials used for the administrator accounts on the two trees are identical.

Question 44

A university with a total of 15,000 students, faculty, and staff is located on a single campus with Fiber Distributed Data Interface (FDDI) links between all sites. Every user has a workstation, and Z.E.N.works is used for workstation management and application launching. NDS is implemented on NetWare 5 servers that are 133MHz Pentium class machines with 64MB of RAM each. How many partitions should the NDS designer create?

○ a. 1

○ b. 5

○ c. 10

○ d. 20

Question 45

In an IPX-only network, which command can you use to ensure that time up-dates are received only from other servers in the same tree as a server?

- ○ a. **SET Directory Tree Mode=ON**
- ○ b. **SET Time From This Tree Only=YES**
- ○ c. **SET Configured Sources=ON**
- ○ d. **SET Synchronization Radius=TREE**

Question 46

In an IPX-only network, from which server types can secondary time servers receive time? [Choose the four best answers]

- ❑ a. Reference
- ❑ b. Single reference
- ❑ c. Primary
- ❑ d. Secondary
- ❑ e. Single primary

Question 47

You want members of the help desk staff to be able to change passwords and password requirements, such as the number of grace logins. Which of the following is the best approach?

- ○ a. Make the HelpDesk Organizational Role a trustee of the containers the staff needs to manage with Supervisor property rights with the All Properties option.
- ○ b. Make the HelpDesk Organizational Role a trustee of the containers the staff needs to manage with Read and Write access rights to the Password Management property.
- ○ c. Choose the individual User objects and assign rights for the Organizational Role to the Password Management property.
- ○ d. Make the HelpDesk Organizational Role a trustee of the containers the staff needs to manage with Read, Write, and Inheritable access rights to the Password Management property.

Question 48

Jeanne is setting up time synchronization in her network. There are 22 servers in the Montreal office and 5 in the New York office. The 2 sites are connected with a 128Kbps link. Which method of time provision should she use?

- ○ a. Default time-synchronization configuration
- ○ b. Configured sources, with one time provider group
- ○ c. Configured sources, with two time provider groups
- ○ d. TIMESYNC.NLM
- ○ e. NTP.NLM

Question 49

In an IPX-only network, when a reference server's time differs from the calculated network time, by how much of the difference does it change its time?

- ○ a. 0 percent
- ○ b. 50 percent
- ○ c. 75 percent
- ○ d. 100 percent

Question 50

In an IPX-only network, when a primary server's time differs from the calculated network time, by how much of the difference does it change its time?

- ○ a. 0 percent
- ○ b. 50 percent
- ○ c. 75 percent
- ○ d. 100 percent

Question 51

In an IPX-only network, when a time server's time is not in sync with the calculated network time, how often does it poll the other servers?

○ a. Every 2,000 milliseconds

○ b. Every 10 seconds

○ c. Every minute

○ d. Every 10 minutes

Question 52

Which project team member is most likely to be responsible for discovering the resource access needs of the user departments and management?

○ a. Project manager

○ b. NDS expert

○ c. Application specialist

○ d. Connectivity specialist

○ e. Server administrator

Question 53

The responsibilities of the server administrator include which of the following tasks? [Choose the two best answers]

❏ a. Plan the location of servers in the NDS tree

❏ b. Ensure server communications over the WAN link is efficient

❏ c. Decide how servers should be added to and removed from the tree

❏ d. Design the strategy for partitioning and replication

Question 54

Bill wants to set up the Network Time Protocol (NTP) on his network and create the NTP.CFG file to show from where his network will receive its time. He has decided that he would like to use the time server bitsy.mit.edu, whose IP address is 18.72.0.3. Which entries are valid for his NTP.CFG file? [Choose the two best answers]

- ❑ a. server bitsy.mit.edu
- ❑ b. peer bitsy.mit.edu
- ❑ c. server 18.72.0.3
- ❑ d. peer 18.72.0.3

Question 55

In an IPX-only network, which file holds time-synchronization configuration parameters?

- ○ a. TIMESRCE.CFG
- ○ b. NTP.CFG
- ○ c. TIMESYNC.CFG
- ○ d. NETTIME.SET

Question 56

Laura is setting up time synchronization in her network. There are 12 servers in the Montevideo office and 5 in the Adelaide office. The 2 sites are connected with a 56Kbps link that is not always up. Which method of time provision should she use?

- ○ a. Default time-synchronization configuration
- ○ b. Configured sources—with one time provider group
- ○ c. Configured sources—with two time provider groups

Question 57

Yoko needs to set up configured lists on her Adelaide-based secondary servers so they will receive their network time from the correct servers. The nearest time server, named FS-ADE-A, is to be attempted first and another server, named FS-ADE-B, is next. How should she configure the TIME SOURCES statement in the TIMESYNC.CFG file?

○ a. **TIME SOURCES = FS-ADE-B, FS-ADE-A**

○ b. **TIME SOURCES = FS-ADE-A; FS-ADE-B**

○ c. **TIME SOURCES = FS-ADE-A; FS-ADE-B;**

○ d. **TIME SOURCES = FS-ADE-B; FS-ADE-A;**

Question 58

You want your roaming users to be able to log in from any location on the network, but in your experience, it has been difficult to teach users to log in using their distinguished names. Which of the following should you implement? [Choose the two best answers]

❏ a. Knowledgeable user login

❏ b. Alias objects

❏ c. Roaming logins

❏ d. Contextless login

Question 59

In a newly implemented NDS tree, user logins take a long time and sometimes don't complete at all. In addition, when a User object is created in one location, it may be hours before that object is usable in other parts of the tree. Which members of the NDS project team need to review their work? [Choose the two best answers]

❏ a. The project manager

❏ b. The server administrator

❏ c. The workstation expert

❏ d. The NDS expert

❏ e. The connectivity specialist

Question 60

You are a consultant for a large NetWare 5 enterprise. You find that login scripts are being changed improperly and that help desk personnel are able to create and delete all object types. Which part of the NDS project was not carried out well?

○ a. Designing a partitioning plan

○ b. Implementing the Service Location Protocol

○ c. Creating the accessibility needs document

○ d. Creating administrative strategy

Question 61

As part of creating the administrative strategies for the user environment, which of these items should you consider? [Choose the best answers]

❏ a. How to design login scripts

❏ b. How mobile users will access the system

❏ c. Which Z.E.N.works Policy Packages will be implemented

❏ d. How to implement system access security

Question 62

In an IPX-only network, when a time server's time is in sync with the calculated network time, how often does it poll the other servers?

○ a. Every 2,000 milliseconds

○ b. Every 10 seconds

○ c. Every minute

○ d. Every 10 minutes

Question 63

After a merge has occurred, which parts of the original NDS design might have to be revisited? [Choose the best answers]

- ❑ a. Time synchronization
- ❑ b. WAN traffic management
- ❑ c. Administration strategies
- ❑ d. Replica placement

Question 64

Which member of the NDS project team is responsible for the management of costs and timelines?

- ○ a. The project manager
- ○ b. The server administrator
- ○ c. The workstation expert
- ○ d. The connectivity specialist

Question 65

Christine is a new NetWare administrator who is concerned about the fault tolerance of her NDS tree's replicas, as shown in the following table. What can she do to improve her tree's fault tolerance? [Choose the four best answers]

	[Root]	Paris	Sales	NYC	Rio
FS1	M	M	M	R/W	
FS2	R/W	R/W		M	R/W
FS3					R/W
FS4		R/W		R/W	M

❑ a. Add a read/write replica of [Root] to FS3

❑ b. Add a read/write replica of [Root] to FS4

❑ c. Add a read/write replica of Sales to FS2

❑ d. Add a read/write replica of Sales to FS3

❑ e. Move the read/write replica of Rio from FS3 to FS1

Question 66

An enterprise with two sites connected by a heavily used WAN link is concerned that NDS traffic from time-synchronization and replica-synchronization tasks is slowing important database transactions. Which of the following initiatives would improve the situation? [Choose the three best answers]

❑ a. Implement separate time provider groups in each site.

❑ b. Remove all replicas of partitions on the far side of the WAN link, other than [Root].

❑ c. Implement WANSPEED.NLM.

❑ d. Use WTM.NLM to delay low-priority synchronization traffic until late at night.

Question 67

Which replica types contain complete copies of the partition information?
[Choose the three best answers]

❏ a. Subordinate reference

❏ b. Master

❏ c. Read-only

❏ d. Read/write

❏ e. All of the above

Question 68

In an IPX-only network, when a secondary server's time differs from the calculated network time, by how much of the difference does it change its time?

○ a. 0 percent

○ b. 50 percent

○ c. 75 percent

○ d. 100 percent

Answer Key

1. c, e	19. b, d	37. c	55. c
2. a	20. b	38. a	56. c
3. a, c, d	21. d	39. a	57. c
4. b, d	22. c	40. d	58. b, d
5. b	23. b	41. a, b, f	59. d, e
6. a, c	24. a, b, d	42. b, c	60. d
7. e	25. b, d	43. a, b, c, d	61. a, b, c, d
8. a, b, d	26. b	44. d	62. d
9. d	27. d	45. a	63. a, b, c, d
10. a, c, d, e	28. a	46. a, b, c, d	64. a
11. b	29. c	47. d	65. a, b, c, d
12. a, d	30. a	48. b	66. a, b, d
13. b, c, d	31. d	49. a	67. b, c, d
14. c	32. d	50. b	68. d
15. b, e	33. b	51. b	
16. c	34. c	52. b	
17. d	35. d	53. a, c	
18. b, c	36. a, c, e	54. a, c	

Question 1

The correct answers are c and e. NDS places subordinate references on a server where the parent is, but the child is not. Paris is the parent of Sales and a replica of the Sales partition is not present on FS2, so a subordinate reference for this partition will be placed there. Therefore, answer c is correct. [Root] is the parent of Rio and a replica of this partition is not present on FS2, so a subordinate reference for the Rio partition will be placed there. Therefore, answer e is correct. Replicas of [Root], Paris, and NYC exist on FS2. Therefore, answers a, b, and d are incorrect.

Question 2

The correct answer is a. NDS Manager is used to create new partitions at container objects and then move the containers. PARTMGR.EXE was used for this purpose in NetWare 4, but this tool does not exist in NetWare 5. Therefore, answer b is incorrect. NetWare Administrator can be used to move leaf objects, but not containers. Therefore, answer c is incorrect. DSMERGE.NLM does not have a move container function. Therefore, answer d is incorrect.

Question 3

The correct answers are a, c, and d, because they result from good NDS design. Low paging rates on workstations would be attributable to good workstation configuration, not good NDS design. Therefore, answer b is incorrect.

Question 4

The correct answers are b and d, because they are characteristics of a successful design process. Innovative design strategies are interesting, but the accepted design methods should be followed because they have worked in a large number of projects. Therefore, answer a is incorrect. Although an individual's experience may be very valuable, projects that are the result of a team's effort and knowledge have a greater chance of succeeding. Therefore, answer c is incorrect.

Question 5

The correct answer is b. Although we don't know for sure that naming standards are in place, the name HP4ACCTG suggests that a standard exists, made up of the type of printer and the department by which it's used. Therefore, answer a is incorrect. And although the local users may know what their printer names mean, users from other containers, and administrators from elsewhere in the tree, may have difficulty finding the printer they need from these names. Therefore, answer c is incorrect.

Question 6

The correct answers are a and c, because knowledge of the enterprise's network layout is used in designing the upper layers of the NDS tree and the enterprise's administrative structure is used in designing the lower layers of the NDS tree. The design of the NDS tree is not impacted by knowledge of the data flow of the enterprise's major production systems or of the enterprise's corporate policies and procedures. Therefore, answers b and d are incorrect.

Question 7

The correct answer is e, because in a smaller enterprise, the server administrator usually handles the role of printing specialist. The other four roles are generally found in all NDS design projects. Therefore, answers a, b, c, and d are incorrect.

Question 8

The correct answers are a, b, and d. All these requirements should be considered in developing the accessibility needs document. Partitioning of the NDS tree is a consideration of the partitioning and replica strategy phase. Therefore, answer c is incorrect.

Question 9

The correct answer is d. When creating the administrative strategy, the designers should have handled how mobile users would access local printers and applications and how they would access their home directories. Designing a partitioning plan would not affect users' login times. Therefore, answer a is incorrect. Implementing the WAN Traffic Manager determines when NDS updates replicas and is not related to the problems described. Therefore, answer b is incorrect. The accessibility needs document would have described the resources the users would need to access, not how to provide them. Therefore, answer c is incorrect.

Question 10

The correct answers are a, c, d, and e, because they are all responsibilities of the project manager (training the users and administrators might be handled by a training coordinator, if one has been assigned to the team). Documentation of the NDS tree design is the responsibility of the NDS expert. Therefore, answer b is incorrect.

Question 11

The correct answer is b. The server administrator is responsible for server time. The project manager is responsible for project timelines, not server time. Therefore, answer a is incorrect. The NDS expert designs the time-synchronization strategy, and the connectivity specialist ensures the WAN links will handle the time-synchronization traffic, but neither implements the strategy. Therefore, answers c and d are incorrect.

Question 12

The correct answers are a and d. NTP defines just two time provider types: peer and server. Secondary and primary servers do not exist in NTP. Therefore, answers b and c are incorrect.

Question 13

The correct answers are b, c, and d, because they are all in the area of responsibility of the connectivity specialist. Designing coordinated login scripts is the responsibility of the NDS expert. Therefore, answer a is incorrect.

Question 14

The correct answer is c. Determining a partition and replica strategy follows the completion of the NDS design. Answers a, b, and d do not reflect the next step in the project and are therefore incorrect.

Question 15

The correct answers are b and e. NDS places subordinate references on a server where the parent is, but the child is not. [Root] is the parent of Paris and Rio, and replicas of these partitions are not present on FS2, so subordinate references for these partitions will be placed there. Sales is not the child of [Root] or of NYC. Therefore, answer c is incorrect. Replicas of [Root] and NYC exist on FS2. Therefore, answers a and d are incorrect.

Question 16

The correct answer is c. The design phase is the second phase of the NDS project and comes after the project-approach phase. The tree-design phase is carried out in every NDS implementation. Therefore, answer a is incorrect. Time synchronization and user planning are part of the design phase. Therefore, answers b and d are incorrect.

Question 17

The correct answer is d. You need to generate the distinguished name .LJ5.CAIRO.ABC, and LJ5.CAIRO.. combined with the current context of Sales.Paris.ABC generates this name. LJ5. results in the distinguished name .LJ5.PARIS.ABC. Therefore, answer a is incorrect. CAIRO.LJ5. results in the distinguished name .CAIRO.LJ5.PARIS.ABC. Therefore, answer b is incorrect. LJ5.CAIRO. results in the distinguished name .LJ5.CAIRO.PARIS.ABC. Therefore, answer c is incorrect.

Question 18

The correct answers are b and c. Both procedures are only carried out in special circumstances. Tree design and user-environment planning are carried out in every NDS implementation. Therefore, answers a and d are incorrect.

Question 19

The correct answers are b and d. Only master and read/write replicas can handle login authentication. Subordinate reference and read-only replicas cannot be used for login authentication. Therefore, answers a and c are incorrect. Because only answers b and d are correct, answer e is incorrect.

Question 20

The correct answer is b. The four phases of the NDS design process are project approach, design, implementation, and analysis of current NDS design. Preparing for NDS design, designing an NDS tree, and determining a partition and replication strategy are the first three procedures in the project approach and design phases. Therefore, answer a is incorrect. Designing an NDS tree, determining a partition and replication strategy, and planning time-synchronization strategy are the first three procedures in the design phase. Therefore, answer c is incorrect. Answer d contains the correct phases, but they are in the wrong order. Therefore, answer d is incorrect.

Question 21

The correct answer is d. Planning time-synchronization strategy is a separate procedure, not part of the first step—designing the NDS tree. Answers a, b, and c are part of the first step of the design phase and are therefore incorrect.

Question 22

The correct answer is c. The program used to actually carry out the merge is DSMERGE.NLM. NDS Manager can be used before the merge to synchronize the schemas, but not to do the merge. Therefore, answer a is incorrect. NetWare Administrator can be used after the merge to move leaf objects to their final destination, but not to do the merge. Therefore, answer b is incorrect. DSREPAIR.NLM can be used before and after the merge to ensure any errors are cleaned up, but not to do the merge. Therefore, answer d is incorrect.

Question 23

The correct answer is b. Of all the trustees who had Supervisor object rights to the root of the source tree, only the one whose credentials were used to carry out the merge received Supervisor object rights to the root of the target tree. The merge process doesn't delete User objects. Therefore, answer a is incorrect. Container trustees of the source tree, whose rights came from trustee assignments to containers below the root, would retain those rights through the merge. Therefore, answer c is incorrect. There is no option called Retain Administrator Rights in NDS Manager. Therefore, answer d is incorrect.

Question 24

The correct answers are a, b, and d, because they result from good NDS design. Fast response to database queries would be attributed to good database design and network configuration, not good NDS design. Therefore, answer c is incorrect.

Question 25

The correct answers are b and d. Good naming standards allow administrators and users to recognize the names of the objects they see in the tree and to know what to look for. Efficient time-synchronization implementation is a result of good time-synchronization design and good WAN connectivity. Therefore, answer a is incorrect. Fast synchronization of replicas across the WAN links is a result of good partitioning and replication strategy and good WAN connectivity. Therefore, answer c is incorrect.

Question 26

The correct answer is b. The default synchronization configuration is a single reference server providing time to secondary servers. Answers a, c, and d do not represent the default synchronization configuration and are therefore incorrect.

Question 27

The correct answer is d. There is no limit to the number of child partitions a parent partition can have. However, Novell suggests no more than 35 child partitions for a single parent partition. Answers a, b, and c give specific values, and because the number of child partitions is unlimited, they are incorrect.

Question 28

The correct answer is a, because a partition can be a child of only one parent partition. Answers b and c contain incorrect values and are therefore incorrect. Because answer a is correct, answer d is incorrect.

Question 29

The correct answer is c. Server configuration is the responsibility of the server administrator. Responsibilities of a project manager include organizing meetings, enabling communications, and educating the enterprise's staff on the effects of an implementation. Therefore, answers a, b, and d are incorrect.

Question 30

The correct answer is a. The server administrator is responsible for implementing the time-synchronization strategy. If the workstations were not receiving network time correctly from a properly functioning time server, the workstation expert would be involved. Therefore, answer b is incorrect. The connectivity specialist gets involved if the WAN links aren't working properly. In that case, there would be more severe problems than time synchronization. Therefore, answer c is incorrect. The NDS expert is concerned with the NDS tree design, including time-synchronization design, but it's up to the server administrator to ensure that it's logical and properly implemented. Therefore, answer d is incorrect.

Question 31

The correct answer is d. Mark cannot change the current replica type to a subordinate reference replica. He can change the current replica to a master, read/write, or read-only replica. Therefore, answers a, b, and c are incorrect.

Question 32

The correct answer is d. On each server, NDS will place a subordinate reference to each of the partitions for which a replica is not present. Answers a, b, and c are incorrect, because they represent incorrect values.

Question 33

The correct answer is b. First, the accessibility needs document is created, then the accessibility guidelines, and finally, the administrative strategy is designed. Answers a and c represent the incorrect order and are therefore incorrect. Answer d is missing the create an accessibility needs document step and is therefore incorrect.

Question 34

The correct answer is c. On each server, NDS will place a subordinate reference to the partition for which a replica is not present. Answers a, b, and d represent incorrect values and are therefore incorrect.

Question 35

The correct answer is d. The recommendation is that three replicas exist of each partition. Therefore, each server must have a replica of all 4 partitions, for a total of 12. The other answers do not provide sufficient fault tolerance. Therefore, answers a, b, and c are incorrect.

Question 36

The correct answers are a, c, and e. Partitioning is necessary if there are more than 3,500 objects in the tree, if there are servers in more than one geographical location, and if there are more than 15 servers holding replicas. Answers b and d are incorrect, because they don't exceed the thresholds.

Question 37

The correct answer is c. The name of the top-level object has changed for users in the source tree and their old login context is now invalid. Merges do not merge containers, so there is no concern about duplicate User objects. Therefore, answer a is incorrect. There's no need for files on the source servers to be copied to the target servers after a merge. A tree merge does not affect the file system on any of the servers in either the target or the source tree. Therefore, answer b is incorrect. Merges cannot proceed when there are time-synchronization problems. Therefore, answer d is incorrect.

Question 38

The correct answer is a. Implementing WAN Traffic Manager adds the LAN Area Membership, WAN Policies, and Cost pages to the Server object details, and adds a new object type, LAN Area, to the schema. NetWare 5

Accounting does not add these entries to the schema. Therefore, answer b is incorrect. LAN-WAN Synchronization Services does not exist. Therefore, answer c is incorrect. You can only create a LAN Area object in NetWare Administrator after WAN Traffic Manager has been installed. Therefore, answer d is incorrect.

Question 39

The correct answer is a. The **1-3AM, NA** policy only restricts background traffic, such as the checking of backlinks, external references, and login restrictions, to the 1 A.M. to 3 A.M. time period. Therefore, answer b is incorrect.

Question 40

The correct answer is d. NDS Manager is the tool to use for partitioning operations, and moving a container requires first creating a partition at the container to be moved. DSMERGE.NLM is a tool for renaming and merging trees, not moving containers. Therefore, answer a is incorrect. DSREPAIR.NLM is a tool for repairing the NDS database, not moving containers. Therefore, answer b is incorrect. NetWare Administrator is used for many functions in NDS, but not moving containers. Therefore, answer c is incorrect.

Question 41

The correct answers are a, b, and f. Server FS1 holds a replica of [Root], but not of its child partition, Rio. Therefore, answer a is correct. Server FS2 holds a replica of Paris, but not of its child partition, Sales. Therefore, answer b is correct. Server FS4 holds a replica of [Root], but not of its child partitions, Paris and NYC. Therefore, answer f is correct. On FS3, there are no situations where the parent is, but the child is not, so it holds no subordinate references. Therefore, answers c and d are incorrect. Although answer e correctly indicates that FS4 will contain a subordinate reference, answer f is the best answer because it indicates the correct number of subordinate references that will end up on server FS4. Therefore, answer e is incorrect.

Question 42

The correct answers are b and c. Because subordinate references are placed by NDS on servers where the parent is, but the child is not, you either have to remove the replica of the parent partition, as in answer c, or add a replica of the child partition, as in answer b. Subordinate references cannot be deleted using NDS Manager or NetWare Administrator. Therefore, answers a and d are incorrect.

Question 43

The correct answers are a, b, c, and d. Synchronizing the time on the two trees, synchronizing the schemas on the two trees, and ensuring the top-level objects in the two trees have different names are required actions before merging trees. Backing up the two trees prior to the merge in case of computer or power failure during the merge is good professional practice. Therefore, answer c is correct. It's not necessary that the credentials used for the administrator accounts on the two trees be identical, just that both the accounts have Supervisor object rights to the [Root] of the tree. Therefore, answer e is incorrect.

Question 44

The correct answer is d. Assuming there are about 32,000 objects in the NDS tree (15,000 User, 15,000 Workstation, and 2,000 Application and other objects), the recommended number of objects in partitions on low-end servers is 1,500, resulting in 21 partitions. Creating 1, 5, or 10 partitions would result in unacceptable NDS performance. Therefore, answers a, b, and c are incorrect.

Question 45

The correct answer is a. The proper command to use is **SET Directory Tree Mode=ON**. **SET Time From This Tree Only=YES** and **SET Synchronization Radius=TREE** are invalid commands. Therefore, answers b and d are incorrect. **SET Configured Sources=ON** tells the server not to use the default time-synchronization configuration. Therefore, answer c is incorrect.

Question 46

The correct answers are a, b, c, and d. Secondary time servers can receive their time from any time server types. To arrange for secondary time servers to receive their time from other secondary time servers, configured sources must be set up. There is no single primary time server in NetWare. Therefore, answer e is incorrect.

Question 47

The correct answer is d. With the rights stated, occupants of the HelpDesk Organizational Role will be able to change all password-related properties. Making the HelpDesk Organizational Role a trustee of the containers the staff needs to manage with Supervisor property rights with the All Properties option would give the help desk staff too many rights. Therefore, answer a is incorrect. Leaving off the Inheritable right makes the assignment of rights in answer b of no value. Therefore, answer b is incorrect. Choosing the individual User objects and assigning rights for the Organizational Role to the Password Management property would not be possible, because that property is not available on User objects. Therefore, answer c is incorrect.

Question 48

The correct answer is b. With a high-quality link between sites, a single time provider group is sufficient. There are too many servers for the default time-synchronization configuration. Therefore, answer a is incorrect. The network is not large enough or dispersed enough to require multiple time provider groups. Therefore, answer c is incorrect. The network will use TIMESYNC.NLM and NTP.NLM, but they are not time-provision methods. Therefore, answers d and e are incorrect.

Question 49

The correct answer is a. Reference servers do not change their time. Therefore, answers b, c, and d are incorrect.

Question 50

The correct answer is b. Primary servers change their time by half the difference. Therefore, answers a, c, and d are incorrect.

Question 51

The correct answer is b. The time server polls the other servers in its time provider group every 10 seconds when its time is not in sync with the calculated network time. The answers in a and c represent incorrect values. Therefore, answers a and c are incorrect. The time server polls the other servers in its time provider group every 10 minutes when its time is in sync with the calculated network time. Therefore, answer d is incorrect.

Question 52

The correct answer is b. The NDS expert is responsible for providing access to network resources. The other team members will depend on the work done by the NDS expert, but providing access to network resources is not their responsibility. Therefore, answers a, c, d, and e are incorrect.

Question 53

The correct answers are a and c, because these tasks are among those allocated to the server administrator. Ensuring server communications over the WAN link are efficient is the responsibility of the connectivity specialist. Therefore, answer b is incorrect. Designing the strategy for partitioning and replication is the responsibility of the NDS expert. Therefore, answer d is incorrect.

Question 54

The correct answers are a and c. When using NTP, a NetWare 5 server receiving time from the Internet is a client of the stated server, not a peer. Therefore, the hosts listed in NTP.CFG are servers, not peers. Therefore, answers b and d are incorrect.

Question 55

The correct answer is c: TIMESYNC.CFG. TIMESRCE.CFG and NETTIME. SET are not valid default NetWare file names. Therefore, answers a and d are incorrect. NTP.CFG is the configuration file for the Network Time Protocol, which is not used in an IPX-only network. Therefore, answer b is incorrect.

Question 56

The correct answer is c. Because the link between sites is not reliable, two time provider groups should be used. There are two sites, which makes default time-synchronization configuration inappropriate. Therefore, answer a is incorrect. The unreliable link makes a single time provider group inappropriate. Therefore, answer b is incorrect.

Question 57

The correct answer is c. Answer c shows the time servers in the correct order, and there are semicolons after each of the server names. Answer a is incorrect, because it uses a comma as a separator and lacks a terminating semicolon. Answer b is incorrect, because it lacks a terminating semicolon. Answer d is incorrect, because, although it has the correct syntax, the servers are listed in reverse order.

Question 58

The correct answers are b and d. If you have a small number of roaming users, creating Alias objects for them in the contexts of the remote locations they visit is possible. Therefore, answer b is correct. For a larger number of roaming users, enabling contextless logins (which implies implementing Catalog Services) would work well. Therefore, answer d is correct. Knowledgeable user login requires users to log in using their distinguished names. Therefore, answer a is incorrect. The phrase *roaming logins* is not defined for NetWare. Therefore, answer c is incorrect.

Question 59

The correct answers are d and e. The efficiency of the NDS design and the workings of the WAN should be investigated; therefore, the NDS expert and the connectivity specialist should be involved. The project manager was responsible for the on-time, on-budget implementation of the new network, but not at the level of design efficiencies. Therefore, answer a is incorrect. The server administrator may be consulted if additional replicas need to be created, but is not responsible for the problems in this question. Therefore, answer b is incorrect. The workstation expert would not be involved in this problem review. Therefore, answer c is incorrect.

Question 60

The correct answer is d, because part of the administrative strategy document is implementing a series of levels of administrative Organizational Roles with clearly defined capabilities. Designing a partitioning plan would not affect administrative access. Therefore, answer a is incorrect. Implementing the Service Location Protocol affects accessibility to services and is not related to the problems described. Therefore, answer b is incorrect. The accessibility needs document would have described the resources the users would need to access, not administrative rights. Therefore, answer c is incorrect.

Question 61

The correct answers are a, b, c, and d. All the identified items must be considered in designing the administrative strategies.

Question 62

The correct answer is d. The time server polls the other servers in its time provider group every 10 minutes when its time is in sync with the calculated network time. The time server polls the other servers in its time provider group every 10 seconds when its time is not in sync with the calculated network time. Therefore, answer b is incorrect. Answers a and c represent incorrect values and are therefore incorrect.

Question 63

The correct answers are a, b, c, and d. With additional servers in the tree, there may now be too many time provider servers for efficiency. Therefore, answer a is correct. The merged trees may produce additional traffic on the WAN links, so WAN traffic management may become more important than ever. Therefore, answer b is correct. The administration strategies of the two trees may have been sufficiently different to cause confusion. Therefore, answer c is correct. It may be possible, or necessary, to change the placement of replicas from the default placement caused by the merge process. Therefore, answer d is correct.

Question 64

The correct answer is a. The project manager has overall responsibility for the costs and schedules of the project. The server administrator, the workstation expert, and the connectivity specialist have other responsibilities. Therefore, answers b, c, and d are incorrect.

Question 65

The correct answers are a, b, c, and d. The [Root] partition should be replicated wherever possible. Therefore, answer a is correct. There should be at least three replicas of each partition and at least one of them should be in another site. Therefore, answers b, c, and d are correct. Moving the read/write replica of Rio from FS3 to FS1, although it may speed up access of Paris users to resources in the Rio partition, is not necessary for improved fault tolerance. Therefore, answer e is incorrect.

Question 66

The correct answers are a, b, and d. Separate time provider groups in each site, each one synchronized to an atomic clock, would keep nearly identical times without any WAN traffic. Therefore, answer a is correct. Removing all replicas of partitions on the far side of the WAN link, other than [Root], would reduce replication traffic, but there would be an increase in traffic because of references made across the link that otherwise would have been satisfied locally. This initiative might not be beneficial, depending on how much of this additional traffic is experienced. Therefore, answer b is correct. Using WTM.NLM to delay low-priority synchronization traffic until late at night would certainly help. Therefore, answer d is correct. WANSPEED.NLM does not exist. Therefore, answer c is incorrect.

Question 67

The correct answers are b, c, and d. Master, read-only, and read/write replicas contain complete copies of the partition information. Subordinate reference replicas do not contain complete copies of the partition information. Therefore, answer a is incorrect. Because answers b, c, and d are correct, answer e is incorrect.

Question 68

The correct answer is d. Secondary servers change their time by the full amount of the difference. Therefore, answers a, b, and c are incorrect.

Appendix A
Management Tools
For NDS

In this appendix, you'll learn the basics of managing NDS with the three tools Novell provides with NetWare 5: NetWare Administrator, ConsoleOne, and NDS Manager. In addition, you'll see how to use these tools to create container objects, such as Country, Organization, and Organizational Unit objects, and leaf objects, such as User, Group, Organizational Role, and Application objects.

NetWare Administrator

NetWare Administrator is the primary tool used to manage NDS. Almost everything associated with managing the NetWare 5 network is accomplished with NetWare Administrator. For example, you can use NetWare Administrator to create User and Group objects, determine which users will be able to use which applications, set up printing with Novell Distributed Print Services (NDPS), and manage a remote workstation with Z.E.N.works (which stands for Zero Effort Networks). In the following sections, you'll become more familiar with NetWare Administrator by learning how to start NetWare Administrator, recognize the various parts of the NetWare Administrator window, create Organizational Unit containers and User and Organizational Role objects, assign trustee rights, and check effective rights.

Starting NetWare Administrator

If you're logged in as Admin or a user with administrator rights (which you need to be if you want to manage NDS), you'll find a shortcut to NetWare Administrator in the Novell Delivered Applications window that opens on your desktop when the Novell Application Launcher (NAL) runs. If this window is not available, click Start|Run, type "NAL", and click on OK or hit

289

Enter to make it run. Alternatively, you can run NWADMN32.EXE from the SYS:\PUBLIC\WIN32 directory to start NetWare Administrator.

 You'll find you use NetWare Administrator a lot, so create a short-cut to it on your Start menu. Using Windows Explorer, locate the NWADMN32.EXE file in the SYS:\PUBLIC\WIN32 folder, then click and drag NWADMN32.EXE to the Start button. The next time you click the Start button, you'll see a shortcut to the NetWare Administrator program at the top of your Start menu.

When NetWare Administrator starts, you'll see the browse window for the tree to which you're attached. If no browse window is open, you can choose File|Browse and navigate to the tree and container you want to manage. In Figure A.1, you can see NetWare Administrator with the browse window for OU=VAN.O=MUNSON open.

Note: You can "mouse" your way through NetWare Administrator if you want, but many experienced administrators find that using the keyboard is often faster. In this appendix, we provide many keyboard-based instructions.

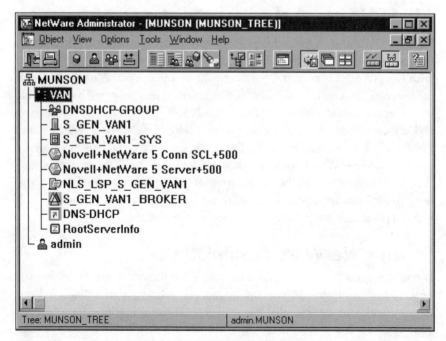

Figure A.1   The NetWare Administrator browse window.

Getting To Know The NetWare Administrator Window

The NetWare Administrator window's title bar shows the program name (NetWare Administrator) and, if the browse window is maximized as in Figure A.1, the name of the top object in the browse window (MUNSON) and the name of the tree (MUNSON_TREE). If the browse window is not maximized, the name of the top object in the browse window (MUNSON) and the name of the tree (MUNSON_TREE) are shown in the title bar of the browse window, not in the title bar of NetWare Administrator.

The menu bar shows the following list of menus available to users:

➤ Object

➤ View

➤ Options

➤ Tools

➤ Window

➤ Help

The toolbar also shows icons that provide access to the most commonly used commands. If the View|Show Hints command is selected, holding the mouse pointer over an icon will result in a description of the command icon replacing the contents of the program's title bar. If the View|Show Quick Tips command is selected, a Quick Tip box will appear when you hold the mouse pointer over the command icon. The Quick Tip box contains a short description of the icon's purpose.

Below the toolbar is the window in which the browse window is shown. You might find it useful to maximize the browse window for easy viewing.

Creating An Organizational Unit Container Object

We'll assume you have installed the first server in the Munson Publishing organization, S_GEN_VAN1, in the container OU=VAN.O=MUNSON. The process of installing the first server caused both the Organization and the Organizational Unit objects to be created. As our first task, let's create the other geographical container for Munson Publishing, OU=DAL:

1. Scroll to the top of the browse window, and select the O=MUNSON container object. (If the top object you can see is OU=VAN, you can go up the tree by pressing the Backspace key on your keyboard.)

2. Choose Object|Create, and choose Organizational Unit from the list. The Create Organizational Unit dialog box appears.

3. Type the name of the Organizational Unit (DAL) into the Organizational Unit Name box and click on Create.

Creating A User Object

Now, let's create a User object for Mary Thompson, who will be one of the administrators for the VAN container:

1. Click on the OU=VAN container object to show where you want the object to be created.

2. Then (because you're already using the mouse), click on the Create User Object icon on the toolbar (see Figure A.2).

Figure A.2 labels commonly used toolbar icons. These icons are used to create several types of objects.

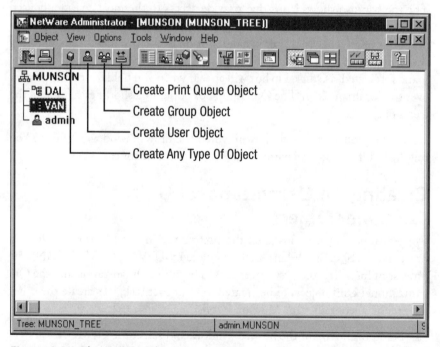

Figure A.2 The Create Object toolbar icons.

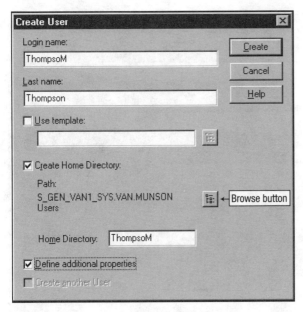

Figure A.3 The Create User dialog box.

3. The Create User dialog box appears, as shown in Figure A.3. Type the new user's ID (ThompsoM) into the Login Name box and her surname (Thompson) into the Last Name box. Check the Create Home Directory checkbox, then click the browse button located to the right of the Path location to specify the path where the home directories are created (SYS:\Users, in this example). Then check the Define Additional Properties checkbox to show you want to provide additional information, and click on Create.

4. You'll now see the User : ThompsoM property pages, as shown in Figure A.4. You can see that the Identification property page tab on the right side of the dialog box is depressed, indicating that you're configuring the Identification group of properties. Enter the required identifying information as specified in the properties standards. Then, click on the Password Restrictions tab to go to that page.

 If you're keyboard-oriented, the Ctrl+PgDn keystroke combination takes you from page to page in any object details dialog box. If you're using the mouse, a right-click anywhere on the dialog box will open a context menu listing all the available pages.

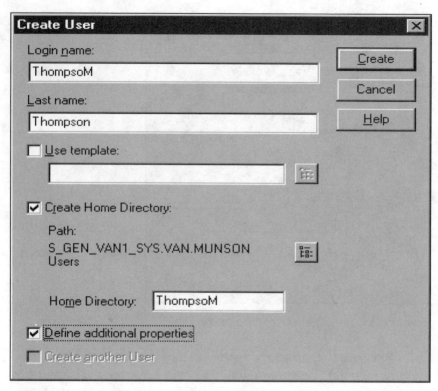

Figure A.4 The User : ThompsoM property pages.

5. The Password Restrictions page appears, as shown in Figure A.5. To set the password, click on the Change Password button and then type and confirm the password you want to use. Note that you should set the password to expire on the current date. This ensures that the user will have to change the password the first time he or she logs in. Therefore, you, as the administrator, won't know the user's password after the first login. You can also use this properties page to specify such properties as whether the password is forced to expire every *n* days and the minimum password length.

 As you can see in Figure A.5, the "dog-ear" on the Identification and Password page tabs are black. This is a quick indication that these pages have been changed.

6. When you're done setting properties for the User object, click on OK at the bottom of the page.

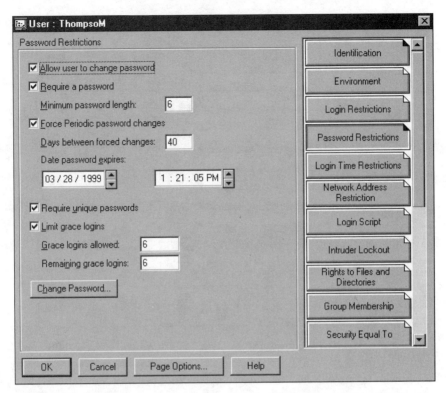

Figure A.5   The Password Restrictions properties page.

The object is created—you can see it directly below the object for the container in which you created it. To see the object sorted with other objects of the same type, close and reopen the container by double-clicking on the container object's icon.

Creating An Organizational Role

Mary Thompson will be an administrator, but currently her User object gives her no administrative rights. To make her an administrator, you create an administrative Organizational Role object called Vancouver Admins and make her an occupant of that role. To do so, follow these steps:

1. With the OU=VAN object selected, click the Create A New Object button, and choose Organizational Role from the list shown.

2. Type the name of the object (Vancouver Admins) in the Name field, and use the Alt+D keystroke combination to check the Define Additional Properties checkbox (or click on the Define Additional Properties checkbox).

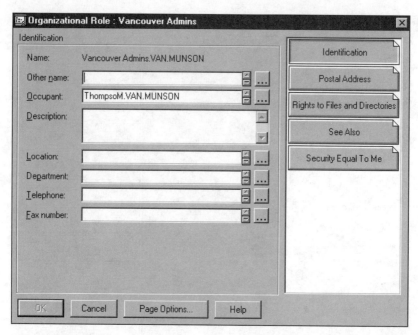

Figure A.6 The Identification properties page for Vancouver Admins.

3. Click on Create. The Identification properties page for Vancouver Admins appears (see Figure A.6).

4. Click on the button to the right of the Occupants field to open the Occupant dialog box.

5. Click on Add and browse to the ThompsoM object. Click on it and then click on OK.

6. Click on OK again.

The ThompsoM User object is now an occupant of the Vancouver Admins Organizational Role object. The rights the Organizational Role has are automatically added to the rights of the ThompsoM User object.

 Browsing for objects in NetWare Administrator is a little unusual. There are two panels of information: the Available Objects on the left and the Browse Context on the right (see Figure A.7). You use the right side to navigate to the correct container (double-click on a container name to move down into the container, and double-click on the upward arrow with two dots to move to the next higher container in the tree), and select the object you're looking for on the left side.

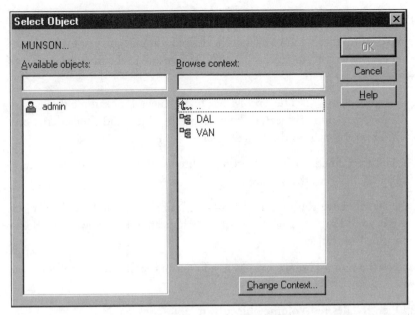

Figure A.7   The Select Object dialog box that appears when you click on the browse button.

Assigning Trustee Rights

The Vancouver Admins Organizational Role object has an occupant, but no rights. To give the occupants of the Organizational Role the ability to manage the OU=VAN container, you need to make the Organizational Role a *trustee* of that container. Here's how you perform this task:

1. Right-click on the OU=VAN object to expose its context menu and choose Trustees Of This Object. The Trustees Of VAN dialog box appears.

2. Click on Add Trustee.

3. Browse to and select the Vancouver Admins Organizational Role object.

4. In the Object Rights section, check the Supervisor checkbox. Giving a trustee Supervisor object rights automatically gives that trustee all object and property rights.

5. Click on OK.

Checking Effective Rights

You can confirm that ThompsoM has the desired administrative rights by checking her effective rights to objects in the NDS tree and in the file system. Here's how:

1. To check the rights ThompsoM has to an object, for example the Vancouver Admins object, right-click on the object and choose Trustees Of This Object from the context menu.

2. Click the Effective Rights button and browse to the ThompsoM User object. Click on OK.

3. In the Effective Rights dialog box (see Figure A.8), you'll see the Object Rights and Property Rights for this user, indicating that they are in effect for this User object.

To check the rights ThompsoM has to a folder in the file system, follow these steps:

1. Open the desired Volume object by double-clicking on it (S_GEN_VAN1_SYS in our case). Then, right-click on the Java folder and choose Details.

2. Click on the Trustees Of This Directory properties page.

3. Click the Effective Rights button and browse to the ThompsoM User object.

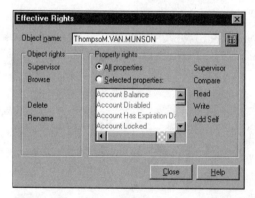

Figure A.8   The Effective Rights dialog box (NDS tree).

4. In the resulting dialog box (see Figure A.9), you'll see that all the file system rights are shown, indicating that they are in effect for this User object.

So far, you've created an Organizational Unit object, a User object, and an Organizational Role object. Further, you've assigned trustee rights to the Organizational Role object. This is just a small sampling of what you can do with the NetWare Administrator program.

 There is good online help for NetWare Administrator. In any dialog box, click on Help to see an explanation of the options available at that point.

ConsoleOne

The newest NetWare tool for NDS management is ConsoleOne, which made its debut with NetWare 5. ConsoleOne is the first graphical user interface (GUI) tool that Novell has provided for managing the NetWare operating system from the server console. In its first release, it's considered to be simply a "proof of concept," showing that the technology works. Compared to NetWare Administrator, ConsoleOne only allows you to perform a limited number of tasks. However, it does provide, a way for the administrator to carry out some basic operations from the server.

Figure A.9   The Effective Rights dialog box (file system).

We understand that the developers at Novell are using the ConsoleOne platform as the basis for future administrative tools, and that we can expect ConsoleOne to replace NetWare Administrator in future releases of NetWare.

Note: ConsoleOne can be run from either the NetWare 5 server console or from a workstation. The screenshots we're using in this appendix are from a workstation. Consequently, they do not show the My Server and Shortcuts folders. Only the icon titled "The Network" and its associated icons are visible under the My World icon when working with ConsoleOne on a workstation.

When run from a workstation, the opening screen of ConsoleOne looks like the one shown in Figure A.10. ConsoleOne has a Windows Explorer–type layout, showing a hierarchy of functions in the left pane and a *contents* selection in the right pane. The "The Network" branch provides you access to the NDS tree, which is what this section addresses.

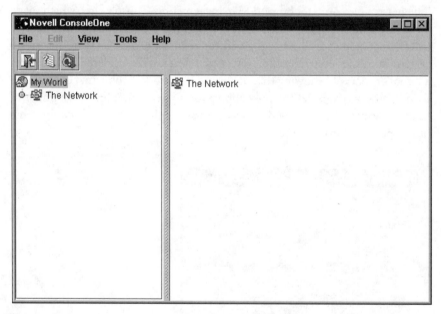

Figure A.10   The opening screen of ConsoleOne on a workstation.

The developers of ConsoleOne must have used a monitor set at 256 colors and 800×600 pixels resolution. If you try to run it on a server screen with 640×480 pixel resolution, you'll see that the contents of the window don't fit on the screen, and you'll often need to scroll the screen contents even to see the OK and Cancel buttons. To make using ConsoleOne easier, click on the Novell button, choose Tools|Display Properties, and choose 800×600 to change the resolution to a usable setting.

When run from a server console, the My Server branch of the tree in the left pane gives the administrator access to the file system, configuration files, and remote management tools. (Remember that the My Server icon and its associated icons are not available when you're running ConsoleOne from a workstation. They are only available on the server.) The Shortcuts branch of the tree in the left pane gives the administrator access to Java applets and important folders in the file system (such as SYS:\SYSTEM, SYS:\ETC, and SYS:\PUBLIC).

Using ConsoleOne is easier when there's a mouse attached to the server. It is *possible* to operate ConsoleOne with keyboard commands, but the process is very awkward and only suggested as a last resort (if, for example, the mouse malfunctions). For instructions on how to move the mouse pointer and how to perform mouse functions using the keyboard, choose Help|Index from ConsoleOne, and search for the term "keyboard".

Choosing A Tree

Several NDS trees might be visible on the network to which a server is attached. Clicking on The Network brings up a selection list of visible trees. When you click on the name of the tree you want to manage, you're prompted to enter your authentication details. After you have done so, the root of the tree appears in the left pane of the ConsoleOne screen.

Double-click on the root to open it, and you'll be able to see the top-level objects in the tree. To view the contents of the container object in which you're interested, double-click on it. The result will be similar to Figure A.11.

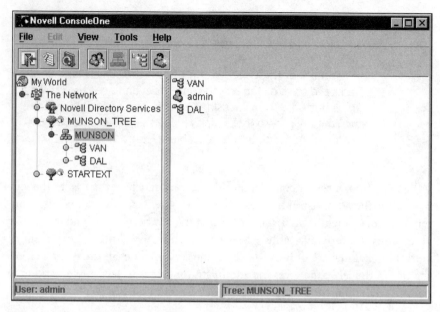

Figure A.11 The top level of the NDS tree.

To see an object's properties, select the object, right-click on it to open the pop-up menu, then choose Properties. You can see and change some of the properties of objects displayed in ConsoleOne. This facility is far from complete in the first release of NetWare 5. For example, you can see and change the trustees of any object, but you cannot change the list of occupants of an Organizational Role object.

Creating Objects

To create an object, select the container in which you want to create the object, then choose File|New. You can only create four types of objects in ConsoleOne: Organization, Organizational Unit, User, and Group. There's an icon on the toolbar for each of these functions.

Creating A User Object

Let's create a User object for Gillian Smith, manager of the Vancouver Web-based training group:

1. Select the VAN Organizational Unit object.

2. Click on the Create User icon.

3. Type the User ID "SmithG" and the last name "Smith". Then check the Define Additional Properties checkbox and click on Create.

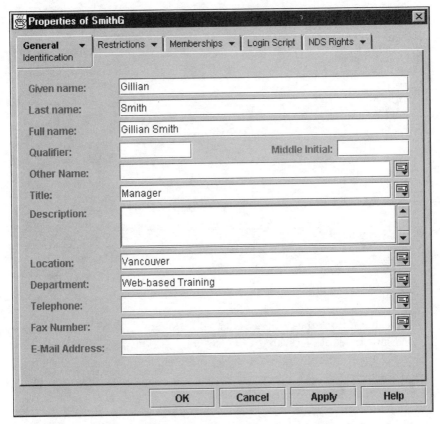

Figure A.12   Properties of a User object.

4. In the Properties Of SmithG dialog box, enter the user's title, location, and department (as shown in Figure A.12) and click on OK.

Creating A Group For An Object

Now, let's create a Managers group and make SmithG a member of that group:

1. Again, select the VAN Organizational Unit object.

2. Click on the Create Group icon.

3. In the New Group dialog box, Group Name section type "Managers". Then check the Define Additional Properties checkbox and click on Create.

4. Click on the Members tab, click on the Add button, and choose the SmithG object (as shown in Figure A.13), then click on OK.

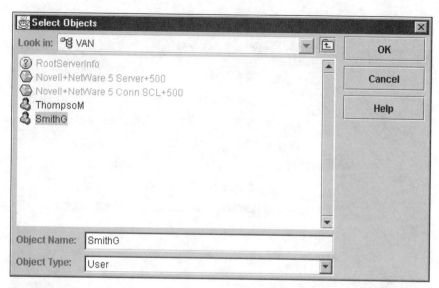

Figure A.13 Selecting an object as a member of a group.

As you can see from the options provided in Figure A.13, ConsoleOne is a limited substitute for NetWare Administrator. It can be used in an emergency to create Organization, Organizational Unit, User, and Group objects and to assign trustee rights. As mentioned earlier, ConsoleOne will become much more important in future releases of NetWare 5.

NDS Manager

The tool to use for all partitioning and replication operations is NDS Manager. With NDS Manager, you can determine which servers hold replicas of the various partitions in the tree and see their status. It's also the only available method for moving containers from location to location in the NDS tree. Let's get to know it.

When using the NDS Manager, we're only interested in containers, partitions, and servers. Therefore, only these objects are shown.

The NDS Manager opens in hierarchical or tree mode. In the left pane, you can see the container hierarchy plus any servers. When a server is selected, the right pane shows the list of all the partition replicas stored on the server, as shown in Figure A.14. Up to this point, we haven't done any partitioning, so the only replica we see is the master replica of the [Root] partition. We have another server in the tree, S_GEN_DAL1, in the DAL Organizational Unit. It has a read/write replica of the [Root] partition.

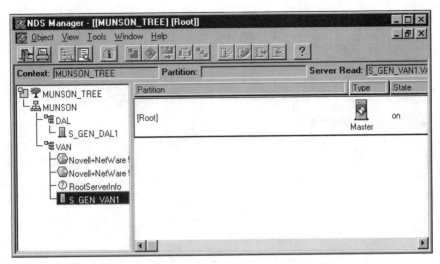

Figure A.14   The NDS Manager screen in tree mode.

As discussed in Chapter 5, the Organization Munson and the Organizational Units VAN and DAL should be three separate partitions. We do this quite easily:

1. Select the Munson container and choose Object|Create Partition.

2. Click on Yes in the two confirming dialog boxes.

3. Click Close in the next dialog box. After a few seconds, the NDS Manager main window reappears, showing the new partition at O=Munson with the master replica on the S_GEN_VAN1 server and the read/write replica on the S_GEN_DAL1 server.

 Whenever you split an existing partition (as we did in creating a Munson partition from the [Root] partition), replicas for the new partition are placed on the same servers that held replicas of the original partition. The replica types will be the same as those in existence for the original partition.

Note that there are four possible replica types, as described in Chapter 5. Figure A.15 shows three of them. The S_ GEN_VAN1 server holds master replicas of the [Root], MUNSON, and VAN.MUNSON partitions, and a read/write replica of the DAL.MUNSON partition. It also holds a subordinate reference replica of the SALES.DAL.MUNSON partition, because a replica of the

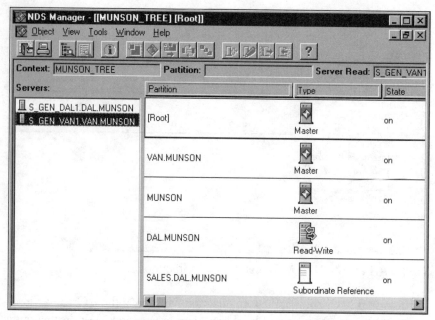

Figure A.15   The S_GEN_VAN1 replicas.

DAL.MUNSON partition is present on the server, but a replica of the SALES.DAL.MUNSON partition is not. This replica was placed on the S_GEN_VAN1 server automatically by NDS and can only be removed by removing the replica of the DAL.MUNSON partition or adding a replica of the SALES.DAL.MUNSON partition.

As you can see in Figure A.15, all replicas stored on the server are in the On state. This is the normal state when a partition and all its replicas are properly synchronized with each other. If a partition is in the process of being created or if another partition operation is underway, the state will be shown as Transition or some other state. The book *Novell's Guide to Troubleshooting NDS* (Peter Kuo and Jim Henderson, IDG Books Worldwide, ISBN 0-7645-4579-5) contains information about the various possible states of partitions.

If the state of the replica is other than On, you can get information about what the reported replica state means by double-clicking on the replica. This opens a description of the state of the replica, which might help you to carry out any necessary troubleshooting steps.

The other view of the NDS Manager window is in partitions mode (choose View|Partitions And Servers). Figure A.16 shows NDS Manager in partitions mode. Here, the NDS Directory tree is shown with only the container objects visible.

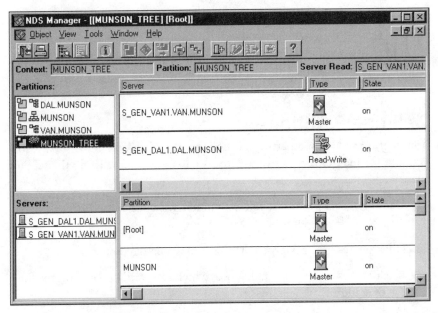

Figure A.16 The NDS Manager screen in partitions mode.

Any container that is a partition root will be shown with the green-and-yellow box next to its icon. Selecting any of the partition root containers causes a list of the servers that hold a replica of that partition to be shown in the right pane. As before, the state of each of the replicas is shown along with the replica type.

Creating Partitions

After you've decided how your tree should be partitioned, you can create partitions by following these steps:

1. Start NDS Manager and navigate to the container object you want to partition.

2. From the Object menu, choose Create Partition. A dialog box appears, giving you a chance to confirm the action.

3. Choose Yes and an informative dialog box appears stating that all conditions have been met for the partitioning operation. You can click on OK at this point and continue with other work.

When the partitioning operation is complete, the container icon changes to include the green-and-yellow box icon that indicates the container is partitioned.

Partitioning operations can take some time, especially on a large tree. It's wise to carry out such operations during low-traffic times. You should also ensure that servers containing all existing replicas of the parent partition are present.

Deleting Partitions

You might decide that a partition is no longer needed. To remove a partition, you join (or merge) the partition with its parent partition. To do this, follow these steps:

1. Click on the partition that you want to remove and choose Partition|Merge from the Object menu.

2. Click on Yes in the Merge Partition dialog box that appears.

3. Click on Yes in the next dialog box, which states that preconditions for the operation have been met.

After the process is complete, you'll see that the green-and-yellow box icon next to the container name has been removed.

Moving Containers

Let's say you want to move an Organizational Unit from its current location to another. Only partitions can be moved; therefore, if the container is not already a partition root, you'll have to make it one. After you've made the container a partition root, follow these steps to move it:

1. Select the partition that you want to move, and choose Object|Partition|Move. The Move Partition dialog box appears.

2. Use the browse feature to select the container to which you want to move the partition and click on OK.

3. Click on Yes in the Move Partition dialog box.

After some time (the more objects in the container, the longer it will take), the container will appear in its new location.

Appendix B
NetWare 5
Command-Line
Utilities

In this appendix, you'll learn about NetWare 5 command-line utilities and NetWare Loadable Modules (NLMs). In NetWare, there are commands that you can execute only at the workstation, and there are commands and NLMs that you can execute only at the server. In the first section of this appendix, you'll discover those NetWare commands that you can execute only at the workstation. Later in this appendix, you'll see how to execute NetWare commands and NLMs that can be run only at the server.

NetWare 5 Commands That Run Only At Workstations

On a workstation that has the appropriate NetWare Client software installed, there are commands you can execute at the DOS prompt to help you perform various NetWare functions. These commands cannot be run in Windows; however, similar functionality is provided within the graphical user interface (GUI) on a Windows client workstation. You can use the following clients to execute the NetWare commands:

➤ DOS

➤ Windows 95/98

➤ Windows NT Workstation

➤ Windows NT Server

The **LOGIN** Command

Because you must log into a NetWare server before you can perform any other commands, you must understand the **LOGIN** command. To execute the **LOGIN** command, follow these steps:

1. From any Windows-based client, go to Start|Programs|MS-DOS Prompt, then enter your network drive letter.

   From a DOS text-based client, enter the correct network drive letter.

 Your first network drive is typically the F: drive, but it could be another drive letter based on the number of devices you have on your system. Because the **LOGIN** command is in the LOGIN directory/folder on a Novell server, you may need to change your directory location to that directory/folder.

2. Type "LOGIN".

3. Next, you'll get a prompt that asks you to enter a valid username. Enter it.

4. After you've entered the valid username, you'll receive a prompt asking you to enter a password. Enter your password (if your username has a password).

5. If you enter the correct username and password (assuming you have a password), you'll see some text displayed on the screen. If you have logged in successfully, you can proceed to enter any other commands. Typically, a few **MAP** statements will appear while you're being logged in. These **MAP** statements provide access to network drives. Figure B.1 shows a successful **LOGIN** command execution.

   Note: Although the LOGIN command is available from the MS-DOS prompt at a Windows client, it would not typically be used. Client32 for Windows 3.x and Windows 95/98 ships with a GUI-based version of the LOGIN command to facilitate the login process from within the Windows interface.

Most NetWare commands have various switches or options that can be added to the end of them. These switches or options modify the command in some fashion. The symbol for switches or options is the forward slash (/)—though

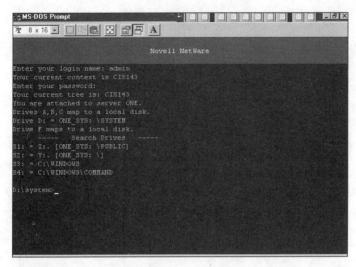

Figure B.1   Successful **LOGIN** command execution.

occasionally, you'll run into various options that do not require the forward slash. One of the most useful options is the option to get help on a command—this is the /? option. For example, to get additional help on the **LOGIN** command, enter the following (the result is shown in Figure B.2):

```
LOGIN /? ALL
```

Figure B.2   The **LOGIN** command's help pages.

Most commands have several help pages. To get all the help pages about a command, use the **ALL** option, as shown in the previous command.

Let's look at some other common ways to execute the **LOGIN** command.

Logging Into A Specific Server

You can use the **LOGIN** command to log into a specific server. For example, to log into a server named MEADORS-1 with the username DixieDoodle, you would type the following:

```
LOGIN MEADORS-1/DIXIEDOODLE
```

> *Note:* *You could also use the backslash (\) instead of the forward slash (/) to separate the server and username.*

Remember that the server name comes first, followed by the username, as follows:

```
LOGIN server name/username
```

Logging Into The Correct Context

In Novell, the Novell Directory Services (NDS) Directory is designed to hold a User object, which is called a leaf object, within a container object. A leaf object is analogous to a file in the DOS directory structure, and a container object is similar to a directory or folder. To log in as a user, you must be in the correct container object that holds the User object. This is known as the *context*. Assume a User object named Todd exists in the Organization CIS143 and wants to log into server ONE. He would enter the following command from within the Organization CISI43:

```
LOGIN ONE\.TODD.CIS143
```

> *Note:* *Remember that when referring to a user's context, the username comes first and then the container. Therefore, it's correct to state .TODD.CIS143, but not .CIS143.TODD.*

You need to provide NDS with the correct context, because there could be multiple users in the tree with the same name. For example, let's say that you have two users named Todd: one in OU=DAYCLASS and the other in O=CIS143. Todd from O=CIS143 will need to provide the correct context so

NDS knows which "Todd" is logging in. Of course, their passwords are probably not the same, so there's not much of a security concern. If Todd from O=CIS143 tries to log into the OU=DAYCLASS context, he would receive an error resulting from providing an incorrect password.

The **CX** Command

The **CX**, or change context, command allows you to display either leaf and container objects in your current context in the NDS tree or set your current context to another container location in NDS. In this section, we'll discuss traversing the NDS tree with the **CX** command and also displaying container and leaf objects with the **CX** command.

Navigating With The **CX** *Command*

To change your current context, enter **CX** *container_name*. To see your current context, simply type "CX" at a DOS prompt. If you happen to be in a container called PAYROLL_DEPT, **CX** will literally return **PAYROLL_DEPT**.

> *Note: The* **CX** *command is similar to the DOS* **CD** *command. Just like the DOS* **CD** *command allows you to navigate the file system directory structure, the* **CX** *command allows you to navigate the NDS Directory structure.*

Suppose you want to change to another location in the NDS tree. Figure B.3 shows a list of leaf and container objects (this was performed with the **CX /A/**

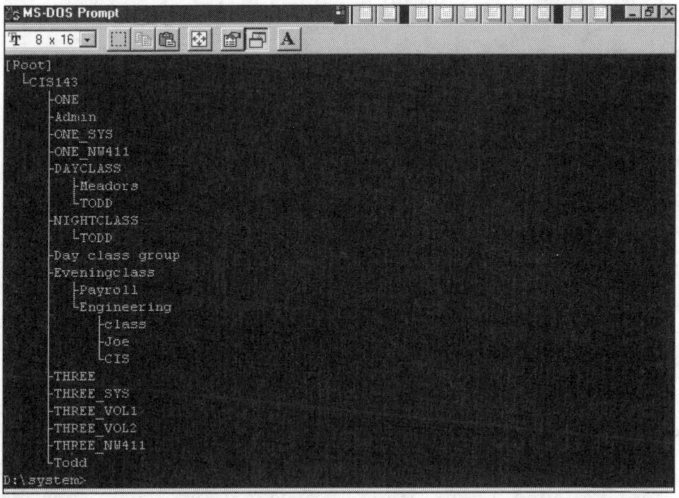

Figure B.3   A listing of container and leaf objects in the NDS tree.

R/T command, which will be discussed later in this section). You can only **CX** to container objects. For example, let's say your current context is CIS143, and you want to change your context to NIGHTCLASS, which is a child object of CIS143. To accomplish this, you would enter the following command:

```
CX NIGHTCLASS
```

Now, reissuing the **CX** command would return NIGHTCLASS.CIS143 as your current context. If you want to change back to the parent container, you use the **CX** command followed by a space and a period, as shown in the following statement:

```
CX .
```

The period, or dot, after the **CX** command tells **CX** to go up one level in the tree to the parent object. (There must be a space *before* the period.) If you want to move up two levels, you would enter the following:

```
CX ..
```

You could go up three levels by having three dots, four levels by having four dots, and so on.

Now, let's suppose you want to go to a *sibling container*. A sibling container is one that is a peer container. In Figure B.3, the container object CIS143 is the parent of the DAYCLASS and NIGHTCLASS containers. DAYCLASS is a sibling container to NIGHTCLASS. If your current context is .DAYCLASS.CIS143, then you could go to NIGHTCLASS by typing the following:

```
CX NIGHTCLASS.
```

This uses what is known as a *relative name*, because you're telling NDS the object's location relative to your current context. A relative NDS name does not begin at the [Root], but at your current context. For each trailing period, you effectively move up the tree one level. In contrast, the following shows a *distinguished name*:

```
CX .NIGHTCLASS.CIS143
```

A distinguished name references all containers all the way to the top of the NDS tree. The period after the **CX** command makes the preceding example a distinguished name. It's called distinguished because it fully distinguishes the name from any other NDS name in the tree. For example, there could be a

NIGHTCLASS object in [Root], but its distinguished name would be .NIGHTCLASS. This differs from the NIGHTCLASS object located in CIS143, whose distinguished name is .NIGHTCLASS.CIS143. In other words, you're referring to the container based on its location compared to [Root].

The next variation of the **CX** command is to use it to go to the [Root], or top level, container object. For example, let's say that you're two levels down from [Root] in the NIGHTCLASS Organizational Unit, which exists below the Organization CIS143. You can get to the [Root] object using one of two methods: **CX ..** (you would have to specify the appropriate number of periods) or **CX /R**. To use **CX** with the period operator to move up the tree, you need to use two periods, or dots, because [Root] is two levels up. Therefore, you would type the following:

```
CX ..
```

To go back to the [Root] container using the second method, you would type the following text:

```
CX /R
```

The option **/R** means to go straight to the [Root] container no matter where you are in the NDS tree.

Displaying Objects With The **CX** Command

You can use the **CX** command with the **/T** option to display a list of container objects in an NDS tree; it also displays a hierarchical picture view so you can see the parent and child relationships. Simply type the following code to use the **/T** option:

```
CX /T
```

The next option of the **CX** command is **/A**. It's typically used in conjunction with the **/T** option to display all objects, whether they are containers or leafs, in a given context. In Figure B.4, you see how the context has been changed using **CX .EVENINGCLASS.CIS143**. By typing "CX /A/T", you can see all NDS objects in the NDS tree in the context .EVENINGCLASS.CIS143 (also shown in Figure B.4).

The **MAP** Command.

The **MAP** command is an extremely useful command because it points, or maps, drive letters to physical drives somewhere on a network server. Just as

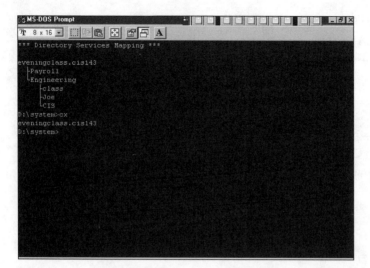

Figure B.4 Screenshot of the **CX /A/T** command showing all objects in a given context.

A: and C: point to local DOS devices, the **MAP** command allows you to create a logical drive; for example, an F: drive that points to network file system resources. You could map a drive on your workstation that actually refers to an application's database. You don't have to load the data on your workstation's hard disk, but you could load it on a server drive to be shared by other workstations. Typing the **MAP** command with no options, or switches, displays your currently mapped drives. However, to map the next available drive letter to a directory called MEADORS, for example, on the SYS volume of a server called THREE, you would enter the following:

```
MAP NEXT THREE_SYS:\MEADORS
```

Note: DOS allows up to 26 logical drive letters, from A: through Z:.

Figure B.5 shows a screenshot of the **MAP** command. As you can see, in this case, the next available drive letter chosen was E:.

You can also specify a particular drive letter instead of picking the next available one. For example, to create a drive mapping for logical drive letter H: to server ONE's SYS volume PUBLIC directory, you would type the following statement:

```
MAP H:=ONE_SYS:\PUBLIC
```

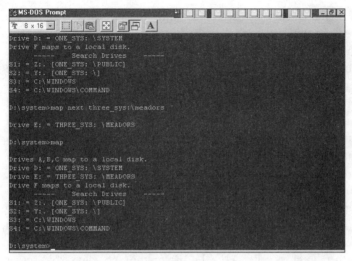

Figure B.5   Mapping to the next available drive letter with the **MAP** command.

Now, suppose you want to delete a certain mapping. Maybe the application data that was stored on a server is no longer needed. To delete a drive mapping, type the following command at a workstation:

```
MAP DEL H:
```

Figure B.6 shows the **MAP** listing both before and after the **MAP DEL** command.

Figure B.6   A screenshot demonstrating the use of the **MAP DEL** command.

The **MAP** command can also be used to set up what is known as search drive mappings. These mappings refer to directories that have executable programs, and the search drive mappings are inserted into the DOS **PATH** statement. You can have 16 of your 26 mappings made up of search drive mappings. These types of drive mappings are typically set up to refer to the directory where an application program or batch file resides. To set a search mapping, you would need to refer to the drive as *Snumber:*, where *S* stands for search drive and *number* is a numeric value from 1 to 16 (remember that you can only have 16 search drive mappings). Novell suggests you insert a search drive at the end of the DOS **PATH** statement using the **MAP INS S16:** command. By specifying **S16**, you tell the **MAP** command to place the mapping at the end of the search list. This is a good idea because the drives are searched in order from left to right. Placing a new search drive at the beginning of the list alters the search order and is accomplished with the **MAP INS S1:** command. To set a search drive mapping to a directory called MEADORS on the SYS volume of a server called THREE, you would enter the following:

```
MAP INS S16:=THREE_SYS:\MEADORS
```

The **NDIR** Command

Another useful command-line utility is the **NDIR** command. It's very similar to the DOS **DIR** command; however, **NDIR** lists the ownership of files, whereas the DOS **DIR** command does not. In Figure B.7 you can see the execution of the **NDIR** command, which shows the owner column. This is

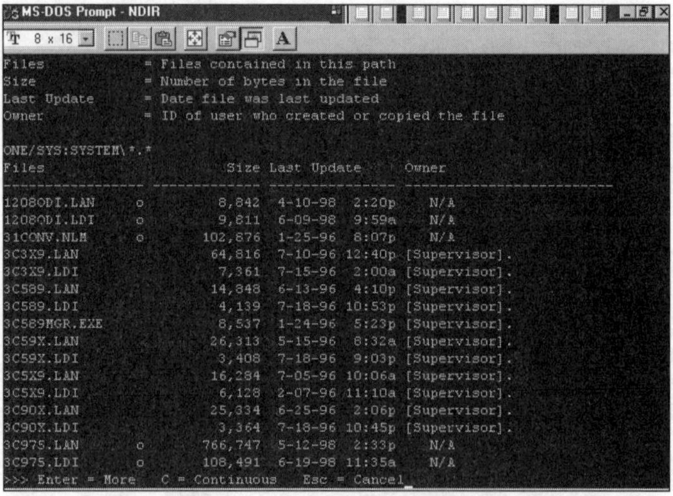

Figure B.7   A screenshot of the **NDIR** command showing the ownership of files.

very important in terms of security, because you're dealing with shared files and you can see who owns certain files.

NDIR has numerous available options. The following examples show a few of the **NDIR** options and their respective tasks. To see all the files owned by a user, such as Admin, use the following command:

```
NDIR /OW EQ ADMIN
```

To see all the files except those owned by a particular user, such as Admin, use this command:

```
NDIR /OW NOT EQ ADMIN
```

Use the next command to see all the files sorted (larger to smaller) by size:

```
NDIR /SORT SI
```

Finally, to see all the files sorted in reverse order (smaller to larger) by size, use the following command:

```
NDIR /REV SORT SI
```

The preceding commands represent only some of the options available with the **NDIR** command. Use the **NDIR /? ALL** command to see all the options of **NDIR**.

The **NLIST** Command

The **NLIST** command provides you with information about certain objects that exist in your NDS tree. Some of the objects you can find information on are Server, Volume, Organizational Unit, and Printer objects. In its simplest form, you execute **NLIST** with the wildcard (*) symbol as follows:

```
NLIST *
```

This provides you with a list of all the object types in a given container context. Figure B.8 shows the various object types in the CIS143 container.

To use the **NLIST** command to get additional information about Server objects (such as the server's network address and the network segment address), use the following command:

```
NLIST SERVER
```

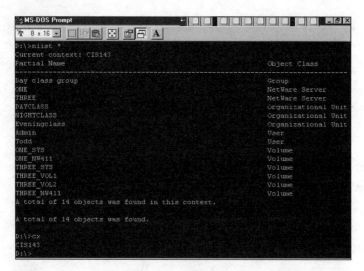

Figure B.8 An **NLIST** listing of all the objects in the CIS143 container.

To get details about Volume objects, enter the following:

NLIST VOLUME

If you want to see more information regarding User objects, type the following:

NLIST USER

There are many variations of the **NLIST** command, and you can review them by issuing the **NDIR /? ALL** command.

The **CAPTURE** Command

The **CAPTURE** command is a text-based utility that allows you to "fool" your local printer port on your workstation into thinking it has a printer. The printer could actually be physically connected to a server, to another workstation, or directly plugged into the network. Instead of the print request being printed locally, it's really printed on a network printer. In Novell, for non-NDPS printing (queue-based printing), you have three required printer objects:

➤ **Print Server object** The server that manages the whole print connection.

➤ **Printer object** A software representation of an actual physical printer.

➤ **Print Queue object** A directory that temporarily holds the print requests until they are printed.

You can use the **CAPTURE** command to send print jobs to a print queue or a logical printer. To send a print job to a server named ONE with a print queue named TODD-PQ-LOCAL, you would enter the following command:

```
CAPTURE S=ONE Q=TODD-PQ-LOCAL
```

In Figure B.9, you can see that the command worked properly.

 By default, LPT1 is the printer port that is captured. To choose a different port, you would add the **L=port_number** option to **CAPTURE**.

To redirect or capture local printer port 2, or LPT2, for a server named MEADORS-1 to a printer name PAYROLL_LASER, you would type the following:

```
CAPTURE L=2 S=MEADORS-1 P=PAYROLL_LASER
```

Another item to point out in Figure B.9 is the **CAPTURE SHOW** command. You use this to display captured printer ports. To delete the captured port, you would enter:

```
CAPTURE EC
```

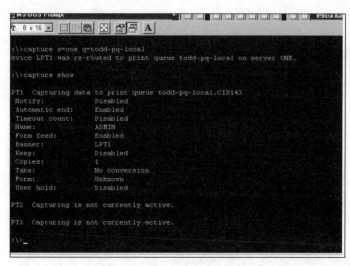

Figure B.9 Using the **CAPTURE** command to redirect a local print request to a network printer.

The EC option indicates that the **CAPTURE** command should end the capture of the printer port.

The **RIGHTS** Command

The **RIGHTS** command is a Novell command-line utility that allows you to change or view the security rights to a file or a folder. You can add and remove User object rights, as well. The rights that can be added and removed are as follows:

➤ **Supervisor (S)** Allows a user to have all the rights to a file or folder.

➤ **Read (R)** Gives the user the ability to read files in a folder and open files in a folder.

➤ **Write (W)** Allows the user to open and write to files in a folder.

➤ **Create (C)** Gives the user the ability to create files and folders in a given folder.

➤ **Erase (E)** Allows the user to remove files and folders.

➤ **Modify (M)** Allows the user to change the name of files and folders and change the attributes of a file.

➤ **File Scan (F)** Allows the user to search and view files and folders.

➤ **Access Control (A)** Allows the user to use the **RIGHTS** command to change rights for other users.

Let's take a look at a few examples. To give a user named Jessie the Read, Write, and File Scan rights to the file called PAYROLL.DAT, you would enter the following statement:

```
RIGHTS PAYROLL.DAT R W F /NAME=.JESSIE.PAYROLL.MEADORS-ENTERPRISES
```

You can also view the Inherited Rights Filter (IRF) for a user using the /I option. IRF is a security technique used to filter out and disallow certain rights for users. To view the IRF for a user named Zac, you would type the following:

```
RIGHTS FOLDER-A /NAME=ZAC /I
```

You can use the **REM** option of the **RIGHTS** command to remove a user. The following code uses a distinguished name on the /**NAME** option:

```
RIGHTS SYS:USERS REM /NAME=.MICKI.WRITING
```

You can also add a right to a user's list of existing rights. For example, let's say Todd already has the Read and File Scan rights to a file named NET2.DAT, and you want to give him the Write right to this file. To do this, you would enter the following:

```
RIGHTS NET2.DAT +W /NAME=TODD
```

Conversely, you can take away a right from the current rights of a User object by executing this statement:

```
RIGHTS RESUME.DOC -W /NAME=DIXIE
```

The **FLAG** Command

Novell has added attributes to the common DOS attributes and allows you to use the **FLAG** command to take advantage of these. The attributes are divided into a few groups: status flags, file attributes, and directory attributes. The attributes and descriptions are shown in Table B.1.

Table B.1	The FLAG command attributes.		
Attribute	**Abbreviation**	**Type**	**Description**
Archive needed	A	File	This attribute means the file has been changed since the last back-up and it needs to be archived or backed up at the next backup cycle.
Can't Compress	Cc	Status flag	This indicates the file cannot be compressed. The file will not provide any disk space savings by being compressed, so it won't compress it and consume CPU time unnecessarily.
Compressed	Co	Status flag	This attribute indicates the file has already been compressed.
Copy Inhibit	Ci	File	This attribute is only used for Macintosh files on a MAC name space volume. It prevents the file from being copied.
Don't Compress	Dc	File/ Directory	This attribute stops a file or directory from being compressed— even if the volume or directory is set for compressed.

(continued)

Table B.1 The FLAG command attributes (continued).

Attribute	Abbreviation	Type	Description
Delete Inhibit	Di	File/ Directory	This attribute prevents a file or directory from being removed or erased.
Don't Migrate	Dm	File/ Directory	This attribute prevents files or directories from being migrated to a near-line storage system.
Don't Suballocate	Ds	File	This attribute prevents a file from being suballocated. (Suballocation occurs when disk blocks are allocated in small chunks of 512 byte blocks.)
Hidden	H	File/ Directory	With this attribute, you cannot see a file or directory with the DOS **DIR** command. Also, the hidden attribute prevents the file or directory from being removed or copied.
Immediate compress	Ic	File/ Directory	This attribute forces compression on a file or directory.
Migrated	M	Status flag	This attribute indicates the file has already been migrated.
Normal	N	File/ Directory	For a file, it indicates the Read Write (Rw) attribute is set; for a directory, no attributes are specified.
Purge	P	File/ Directory	This attribute removes the file or directory immediately if it has been deleted.
Rename Inhibit	Ri	File/ Directory	This attribute prevents the file or directory from being renamed.
Read Only	Ro	File	This attribute only allows you to read a file. You cannot write to the file or delete it. **Ro** also sets the **Ri** and **Di** attributes.
Read Write	Rw	File	Gives you the ability to read and write to a file.
Shareable	S	File	With the shareable attribute, more than one person can use a file at the same time.

(continued)

Attribute	Abbreviation	Type	Description
			Table B.1 The FLAG command attributes (continued).
System	Sy	File/ Directory	The system attribute indicates that the file or directory is used by the system and it cannot be removed or copied. It cannot be seen with the **DIR** command.
Transactional	T	File	When set, Transaction Tracking System (TTS) protects the file by rolling back the transactions within the file in the event of server power loss.
Execute Only	X	File/ Directory	This attribute gives a file protection from being deleted or copied over. It can only be set for machine-executable programs that have .COM and .EXE extensions.

Now, you'll see how the **FLAG** command is used. To display the attributes for all files in a given directory, run the following command:

```
FLAG *.*
```

To add the Read Write and Immediate compress attributes to the current attributes, enter:

```
FLAG SYS:USERS\FILENAME.TXT +Rw Ic
```

To remove the Read Only attribute from the current attributes, type:

```
FLAG FILE2.TXT -Ro
```

NetWare 5 Commands That Run Only At The Server

There are numerous commands and NLMs that can only be run at the NetWare server. We'll cover some of the most important commands and NLMs in this section. Console commands are internal to the NetWare kernel (SERVER.EXE), and NLMs are external executable modules. You can see all the available console commands and NLMs by simply typing "HELP" at the server console.

Commands

As mentioned, the console commands are internal to the NetWare kernel. Some of the more common console commands are discussed in the following sections.

The SET Command

The SET command is used for changing parameters on your server. A SET command can either be put in the server's startup file, AUTOEXEC.NCF, or executed at the server console. You know you're at the server console when you have the server name followed by a colon symbol. To see a list of the SET command's major categories, type "SET" at the server console. The following statement runs the SET command from a server named TWO:

```
TWO: SET
```

Figure B.10 shows the output of the SET command.

The **SET** command statements generally take one of two forms. You can set the parameter to a numeric value that is in a given range. For example, **SET MINIMUM DIRECTORY CACHE BUFFERS = 160** changes the value to a number. Or, you can set a value to either on or off. **SET ALLOW UNENCRYPTED PASSWORDS = ON** toggles a parameter on; you could also use **OFF** to toggle it off.

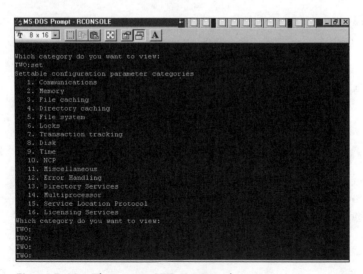

Figure B.10   The server **SET** command.

Some of the major categories of the SET command are as follows:

➤ **Communications** Allows you to optimize variables related to server communication.

➤ **Directory Caching** Allows you to tune directory caching parameters.

➤ **Directory Services (NDS)** Allows you to optimize NDS.

➤ **Disk** Allows you to modify server hard disk parameters.

➤ **Error Handling** Allows you to handle the size of log files.

➤ **File Caching** Allows you to modify file caching parameters. By default, after the network operating system loads on a server, all other memory is set aside for caching.

➤ **File System** Allows you to control performance tuning of the NetWare file system.

➤ **Locks** Allows you to modify file- and record-locking parameters. Locking is a concept where a record cannot be updated by multiple users concurrently; without record locking, there could be data inconsistency problems.

➤ **Memory** Allows you to optimize memory parameters.

➤ **Multiprocessor** Allows you to modify parameters when using multiple CPUs.

➤ **NCP** Allows you to manage the NetWare Core Protocol (NCP) and Internetwork Packet Exchange (IPX)-related parameters.

➤ **Time** Allows you to modify time-synchronization values and also the server time.

➤ **Transaction Tracking** Allows you to modify Transaction Tracking System (TTS) values. TTS is used for transaction recovery to rollback transactions in a database file if a server problem occurs. If there are no problems, TTS will commit the transaction to the database.

The SWAP Command

You can execute the **SWAP** console command to display the amount of swap space your server is using or to add more swap space to your server. *Swap space* is a concept of virtual memory where the computer's disk space is used as an overflow area for RAM. Programs get swapped in and out of the swap space (disk volume area) to and from RAM as needed. This is how a CPU handles multiple tasks. You can add or delete swap space from a volume. To see how

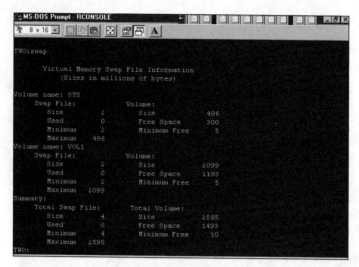

Figure B.11 Using the **SWAP** command to display the amount of swap space.

much swap space is being used, type "SWAP" at the server console. You'll see a screen similar to Figure B.11.

You could add a swap file to a volume called VOL1 to server TWO by typing the following:

```
TWO: SWAP ADD VOL1
```

If you don't specify a parameter, the default values are used. The parameters and their defaults are **MAX** (free volume space), **MIN** (2), and **MIN FREE** (5).

The **BIND** And **UNBIND** Commands

To allow a protocol to work with a given network board, the protocol must be bound to the LAN driver appropriate for the network card. The **BIND** command is used to accomplish this task. The following is an example of the **BIND** console command:

```
BIND IPX TO SMC9432 FRAME=Ethernet_802.2 NET=A
```

 To bind the protocol to the network board, you must install the network board, load the corresponding LAN driver, and then bind the correct protocol, such as IPX or IP.

If you no longer need the protocol bound to the network board, you can issue the **UNBIND** command. If you do this, you can no longer use the network board to communicate on the network.

The **VERSION** Command

The **VERSION** console command allows you to see what version of NetWare you're running. In addition, it shows you the date it was installed and the copyright information.

The **MODULES** Command

Typing "MODULES" at the server console allows you to see which NetWare Loadable Modules (NLMs) are loaded on the server. Figure B.12 shows sample output of the **MODULES** console command. Notice the version of each module is also displayed.

The **VOLUMES** Command

You use the **VOLUMES** command to see which volumes are mounted and what type of name space they have loaded. Name space is a term used to define the ability of a NetWare volume to store file names of other operating systems. Examples are DOS, MAC, NFS (Unix), and LONG.

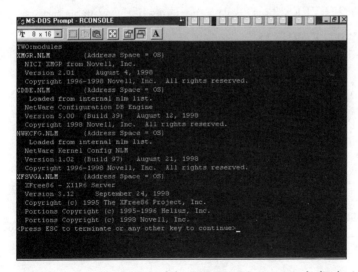

Figure B.12   The output of the **MODULES** command, displaying the NLMs running on the server.

The **DOWN** Command

This console command brings the server down. It'll warn you if users are attached. It's important to bring a server down properly instead of just powering off the computer.

The **TRACK ON** And **TRACK OFF** Commands

The **TRACK** command can be used to display packet activity between server and workstation. You either turn **TRACK ON** or turn **TRACK OFF** at the server. Typically, there are two types of packets that can be viewed: Routing Information Protocol (RIP) traffic and Service Advertising Protocol (SAP) traffic. There are IN packets, which are sent when a server is receiving inbound packets, and there are OUT packets, which are sent when a server is broadcasting outbound packets.

The **DISPLAY** Command

There are several useful variations of the **DISPLAY** command. They are as follows:

➤ **DISPLAY NETWORKS** This displays what networks are known.

➤ **DISPLAY PROCESSORS** This displays the CPU number and status.

➤ **DISPLAY SERVERS** This displays the names of the available servers.

➤ **DISPLAY INTERRUPTS** This displays the interrupts of different server hardware components.

➤ **DISPLAY ENVIRONMENT** This displays several pages of the **SET** variables that you have on your server.

➤ **DISPLAY MODIFIED ENVIRONMENT** This displays only those **SET** variables you've modified from the default values.

Figure B.13 shows samples of some of these commands.

 DISPLAY MODIFIED ENVIRONMENT is a useful tool to see which **SET** variables have been altered on your server.

The **SPEED** And **CPUCHECK** Commands

The **SPEED** command displays the CPU's speed, and the **CPUCHECK** command displays the speed of the server's CPU, the model type, and other

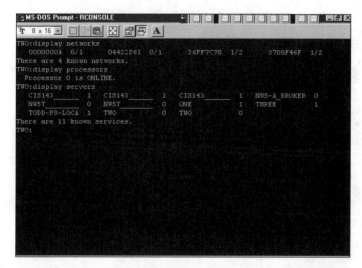

Figure B.13   The **DISPLAY NETWORKS**, **DISPLAY PROCESSORS**, and **DISPLAY SERVERS** commands.

information. To view the speed and CPU information of a server named TWO, type the following:

```
TWO: SPEED
TWO: CPUCHECK
```

The LIST DEVICES Command

The **LIST DEVICES** console command allows you to see the hardware devices on your system that NetWare recognizes. **LIST DEVICES** displays information such as the quantity and size of hard disks and CD-ROM devices.

The FILE SERVER NAME Command

The **FILE SERVER NAME** command lets you see or set the name of the file server. **FILE SERVER NAME** can also be set in the AUTOEXEC.NCF server boot file.

The NCP ADDRESSES Command

The **NCP ADDRESSES** command tells you the address of services for the server. For Transmission Control Protocol/Internet Protocol (TCP/IP), it gives you the IP address followed by the port number. For a server named TWO, you would enter the following:

```
TWO: NCP ADDRESSES
```

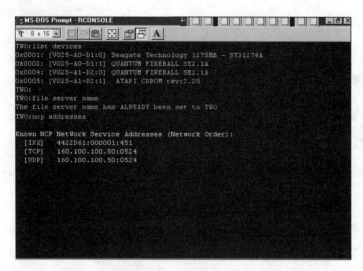

Figure B.14 The **LIST DEVICES**, **FILE SERVER NAME**, and **NCP ADDRESSES** commands.

Figure B.14 shows examples of the **LIST DEVICES, FILE SERVER NAME,** and **NCP ADDRESSES** commands.

The **ADD NAME SPACE** Command

The **ADD NAME SPACE** command allows you to store files for other operating systems on a NetWare volume. Figure B.15 shows an example of the

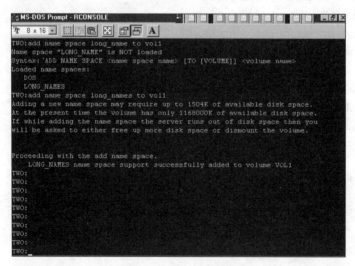

Figure B.15 The **ADD NAME SPACE** command's output.

ADD NAME SPACE command. To add the LONG name space to a server named TWO, you would enter the following:

```
TWO: ADD NAME SPACE LONG_NAMES TO VOL1
```

To add the MAC name space to a volume named MIS to store Macintosh files on a NetWare server named TWO, you would enter:

```
TWO: ADD NAME SPACE MAC TO MIS
```

 A word of caution: Adding name space causes the volume to use additional disk space to store the file names.

The **TIME** And **SET TIME ZONE** Commands

The TIME command allows you to see the time zone and time-synchronization information about a server. The SET TIME ZONE command displays the current time zone or changes it.

The **MOUNT** And **DISMOUNT** Commands

The MOUNT command mounts the NetWare volumes so they are available for use. Use MOUNT ALL to mount all volumes and MOUNT *Volume_name* to mount a specific volume.

To make volumes unavailable to users, you can run the DISMOUNT command. However, no users will be able to use any files or directories on that volume. To run a volume repair operation (VREPAIR), you must DISMOUNT the volume.

> *Note:* By default, all hard disk volumes are mounted when the server boots.

NLMs

As mentioned, NLMs are external executable modules (also called utilities) that consist of substantial code that adds functionality to the server. For many NLMs that are loaded at the server, there are management screens and menu options that become available once they are loaded. In the following sections, we discuss some of the more common NLMs.

The NWCONFIG NLM

In NetWare 5, there's an NLM—NWCONFIG (NetWare Configuration)—that replaces the INSTALL.NLM of previous NetWare versions. After NWCONFIG is loaded, it brings up a text-based menu screen. To load NWCONFIG on a server named TWO, you would type the following at the server console:

```
TWO: NWCONFIG
```

> *Note: In NetWare 5, you don't have to specify the LOAD option as you did in NetWare 4.x. Now, you just type in the name of the NLM.*

See Figure B.16 for a sample screenshot of NWCONFIG. NWCONFIG allows you to perform the following activities:

➤ Unload and load server disk drivers and network board drivers.

➤ Manage volumes and partitions and create disk mirrors.

➤ Manage Novell Storage Services (NSS) volumes, which are mass storage devices.

➤ Add and remove licenses on a server.

➤ Copy NetWare system files from a CD.

➤ Install and remove NDS on a server.

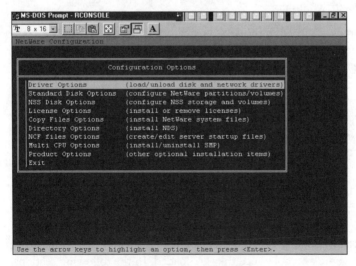

Figure B.16 The NWCONFIG initial screen.

➤ Modify the STARTUP.NCF and the AUTOEXEC.NCF server boot files.

➤ Manage servers with multiple CPUs.

➤ Add other products, such as Unix print services, or languages to the server.

The VREPAIR NLM

You use the VREPAIR NLM to fix a volume or to remove the name space from a volume. Typically, you need to run VREPAIR on the server if there's a sudden power loss or disk failure. The Directory Entry Table (DET), which locates directories on disk, and the File Allocation Table (FAT), which locates files on disk, may become corrupt if the server has a sudden loss of power. VREPAIR is similar to the DOS **CHKDSK** or **SCANDISK** command. To run the VREPAIR NLM on a server named TWO, you would type the following:

```
TWO: VREPAIR
```

You'll be presented with a menu that allows you to repair the volume or set volume options.

The Directory Services Related NLMs

There are several Directory Services–related NLMs. They are DSMERGE, DSREPAIR, DSDIAG, and DSTRACE:

➤ **DSMERGE NLM** Allows you to do the following:

➤ Check servers in the tree

➤ Check time synchronization

➤ Merge two NDS trees

➤ Rename an NDS tree

➤ **DSREPAIR NLM** Used to repair problems related to NDS database objects. Problems can occur because of disk failures or sudden power outages. With DSREPAIR, you can perform the following operations:

➤ Repair the NDS database in unattended mode

➤ Repair time synchronization

➤ Report synchronization status

➤ View the repair log

➤ **DSDIAG (Directory Services Diagnostics) NLM** Generates reports about the NDS tree, partitions, and servers. It can also help you troubleshoot NDS problems.

➤ **DSTRACE** Can be used to watch for Directory Services problems. It shows Directory Services traffic similar to the way in which **TRACK ON** shows RIP and SAP traffic.

The REMOTE And RSPX NLMs

For a client workstation to connect to the server remotely over a LAN, you must install the REMOTE and RSPX NLMs on the server. REMOTE provides remote administrator access from a workstation. RSPX is the required transport protocol. To run the REMOTE NLM at the server console of a server named TWO, you would enter:

```
TWO: REMOTE
```

REMOTE will prompt you for a password. This is a security measure so not just anyone can access the server remotely. The server can be downed with the **DOWN** command from a remote workstation. After the REMOTE NLM is installed, you can see it with the **MODULES** command.

To install the RSPX module, type "RSPX". Now, you can go to a workstation and run the RCONSOLE utility. You must enter the correct password for the REMOTE NLM you loaded on the server.

 For more information on any of the console commands and NLMs mentioned in this appendix, and to view any additional commands or NLMs, see the Novell Online documentation Utilities Reference section. This information can also be found on the Web at **www.novell.com/documentation/lg/nw5/docui/ index.html**.

Glossary

access control list (ACL)—A list of objects (trustees) that have been granted or denied rights to perform operations on a particular object. Also called the *Object Trustees property* and the *Object Trustees (ACL) property*.

Alias object—An object that represents, or points to, another object in the Directory tree.

Application object—The fundamental NDS object employed by Application Launcher to efficiently and seamlessly deploy applications to users at workstations in the NDS tree.

AUTOEXEC.NCF—A NetWare server boot file.

backlink—A property value used by NDS to keep track of where the external references of an object are located. Each backlink value is periodically checked to verify that the associated external reference still exists. This creates additional NDS background traffic.

Backup Admin—An Organizational Role object that is created and assigned to the administrator that will perform backups and other administrative functions.

bindery—The flat database used in NetWare 3.x and earlier versions to contain User, Group, Print Server, and Print Queue objects. An NDS container can emulate a 3.x bindery, thus allowing services to establish a bindery connection for backward compatibility.

catalog—A flat-file database that holds information gathered from the NDS database.

child—Any object that receives information from a parent object or resides below a parent object.

common name—The actual name you assign to an NDS leaf object (as opposed to an object's distinguished name).

Compatibility Mode Driver (CMD)—The virtual network driver that implements Compatibility Mode, which is a tunneling technology that puts an IPX stub inside the IP packets to provide IPX application compatibility.

connection management—The process that ensures a highly secure virtual connection for servers in the replica list to communicate across.

connectivity specialist—The person responsible for maintaining the physical aspects of a network.

ConsoleOne—The NetWare management utility that uses a Java GUI environment to allow you to perform basic administrative functions on NDS objects, access the file system, and edit NetWare configuration files in a Java text editor. ConsoleOne can be run on a server or workstation.

Container Admin—An Organizational Role object that is created and assigned to the administrator who will manage a specific container. This role is used to divide NDS management tasks among network administrators to ease overall administration.

container object—An NDS object that can contain or hold other objects—in contrast to leaf objects, which cannot.

context—An object's location in the NDS Directory structure.

Country object—An object that can exist only between the [Root] object and an Organization object. The Country object is used to designate a country as a valid NDS container object for wide area networks (WANs) that employ a geographical NDS design. It can only have a valid two-letter international country code, such as *US*, as its name. Country objects only need to exist in NDS if another X.500 directory system requires it.

current context—A workstation's setting that specifies where in the NDS Directory to "look" for objects. For example, if the workstation context is set to be .OU=RESEARCH.O=ACME and a user logs in as FRED, the system will look for a valid FRED object in the RESEARCH container.

design analysis—The NDS design phase in which the NDS tree is monitored continuously and compared to the operation of the organization.

design phase—The second phase of the NDS design process, which includes designing the NDS tree, designing the partition and replica implementations for the tree, planning the time-synchronization strategy, and planning the user environment.

Directory Map object—An object that contains a reference to a file system directory on a NetWare volume. It can be used with the **MAP** command in login scripts to point to file system resources.

Directory tree—The database of all the resources that can be used in a Novell network. See also *Novell Directory Services (NDS)*.

distinguished name—The complete path from an object to the [Root] of the NDS Directory tree. A distinguished name is a combination of an object's common name and context.

drive mapping—A drive association created using a workstation-based map utility (such as the Novell **MAP** command) that associates a drive letter with a directory or subdirectory on a hard drive. The drive letter association provides a way for the operating system to access files that reside on the hard drives of network file service providers.

DSMERGE—An NLM used to merge NDS trees.

DSTRACE—An NLM that provides monitoring capabilities for NDS events.

dynamic link library (DLL) files—Files that are libraries of executable code linked to applications when the applications are run, rather than being compiled with a program's executable. These files can be shared by several applications, because they're linked dynamically and exist as independent files on the hard drive.

effective rights—The rights you actually have in a given location in NDS or the NetWare file system. They are determined by adding all rights you have received by whatever means and subtracting all rights that have been revoked by the IRF or blocked by explicit assignments.

Enterprise Admin—An Organizational Role object that is created and assigned to the administrator that controls the tree name, partition and replication strategies, and time synchronization. This role will manage the entire Directory tree and should be granted full access to the [Root] object.

Ethernet—A network communications protocol characterized by its contention-based channel access method, network board design, supported physical topologies, and various media types.

external reference—A temporary object ID that is automatically created by NDS to reference objects that are not stored locally. To keep track of external references that are created for a particular object, the multi-valued backlink property for an NDS object points to the external references associated with the object.

fault tolerance—The ability of a computer to work continuously, even when a system failure occurs.

Fiber Distributed Data Interface (FDDI)—A network communications protocol characterized mainly by its use of fiber media for data transmission and high-speed throughput (100Mbps).

firewall—Software and/or hardware that regulates access to the network to protect both information and computers from outside threats.

frame relay—A protocol specification and a type of public data network service that provides efficient Data Link layer functions on permanent and switched virtual circuits.

graphical user interface (GUI)—An operating environment that uses icons and buttons rather than commands to perform certain functions.

Group object—An NDS object designed to represent groups of users in the NDS tree to the NetWare operating system. Changes made to a Group object are passed on to all members of the group automatically.

GroupWise—A popular product developed by Novell that provides email, scheduling, calendar, and workgroup services. GroupWise uses NDS to store configuration information.

heartbeat—The NDS synchronization process that makes NDS Directory objects the same across all replicas in the replica list. This process executes every half-hour, by default.

hostname—The recognizable DNS name of a machine on a TCP/IP network.

implementation phase—The NDS design phase in which the design is set up in a real-world environment and fine-tuned.

Inherited Rights Filter (IRF)—A selection in an object's ACL that is used to block rights and keep them from being inherited by child objects. The IRF ultimately alters what a trustee can do at a lower level in the Directory. An IRF can also be applied to a file or a directory within the NetWare file system.

Internet Protocol (IP)—A DoD Internet layer protocol that provides connectionless, nonguaranteed service to move packets across an internetwork.

Internet Service Provider (ISP)—A commercial organization that provides customers access to the Internet, usually for a fee.

Internetwork Packet Exchange (IPX)—Modeled after Xerox Corporation's Internetwork Packet protocol, XNS, IPX is a protocol that operates at the third layer (Network layer) of the OSI model to move packets across an internetwork.

Internetwork Packet Exchange/Sequenced Packet Exchange (IPX/SPX)—The native protocol stack for NetWare networks. SPX provides reliable connections and operates at the Transport layer of the OSI model, relying on IPX for lower-level network functions.

IP Address object—The object that represents an IP address in NDS.

Java—Sun Microsystems's cross-platform programming language.

Java applet—A program written in Java that runs within a Java-compatible browser.

kernel—The base of most operating systems. The kernel provides just the core functions deemed critical for the operating system. Further functionality is provided by additional program modules.

LAN Area object—An NDS object that is created to contain servers that are physically close to each other on a LAN or need to be grouped together for some reason.

LAN driver—A file containing software code that provides a communication link between the operating system and the network board.

leaf objects—A class of NDS objects that represents actual resources in the NDS tree and does not contain other NDS objects.

legacy device—A component on a NetWare network that is not NDS-aware. Any NetWare 3 resource (or even NetWare 2) is a legacy resource, because it only recognizes the NetWare bindery and not NDS.

License Certificate object—An NDS leaf object that contains information about the software's publisher, product, and version. It also designates the number of licenses the certificate has, licenses in use, and licenses available.

limber—A process that runs five minutes after the server is booted and then once every three hours thereafter. Limber makes sure a server's index pointer table is updated to reflect changes in the server's name and address among the replicas. It also verifies that the NDS tree name is consistent among servers in the replica list or replica ring.

line printer daemon (LPD)—The standard for print services on TCP/IP networks. LPD is analogous to NPRINTER in the NetWare world.

local area network (LAN)—A collection of computers and other networked devices that fits within the scope of a single physical network. LANs provide the building blocks for internetworks and wide area networks (WANs).

login script—A set of instructions that the network client executes during the login process.

master replica—The original copy of a partition that's used for authentication and for partition merging and creation.

mobile user—A person who travels outside of his or her normal physical location and accesses information, applications, and network resources in a local container.

name context—The location in an NDS tree to which a workstation points.

NDS Catalog Services—A NetWare feature that allows quicker access to NDS information by cataloging Directory information in an easily accessible index format. Catalog Services stores the catalog (which is a flat-file database) as an NDS object. This allows administrators to quickly access a snapshot of the complete Directory, as opposed to performing a query across the entire network.

NDS expert—Typically, the person in an organization who has the most experience with NDS or has completed Novell-approved NetWare 5 and NDS training.

NDS Manager—The NetWare application used to partition and replicate an NDS tree. It is executed using the NDSMGR32.EXE utility.

NDS object—Any object in the NDS tree. NDS objects can be divided into the following subtypes: [Root], container, and leaf.

NDS tree—The entire hierarchical Novell Directory Services (NDS) database of objects. If you have access to more than one tree, you must be authenticated to each tree to gain access to its resources.

NetWare Administrator—NetWare's graphical utility for managing NDS databases. Also called *NWAdmin*, although it's not a trademarked term. The executable for NetWare Administrator is NWADMN32.EXE and it's located in the SYS:\PUBLIC\WIN32 directory.

NetWare Loadable Module (NLM)—One of several types of NetWare server executables; the other types include CDM, HAM, LAN, and NAM. Each executable has a specific function, with the NLM being the most common form.

Network Time Protocol (NTP)—An Internet standard for providing time synchronization. This protocol enhancement for TCP uses authoritative time servers to provide network time information through a hierarchy of time servers. NTP is similar, but not identical, to the timesync protocol for NetWare 4, which is still provided for NetWare 5 IPX servers.

Novell Client—The Novell software package that provides connectivity to a Novell network.

Novell Directory Services (NDS)—Novell's Directory service that stores information on the network resources and regulates their access. NDS is a hierarchical distributed database that is X.50x compliant.

Novell Distributed Print Services (NDPS)—A service that provides administrators the ability to control printing through NDS. It also provides bidirectional communications between control points, management applications and workstations, and network printers.

object classes—General types of objects in the NDS tree differentiated by their schema. Organization and Country are two different classes of objects. Each object class has a different set of properties that designates its purpose. The set of properties defines the object class.

object rights—The rights that control the viewing, deleting, and renaming of NDS objects. The object rights are Supervisor, Browse, Create, Delete, and Rename.

Organization object—An NDS container object that contains the subordinate objects that represent the resources of a specific organization.

Organizational Role object—A leaf object that can be created in the NDS tree that represents a specific position in the organization; for example, Server Admin, Enterprise-wide Admin, and so on.

Organizational Unit object—An object in the NDS tree that represents divisions or departments that exist within the overall organization. Organizational Unit objects can only exist in an Organization object or other Organizational Unit objects.

parent—A term for an object that stores other objects. Also called the *parent object*.

partition—A logical portion of the NDS database. A partition is composed of at least a single container object and all the objects that exist within that container object.

partition boundary—A partition boundary is defined by a container object and any object that has that container as its parent. A partition can contain multiple containers; however, all NDS objects in a container belong to the same partition as the container.

partition root object—The top-level container object in a partition.

Password Admin—The Organizational Role object that has some of the most restrictive rights for administrators, such as severely limited property rights to Group and User objects, passwords, and login scripts.

Policy Package object—Z.E.N.works NDS objects that allow you to create and maintain policies within the NDS tree. These policies are grouped into packages according to the types of objects (such as container, User, and Workstation objects) that the policies can be associated with. They control the configuration of such things as remote control settings, client settings, user restrictions, workstation configuration settings, and so on.

polling—A time-synchronization technique in which the time consumer checks with a time provider to determine if the consumer's time is accurate.

primary time server—The time server that synchronizes its time with the other time servers in a network. Primary time servers poll other primary time servers and reference time servers and vote with these time servers to determine the correct network time. The time on a primary time server is corrected 50 percent per polling interval.

print queue—The temporary storage location (logical and/or physical) for documents sent to the printer, but waiting to be printed.

Printer object—An object in the NDS structure symbolizing a physical printer.

Profile object—An NDS object that contains a common login script that executes for a set of users (assigned to the object) that exists in different containers or for a subset of users within a container.

project approach phase—The first phase of the NDS design process in which preparation for the NDS design takes place. This phase of the project involves gathering information pertinent to the NDS design and establishing project scope and schedule.

project manager—The person who is the coordinating and driving force behind the NDS design and implementation process. This role can be filled by a manager at any level of the IS department, preferably a senior manager of the administrators or server support staff.

property rights—The NDS rights that control what the trustee can do to the values stored within the properties of an object. Property rights allow a trustee to view, compare, search, and modify values in a property. The property rights are Supervisor, Compare, Read, Write, and Add Self.

protocol—A set of rules used to define the procedures to follow as data is transmitted or received.

provider—The Novell Storage Services (NSS) application that manages storage objects and scans all the storage devices to locate free space.

read-only replica—A complete copy of an NDS partition that cannot be used for authentication.

read/write replica—A complete copy of an NDS partition. You can have several read/write replicas, and they can be used for authentication.

Redundant Array of Inexpensive Disks (RAID)—Multiple drives linked together via hardware or software, used to increase reliability. There are six recognized levels of RAID, with additional levels being developed. The exact features depend on the RAID level used.

reference time server—The IPX-only time server that gets its time from an external time source and is a time provider to primary and secondary time servers.

relative distinguished name—An object's location relative to the workstation's current context. A relative distinguished name does not begin with a period and does not necessarily reference the [Root].

remote user—A user who uses a dial-up connection to access the network and resources within his or her home container.

replica—A copy of the NDS database that contains the actual data that constitutes the NDS objects within a partition boundary.

replica list—The list of servers that send and/or receive the NDS Directory information for a given partition.

replica ring—The group of servers that stores copies of an NDS partition.

replication—The process of copying an NDS database to other servers in the tree.

[Root] default partition—See *[Root] object*.

[Root] object—The NDS object from which all other objects emerge. The [Root] object is created during installation and cannot be deleted or renamed.

scalability—The degree to which NDS can be broken down into smaller pieces or partitions.

schema—A set of procedures and rules that defines the structure of NDS objects, their properties, and their containment rules.

schema synchronization—A process that occurs once every four hours and is performed to make sure the schema is the same across all partitions. It also ensures that all schema changes are consistent.

secondary time server—A time consumer that gets its time from single reference, primary, or reference time servers. Secondary time servers act as time providers to client workstations and can be configured to act as time providers to other secondary servers.

Sequenced Packet Exchange (SPX)—In the IPX/SPX protocol suite, the protocol that provides reliable data transfer between nodes and is roughly equivalent to the TCP protocol. SPX is characterized by a connection setup, ensuring data receipt and session termination.

Server Admin—An Organizational Role object that is created and assigned to the administrator that will manage a specific server.

server administrator—The person who maintains and configures the server.

server console—The NetWare 5 screen used by the network administrator to interact with and monitor the server.

Server object—An object that's created automatically whenever you install a server into NDS. It represents the physical server as an object in the NDS tree.

Server Status Check—A process that is initiated on a server that does not have a replica. It connects to either a master or read/write replica, and the process runs every six minutes.

Service Advertising Protocol (SAP)—A protocol used by IPX to broadcast information on available services. SAP is characterized by limited scalability countered by easy configuration.

single reference time server—Novell's default type of time server that maintains the master time and propagates the time to secondary time servers and client workstations.

Special Use Admin—An Organizational Role object that is used on servers that the IS department doesn't control.

STARTUP.NCF—One of the two boot files for the NetWare server (the other is AUTOEXEC.NCF).

subordinate reference replica—An incomplete copy of a partition. It's created automatically on servers that have a complete replica of a parent partition, but not its children. It cannot be used for authentication.

Supervisor object right—The NDS right that allows you to perform any and all actions on an object. This right can be blocked by the Inherited Rights Filter (IRF).

Supervisor right—The unrestricted file system right that allows a user to perform any operation on any file or directory for which the right is granted. This right cannot be blocked by the IRF.

synchronization—This is either the time-synchronization process of keeping server time consistent or the process of comparing and updating NDS information.

SYS volume—The mandatory name of the first volume on a NetWare file server. The SYS volume must be a traditional NetWare volume.

TCP/IP (Transmission Control Protocol/Internet Protocol)—A protocol suite created by the Advanced Research Projects Agency (ARPA). This transmission protocol suite is the standard used for Internet communications.

time consumer—A server that gets its time information from another server.

time provider—A server that provides the time to a time consumer, which is either a server or workstation.

time provider group—A method of server time negotiation in which one server acts as the reference time server and two or more servers act as primary time servers.

time radius—The time period in which the internal clock of a server is adjusted and synchronized.

time synchronization—The process of coordinating and maintaining consistent time among all servers in an NDS tree.

TIMESYNC.CFG—The configuration file used to set the parameters for the time-synchronization functions.

TIMESYNC.NLM—The NLM that handles time synchronization.

Traffic Manager—A NetWare 5 tool that allows you to manage NDS synchronization traffic across WAN and LAN links.

transitive synchronization—The process in which servers with differing protocols can synchronize their replicas.

trustees—Objects with the rights to access certain network resources. A trustee is defined as an object in the access control list (ACL) that has access to an object. Six objects are most suited to be designated as trustees: Users, Groups, Organizational Roles, containers, [Root], and [Public].

typeful naming—The naming scheme used to name NDS objects in which the object class is referred to before naming the object (for example, CN=MARYB.OU=AUSTIN.O=ACME). Generally, you only need to use typeful naming when typeless naming is not permitted.

typeless naming—The naming scheme used to name NDS objects in which the object class is not referred to and the syntax of the name is trusted to identify the object correctly (for example, MARYB.AUSTIN.ACME).

Universal Time Coordinated (UTC)—The time used as a standard throughout the world (also called Universal Coordinated Time). UTC is based on Greenwich mean time (GMT), which is 0 degrees longitude on a map.

User object—An NDS object that represents an individual user and contains personal and access right information about the user.

Virtual Loadable Module (VLM)—Utilities or programs that perform communication and other services between workstations and servers. This is the basis of Novell's 16-bit client, which preceded Client32 for access from DOS and Windows clients to the NDS tree.

volume—The fundamental unit of NetWare server storage space.

Volume object—An NDS object that represents the corresponding physical volume.

WAN Traffic Manager—See *Traffic Manager*.

wide area network (WAN)—An internetwork that connects multiple sites where a third-party communications carrier, such as a public or private telephone company, is used to carry network traffic from one location to another. WAN links can be quite expensive and are charged on the basis of bandwidth, so few such links support the same bandwidth as that available on most LANs.

Workstation objects—NDS objects that represent workstations attached to your network and enable you to manage them efficiently.

WTM.NLM—The NLM that is executed on a Novell server to enable the WAN Traffic Manager.

Z.E.N.works (Zero Effort Networks)—A group of utilities and special NDS objects for administrators that is used to increase the ease of most network-management tasks by making them centrally available.

Index

D

CERTIFIED CRAMMER SOCIETY

PHI SLAMMA CRAMMA

A breed apart, a cut above the rest—a true professional. Highly skilled and superbly trained, certified IT professionals are unquestionably the world's most elite computer experts. In an effort to appropriately recognize this privileged crowd, The Coriolis Group is proud to introduce the Certified Crammer Society. If you are a certified IT professional, it is our pleasure to invite you to become a Certified Crammer Society member.

Membership is free to all certified professionals and benefits include a membership kit that contains your official membership card and official Certified Crammer Society blue denim ball cap emblazoned with the Certified Crammer Society crest— proudly displaying the Crammer motto "Phi Slamma Cramma"—and featuring a genuine leather bill. The kit also includes your password to the Certified Crammers-Only Web site containing monthly discreet messages designed to provide you with advance notification about certification testing information, special book excerpts, and inside industry news not found anywhere else; monthly Crammers-Only discounts on selected Coriolis titles; *Ask the Series Editor* Q and A column; cool contests with great prizes; and more.

GUIDELINES FOR MEMBERSHIP

Registration is free to professionals certified in Microsoft, A+, or Oracle DBA. Coming soon: Sun Java, Novell, and Cisco. Send or email your contact information and proof of your certification (test scores, membership card, or official letter) to:

Certified Crammer Society Membership Chairperson
THE CORIOLIS GROUP, LLC
14455 North Hayden Road, Suite 220, Scottsdale, Arizona 85260-6949
Fax: 480.483.0193 • Email: ccs@coriolis.com

APPLICATION

Name:

Address:

Society Alias:

Choose a secret code name to correspond with us
and other Crammer Society members.
Please use no more than eight characters.

Email:

CORIOLIS HELP CENTER

Here at The Coriolis Group, we strive to provide the finest customer service in the technical education industry. We're committed to helping you reach your certification goals by assisting you in the following areas.

Talk to the Authors

We'd like to hear from you! Please refer to the "How to Use This Book" section in the "Introduction" of every Exam Cram guide for our authors' individual email addresses.

Web Page Information

The Certification Insider Press Web page provides a host of valuable information that's only a click away. For information in the following areas, please visit us at:

www.coriolis.com/cip/default.cfm

- Titles and other products
- Book content updates
- Roadmap to Certification Success guide
- New Adaptive Testing changes
- New Exam Cram Live! seminars
- New Certified Crammer Society details
- Sample chapters and tables of contents
- Manuscript solicitation
- Special programs and events

Contact Us by Email

Important addresses you may use to reach us at The Coriolis Group.

eci@coriolis.com

To subscribe to our FREE, bi-monthly on-line newsletter, *Exam Cram Insider*. Keep up to date with the certification scene. Included in each *Insider* are certification articles, program updates, new exam information, hints and tips, sample chapters, and more.

techsupport@coriolis.com

For technical questions and problems with CD-ROMs. Products broken, battered, or blown-up? Just need some installation advice? Contact us here.

ccs@coriolis.com

To obtain membership information for the *Certified Crammer Society*, **an exclusive club for the certified professional.** Get in on members-only discounts, special information, expert advice, contests, cool prizes, and free stuff for the certified professional. Membership is FREE. Contact us and get enrolled today!

cipq@coriolis.com

For book content questions and feedback about our titles, drop us a line. This is the good, the bad, and the questions address. Our customers are the best judges of our products. Let us know what you like, what we could do better, or what question you may have about any content. Testimonials are always welcome here, and if you send us a story about how an Exam Cram guide has helped you ace a test, we'll give you an official Certification Insider Press T-shirt.

custserv@coriolis.com

For solutions to problems concerning an order for any of our products. Our staff will promptly and courteously address the problem. Taking the exams is difficult enough. We want to make acquiring our study guides as easy as possible.

Book Orders & Shipping Information

orders@coriolis.com

To place an order by email or to check on the status of an order already placed.

coriolis.com/bookstore/default.cfm

To place an order through our online bookstore.

1.800.410.0192

To place an order by phone or to check on an order already placed.